AF184185

New Challenges in Change Management

New Horizons in Management Sciences

Edited by Lukasz Sulkowski

Scientific Board:
Prof. Dr. German Chavez
Prof. Dr. Marcela Rebeca Contreras Loera
Prof. Dr. hab. Natalia Czuchraj
Prof. Dr. Geoff Goldman
Prof. Dr. hab. Barbara Kozuch
Prof. Dr. Claude Martin
Prof. Dr. Thomas P. Massey
Prof. Dr. hab. Bogdan Nogalski
Prof. Dr. hab. Roman Patora
Prof. Dr. Americo Salvidar
Prof. Dr. hab. Kazimierz Zimniewicz

Volume 8

PETER LANG

Łukasz Sułkowski / Ewa Grandys (eds.)

New Challenges in Change Management

PETER LANG

Bibliographic Information published by the Deutsche Nationalbibliothek
The Deutsche Nationalbibliothek lists this publication in the Deutsche Nationalbibliografie; detailed bibliographic data is available in the internet at http://dnb.d-nb.de.

Library of Congress Cataloging-in-Publication Data
A CIP catalog record for this book has been applied for at the Library of Congress

This publication was financially supported by the University of Social Sciences in Łódź.

ISSN 2194-153X
ISBN 978-3-631-74113-9 (Print)
E-ISBN 978-3-631-74114-6 (E-Book)
E-ISBN 978-3-631-74115-3 (EPUB)
E-ISBN 978-3-631-74116-0 (MOBI)
DOI 10.3726/b12994

© Peter Lang GmbH
Internationaler Verlag der Wissenschaften
Berlin 2018
All rights reserved.
PL Academic Research is an Imprint of Peter Lang GmbH.

Peter Lang – Berlin · Bern · Bruxelles · New York · Oxford · Warszawa · Wien

All parts of this publication are protected by copyright. Any utilisation outside the strict limits of the copyright law, without the permission of the publisher, is forbidden and liable to prosecution. This applies in particular to reproductions, translations, microfilming, and storage and processing in electronic retrieval systems.

This book is part of an editor´s series of Peter Lang Academic Research and was peer reviewed prior to publication.

www.peterlang.com

Table of contents

Preface

Research into change management and its models is still very relevant in the 21st century. The source of change management issues as faced by researchers, organisational development experts and organisational leaders is the complexity of change and the speed of adjustment it involves rather than its worth or relevancy.

In our turbulent world, where innovation cycles are growing shorter and shorter, change management must engage all employees to be effective, as some changes may affect all functions in organisations as well as industries.

With change being an inherent element of today's world, success is usually with leaders that react in a prompt and responsible manner, but those that can create the future or anticipate it are even more successful, as they play their own game while others only follow them. The survival of an organisation experiencing adaptation problems is questionable.

There are numerous models for making organisational change successful. Winners are quick to act, learn and adapt to the complexity and speed of change, as opposed to losers, who strive to master and control change. The leaders of organisations are responsible for designing and implementing a model of transformation strategy that in addition to making their organisations sustainable will also help them thrive in the near future and beyond. This monograph compares and discusses change models and strategies enabling organisations to anticipate change or respond to it.

Managing change is a tough challenge, partly because experts disagree over factors that have the biggest influence on transformation initiatives.

Change management gurus have recently focused their attention on soft factors, such as motivation, leadership and organisational culture. While these are vital to successful management of change, they are not likely to lead to transformation projects, as their real influence on the results of most change programmes is very limited. Visionary leadership may not always be a prerequisite of transformation projects, but it frequently plays an important role. The same applies to communication with employees. Modifying behaviours and attitudes is not easy, as they are deeply ingrained in people and organisational culture. Motivation and cultural changes can be indirectly assessed by means of interviews and surveys, but a reliable measurement of the degree to which soft factors contribute to them is much more difficult.

Hard factors are apparently given less attention than they deserve. There are three unique attributes that make them special. Firstly, organisations can employ direct and indirect methods to measure them. Secondly, their importance can be easily communicated to the outside and inside of the organisation. Thirdly, and most importantly, organisations can change without much problem. Hard factors not only influence the transformation initiatives but also enable their completion, determine the number of people that are involved in them, as well as their financial outcomes.

The chapters of this monograph have been contributed by Polish authors who present their perspectives on challenges in the science and practice of management.

In chapter 1, on production management issues, Ewa Grandys presents her innovative approach to investigating changes occurring in the course of production. Part 1 of the chapter analyses the production cycle of seasonal products, part 2 considers the role of time and the impact of endogenous and exogenous changes on the process of production and part 3 explains the construction of a production cycle model, a production management model and a method for studying unexpected changes in the production of seasonal products. The chapter was prepared on the basis of the author's long-term empirical investigations that provided data necessary to build the production cycle model and theoretical research that inspired her to create the production management model and the method for examining production changes.

Chapter 2, authored by Mariusz Bednarek and Łukasz Bielawski, provides insights into the practical aspects of Lean Manufacturing.

In chapter 3, Mariusz Bednarek and Marcin Lisowski analyse the digital evolution and revolution of logistics and investigate the role of information in the reconstruction of internal and external organisational forms of logistic issues.

Chapter 4, contributed by Remigiusz Kozłowski, provides a review of various logistic technologies. The need for effective management of technologies is a natural consequence of the global character of logistic business. The author proposes a method for selecting fit-for-purpose technologies, which is the starting point for effective management. The method can be a useful tool for technology managers and executives in logistic companies.

In chapter 5, Łukasz Sułkowski and Dominika Kaczorowska-Spychalska discuss change management in the context of social media, which are very important today as a technological innovation and a factor contributing to the digitalisation of management.

Chapter 6, written by Zofia Patora-Wysocka, introduces "a practice-based approach to organisational change", a relatively new and interesting strand of research within organisational and management studies.

In the last chapter, Małgorzata Rozkwitalska depicts the role of learning based on intercultural interactions as an antecedent of organisational change, setting the discussion in the context of social learning, social cognitive theories, social-cognition models and cognitive dissonance. The chapter stresses the significance of this type of learning for organisations to thrive.

The monograph is intended for managers in modern enterprises as a resource of up-to-date knowledge and practical solutions supporting management functions. It can be also a valuable guide for students aspiring to become managers.

Łukasz Sułkowski
Ewa Grandys

Ewa Grandys
University of Social Sciences

An Innovative Method for Investigating Production Process Changes

Abstract: Short life cycle products belong to a special segment of manufacturing. Following an empirical investigation into the process of their manufacture, a graphic model of the production cycle divided into four subprocesses was created. The subprocesses were illustrated on the example of garment production. The model and its description were used to confirm the hypothesis that the duration of the production process can be determined and that subprocesses are separated by constant time intervals.
Production management has to react to changing exogenous and endogenous factors. A method called the Production Process Control Tree (PPCT) was developed to control the production process and analyse its changes. The method's name refers to its underlying production management model, which is shaped as an inverted tree (graph theory). The method helps to cushion or even eliminate the negative impacts of changing processes which could extend their duration.

Key words: production management, production cycle, product life cycle.

Introduction

The factor which enables the search for new production management methods is the development of knowledge. Among the many questions that knowledge is expected to answer, there is the question of how an organisation can flexibly cope with changes taking place in its environment [Bednarek 2007, p. 30]. This question can only be answered through research. The practical orientation and simplicity of such research are misleading because the pragmatism of management sciences covers in fact complex processes through which the world of organisations [Sułkowski 2012, p. 9], including enterprises, is explored and interpreted. In these circumstances, it seems purposeful to seek production management methods that might enable the identification of unexpected exogenous and endogenous changes affecting production processes. The changes must be recognised early enough to minimise their negative impacts or to use unexpected opportunities to the best possible extent. The methods that are used these days to manage production fell short of meeting the needs of the manufacturers of seasonal products, who must maintain the fast pace of operations and deliver products that have a relatively short life cycle in the market. The awareness that such problems exist led to the formulation of the goals for the research conducted by the author. The goals fall under the category of theoretical and **modelling** research, which is one of the areas explored by management science.

The main objective in the course of writing this chapter was to create a method for investigating changes that might unexpectedly affect the production of seasonal products. To achieve the objective, two intermediate goals were formulated: the construction of a production cycle model and of a production management model. The other model was constructed in the framework of graph theory. Wilson [2000, p. 7] indicates that graph theory is used for the purposes of operational accounting, organic chemistry, genetics, linguistics, IT, geography, sociology and architecture because it helps solve complex organisational problems by means of simple mathematical models (diagrams).

The chapter consists of three parts. Part 1 discusses issues related to the production cycle of seasonal products. The cycle has been divided into subprocesses, which are briefly characterised. Part 2 deals with the role of time and the impacts of endogenous and exogenous changes on production. Regarding the production of seasonal goods, the beginning and end dates of the production process are deterministic. Irregularities may delay the completion of the manufacturing planning and manufacturing subprocess. This reduces the period allocated to the subprocess of distribution or even leaves no time for it, as a result of which the manufacturer's financial result is worse than expected. The most extensive part is Part 3, which explains the construction of the production cycle model, the production management model and the method for investigating unplanned changes in the production of seasonal products. The method allows active control and verification of the production process when there is a risk that the irregularities occurring will cause a delay in its end date. The chapter is based on long years of empirical studies conducted by the author that provided data for building the production cycle model, but it also presents the results of theoretical research that led to the creation of the production management model and the method for investigating changes in the production process.

Part I. The production process cycle for seasonal goods

1. Introduction

Some notions used in management sciences lack clear definitions. This field of knowledge is still relatively new and its academic identity is less distinct compared with other disciplines of social sciences [Sułkowski 2005, pp. 66–76]. Let us therefore start by explaining the terms used in the title of this part of the chapter to avoid interpretation problems. The term **'cycle'** derives from a Greek word denoting a circle or a disc, which makes it very useful in describing sequences of events appearing at regular intervals. The word has been used to form many compounds operating in economic sciences, such as an economic cycle, a business cycle, a product lifecycle, etc. As far as 'production **process**' is concerned, the word 'process' must be dealt with first. It comes from the Latin word *processus* ('to advance'), which denotes changes occurring as successive stages of development are reached. Because of the breadth of this definition, Bitkowska [2013, pp. 29–30] created a list of definitions (all applying to economics) of the word 'process' developed by sixteen authors and then made a comparative analysis which showed the existence of definitional discrepancies. As a result, the author of this chapter decided against any further exploration into this area and assumed that for the purposes of this work the word 'process' would be interpreted as proposed by Adair and Murray [2002, p. 27], who view a process as a set of tasks or phases that on the input end receives "raw materials" (physical resources, information, humans, machines, methods, etc.) and on the output end delivers a product (a physical product, information, service) for a specific recipient to use. The fact that Adair and Murray have given such a broad definition to "raw materials" implies that they consider the word 'process' to be universally applicable.

Given the purpose of this chapter, the term 'production process' must be defined as well. The Polish terminology within management theory partly derives from the English language. For instance, Waters defined the terms 'operations management' and 'a business process' [Waters 2001, pp. 15, 20]. Sudoł [Godziszewski, Haffer, Stankiewicz, 2011, pp. 359–360] explains that the former encompasses all vertical structures and units in the organisation that have some role in management processes. This explanation is consistent with how the term is understood by Waters [Waters 2001, p. 10], who made a point of not equating operations management with the lowest level of management in the organisation. Waters indicates that because the early studies aimed to boost productivity in factories their focus was on the manufacture of physical goods. It was not until much later that their scope was extended to services. Because now the two types of economic activities are understood to have the same scope, wider definitions are needed to describe them: operations management and a business process. For Waters, a **business process** is sequences of actions called key processes that are directly or indirectly related to the delivery of physical goods or services that create value for customers or other interested parties. Because in this chapter the focus is on the manufacturers of physical goods, a narrower term – **a production process** – will be used henceforth.

An analysis of the views of researchers representing various schools of economics shows that value and its determinants are understood differently. Even so, a more general conclusion can be drawn that the concepts of value developed by particular schools concentrate on philosophical value and economic value (utilitarian and measurable) [Michalczuk 2013, p. 9]. When the scope of analysis is limited to the views of researchers exploring organisation and management problems, we can see that they give priority to economic values. These values can be identified by establishing goals pursued by companies. Rappaport [1999, p. 5] indicates that different entities have different expectations as to what goals companies should work towards and proposes a classification of the goals. One of the specific goals is earning profits. Noga [2009, pp. 112–120] argues, however, that the behaviour of companies in today's world cannot be explained only on the grounds of profit maximisation or the traditional neoclassical principle of rational management. While the author of this chapter agrees with this opinion, the scope of the conducted research was limited to this field of economic knowledge that concentrates on the sources and determinants of profits. The amount of profits earned by companies delivering seasonal products depends above all on the **production cycle**, the efficiency of which is measured by units of time that are necessary to complete production. The number of these units is determined by the complexity of the product (which has a bearing on how long technical and technological solutions will be prepared), workers' skills and the organisation of the production process. The length of the production cycle also indicates how long the company's working capital will be tied up, which will not bring profits until the cycle is completed. The model of the production process cycle presented in section 5 has been constructed on the basis of empirical research.

The last notion used in the title to this part of the chapter has been defined by the European Commission. According to the EC, **seasonal products** are goods that are not available to consumers in certain periods or whose volumes are too small for their prices to be observed in certain cyclical periods (these criteria are met by some vegetables and fruits, clothing and footwear) [*Commission Regulation*, 2009]. The presented research focuses on the production of clothing. Clothing is an everyday product, which provides a reason to believe that the research results will prove interesting. The amount of time during which seasonal products can be sold is short not because of the fact that at some point they stop being attractive, but because seasons change external conditions, which means that the producer cannot control them. According to Eurostat data [ec.europa.eu/eurostat], the textile and clothing industry in the Community consists of 220,000 enterprises employing 2,500,000 people (plus those in the so-called grey economy).

The annual output of the industry is estimated at € 190 billion, which constitutes 3 % of value added generated by all industries in the EU. As reported by the British Fashion Council, the total value of goods that the country's clothing industry delivers every year amounts to £ 20.9 billion. Its contribution to UK's GDP is twice as big as that made by the automotive and chemical industries together (approx. £ 10 bn. each) and only slightly smaller than the shares of the telecommunications industry (£ 28.7 bn.) or of the real estate market (£ 26.4 bn.) [Rabij, www.nesweek.l/wiadomoci/busines]. The textile and clothing industry continues, therefore, to be a major manufacturing industry in the EU, which provides a strong argument for making efforts to attain the main objective of this chapter.

2. A process-based approach to the production cycle of seasonal products

Managing a company is based on the processing of internal and external information in order to formulate goals, decisions and tasks [Bednarek 2007, p. 39]. According to Hammer and Stanton, a process-centred enterprise is an optimal organisational formula for the constantly changing world [Hammer, Stanton 2003, p. 99]. The formula focuses on companies' strategies with a view to improving their efficiency and effectiveness, and to making successes sustainable thanks to planning and management systems [Horvath & Partner 2005, p. 4]. Sułkowski [2004, p. 47] indicates that the main advantage of the process-based management is its orientation to changes and its ability to introduce changes as soon as they are necessary. Process-based management consists of planning, organising, managing and controlling changes in processes that create customer value [Engelhardt 2014, p. 38]. The results of the author's own research (see section 4) have also shown that exogenous and endogenous changes may significantly affect production. Hammer and Champy [1994, pp. 32–33], too, concentrate on processes rather than jobs, human resources, structures and functions, which allows them to maintain focus on the main goal of a process instead of following its elements, which are imperceptible for the customer and therefore secondary. In this research, the process-based approach to the production cycle was also adopted to enable the transition from improving the company's functions to improving its processes [Davenport 1993]. That such transition is necessary is stressed by many authors [Grajewki, Nogalski 2004, p. 60; Grunberg 2003]. Krzos [2004, p. 265] argues that this switch in approach involves the replacement of traditional management methods addressing elementary operations with a holistic view of the process and the need to improve it throughout. A process-based approach was a prerequisite for conducting this research. For instance, it enabled the division of clothing production into four subprocesses:

- the preparation of designs and the production of the garment prototype (product creation),
- manufacturing planning (technical, technological, and organisational decisions, required materials and supplies),
- manufacturing and quality assessment of the product,
- sale and customer service.

The above division and the descriptions of particular subprocesses (for details see subsections 2.1, 2.2, 2.3, 2.4) are based on the results of the author's empirical research. The same research provided information necessary to achieve the intermediate goal of constructing a production cycle model for seasonal products (section 5), which preceded the creation of a method for investigating changes in production. The model was built for lack of universal models in the pertinent literature.

2.1. The preparation of designs and the making of a garment prototype

In Tidd and Bessant's [2011, p. 527], the development of a new product is presented as a process of transition from an idea to a successful product, which consists of several stages. In each stage, new problems are solved and uncertainty is reduced. Moreover, as the process moves on from concept generation through the making of decisions about the method of its implementation to choosing the manner of production, the market knowledge and the technological knowledge are put together. A similar approach should be used to create seasonal products, which also need to be made in a structured manner. A useful example of such an approach can be a simplified model drawing on Tidd's and Bodley's [2002, pp. 127–138] four stages that will be described more in detail in this subsection. These stages are the following:

- the generation of a concept (designing),
- the evaluation of designs (designs failing to meet the established criteria are eliminated),
- product development (designs are converted into prototypes),
- commercialisation (the product is put on the market and sold).

Inspiration for new products comes from exogenous and endogenous sources of information. How much each of the two sources contributes to the creation of new designs can be estimated on the strength of the results of a questionnaire survey with 750 directors of firms located in different parts of the world. According to the respondents, a typical research and development activity (R&D) generates only 14 % of innovations in their organisations, while employees and customers account, respectively, for as much as 41 % and 36 % [Peppers, Rogers 2007, p. 13]. These percentages should be treated as specific to this survey.

In her research, the author concentrated on **seasonal collections of clothing** that producers offer to customers such as wholesalers and chains of shops. A collection of seasonal products can be defined as a set of garment prototypes coordinated in terms of style and colour, which is put on the market as fashion and seasons change. The biggest producers of clothing deliver four collections a year, but two collections are much more common: one for the spring / summer season (in shops from early February) and the other for the autumn / winter season (starting early September). By making two collections, firms can minimise the costs of introducing them to the market and make their products more competitive. The term '**garment prototype**' used in the definition above should be understood as denoting a physical representation of the drawings prepared by the designer. Being a creation of an artist, the new garment is protected by copyright. This means that imitations, which are frequent in the case of popular brands of clothing, are punishable under the law. To avoid legal problems, all items constituting a seasonal collection should be 100 % original.

For a seasonal collection to be created, inputs from many sources of information are necessary. The more diverse the information is, the higher the probability of interesting designs being created [Zahay, Gryfin, Fredericks 2004, pp. 658–659]. The types of information necessary to design garments are the following:

- style and colour trends for the new season,
- the results of surveys of the target market segment,
- the rules of garment construction and technology of manufacturing.

Information about style and colour trends for the new season is gathered by agencies that specialise in preparing forecasts. The agencies seek data on the living and working conditions, leisure activities, new developments in art and music and changes in the economy, and then use them to forecast trends for several years ahead. This process is burdened by uncertainties, so the risk of the designers' presenting incompatible seasonal collections is fairly high, though partly mitigated by the fact that the services of consultancies such as WGSN.com or Style.com are used by most firms in the clothing industry. Colour trends have been predicted for more than 10 years now by the *Pantone Color Institute*, which prepares its forecasts using the opinions of designers, manufacturers and the results of consumer surveys. The colour palettes which the Institute proposes are important for many industries, including the clothing industry. The most important source of information on styles is premiere vision shows, which are organised biannually in Milan, Paris and New York with the participation of the most prominent creators of fashion who present their collections there. The shows are also an opportunity for designers and journalists from many countries to purchase the hard or electronic copies of catalogues with specific design guidelines, e.g. the recommended length and fit between the garment and the body, etc., as well as with a wealth of construction drawings. Attending the shows is also a chance to meet with other designers and to participate in panel discussions where information additional to that contained in the catalogues can be obtained. Another group of users of the design guidelines is journalists writing about fashion and thus driving the emergence of new fashion trends. Trendsetters have a similar role because the way they dress is quickly copied and disseminated by increasing groups of followers.

As a source of information, market surveys offer a wider perspective on clothing products [Luca, Atuaehbe—Gima 2007]. Surveys are vital to the domestic economy and transnational corporations because they allow them to adapt their products to the needs of local customers. They are equally important for medium and small-sized enterprises. Market surveys are mainly conducted to render decision making less risky when uncertainty is substantial [Düssel 2010, p. 50] and to build databases containing attractive garment prototypes (in terms of their design, quality and price) in an interaction with the customers. Many methods are used to conduct market surveys [Düssel 2010, pp. 54–61], but they will not be presented as they are outside the scope of this research. Market information is never comprehensive, so premiere vision shows indicating what Zara, H&M or the Polish company Reserved will sell through their chain shops must also be taken into account in designing seasonal collections.

Polish designers learn to construct garments and acquire the knowledge of manufacturing technologies at school. The Department of Fabrics and Clothes at the Łódź Academy of Fine Arts (ASP) and the Department of Clothing Technology at the Łódź University of Technology have entered into cooperation to make this education more effective. This arrangement gives the future ASP graduates a chance to cooperate with professional garment constructors and technologists that have both theoretical knowledge and hands-on experience. When the designer, the constructor and the technologist work together on a garment prototype, there is a great chance of the production process being optimised. Manufacturing methods, machines and equipment evolve with technological progress, meaning that the knowledge of garment construction and manufacturing technologies must be improved on an on-going basis. A breakthrough technology that has substantially changed the way clothing is manufactured has been the partial replacement of stitched joints with adhesive bonding. Not only has this new technology reduced the amount of time needed to manufacture apparel, improved its quality, appearance and comfort of wear, but it has also made articles of clothing more resistant to maintenance and care processes. Adhesive bonding still seems to have plenty to offer and further advances in the technology can be expected. But adhesive bonding is not the only attempt at replacing traditional technologies with solutions that are more up-to-date. As technologies change, modifications are introduced to the construction of machines used in the clothing industry and vice versa: new machines drive the creation of new technologies, such as those enabling the personalisation of clothing. A pertinent example is the Galvo-type laser made by Galaxy, which offers many options of decorating parts of garments (local discolouring, the creation of all sorts of images) without the necessity to prepare costly matrices. The evolution of the clothing industry causes the necessity to constantly update the knowledge of the garment construction rules and of manufacturing technologies. Because barriers hindering the absorption of this knowledge were found to be considerable, the author decided to investigate their nature [Grandys 2008]. Studies undertaken by other authors aimed to facilitate the diffusion of knowledge about innovations and to eliminate obstacles to their implementation [Rogut, Piasecki 2007].

To design garments, a full set of information, a talented designer and the person's ability to convert guidelines of the global fashion creators into a seasonal collection of clothing are necessary. In the next phase, the design of a particular garment (drawings) is used to construct a 3D model called a prototype. This work is performed in the design room, which is a unit within the organisation where the constructors and the designer discuss the decomposition of the design into its structural elements, the fit between the garment and the body, and the characteristics which the fabric should have. This leads to the preparation of master patterns, i.e. templates corresponding to the particular parts of the prototype. Master patterns can be made with the use of a variety of methods [Więźlak, Elmrych-Bocheńska, Zieliński 2009, pp. 104–111], but in most cases, computer systems with software developed on the basis of empirical methods of construction are employed. The best-known computerised patternmaking systems are produced by Gerber (the company pioneered the use of computers in the construction of clothing), Investronica, and Lectra. The systems allow for a considerable reduction of the amount of time necessary to make patterns. To find out if the patterns match the original design, a prototype of the garment is prepared. It is necessary that the prototype should be made by the most skilful workers in the company, with excellent manual skills and capable of creative thinking, as practice shows that they can frequently make valuable suggestions on the construction of the prototype, thus improving the wearability of the final product or facilitating its manufacturing [Szatkowski 2008, p. 76]. The completed prototype is evaluated in terms of its aesthetics, practicality (seam strength, the comfort of wear, pilling, colourfastness, etc.) and economics (the cost of manufacturing). The scope of the evaluation is regulated by the in-house standards, which must be at least as strict as the applicable national and international standards. The approved prototype is added to the seasonal collection of clothing that the manufacturer will sell through its own outlets or chain shops.

2.2. Manufacturing planning – techniques, technologies, supplies and organisation

Manufacturing planning requires substantial knowledge and experience, the extent of which must correspond to the type of the product to be made. The characteristics of the subprocesses constituting this activity will be presented below on the basis of the observations which the author made in the clothing industry. Therefore, manufacturing planning consists of:

- the determination of the sequence of operations needed to make a product,
- the estimation of unit material requirements,
- the calculation of direct costs per unit product,
- the specification of the necessary equipment and machines,
- manufacturing planning.

The technology of manufacturing is developed by a technologist on the basis of their knowledge, experience and intuition. Most companies do not have among their staff skilled technologists who could design a technology consistent with the required optimality parameters [Szatkowski 2008, p. 98]. Some solution to this problem can be dedicated computer-controlled systems, provided that appropriate databases have been created for them beforehand. An example of an advanced system of this type is Computer-Aided Manufacturing (CAM). The author pioneered the implementation of a CAM system in Poland in 1987. The descriptions of this process can be found in her publications from that period. A CAM system can, either automatically or controlled by an operator, perform the following operations:

- grade patterns,
- arrange patterns for all types of fabrics,
- calculate material consumption standards,

- prepare paper markers in the required scale (usually 1:1) or send data to a computerised cutting machine in the cutting room (then fabric, lining, stiffening interlinings, insulating interlining, etc. are cut automatically).

From the perspective of manufacturing planning, it is irrelevant whether the product will be made in-house or outsourced to an external service provider (Polish clothing companies tend to use the latter option to reduce costs) [Grandys, Grandys 2008]. The important factors are the type of materials and supplies, the availability of machines and equipment and workers' skills because all of these have a bearing on what type of manufacturing technology will be implemented. The list of the sequence of activities constituting the subprocess of manufacture depends on the experience of the technologist. The degree to which this experience can be useful in making a new product is determined by the product's similarity to those for which manufacturing technologies have already been developed. Together with the manufacturing plan, the specification of machines and equipment for particular manufacturing operations and their standard times are worked out. The rules for calculating the times can be found in the pertinent literature [Szatkowski 2008, p. 106–108]. The technical and technological documentation is used to organise the work team and to calculate the pay of the piecework workers, direct manufacturing costs, etc.

The specification of activities which constitute the manufacturing subprocess is preceded by the activities preparing the procurement of the necessary fabrics and supplies. These activities are not only important to the company, but also consume substantial amounts of financial resources. Managing the procurement of hundreds of items is a very important task because the consequences of deliveries coming late or in smaller amounts than ordered can be very serious. If, in the course of manufacturing, fabrics are found to have flaws, the company may be exposed to serious losses; the situation is even worse if they are found afterwards by the customer. It is therefore very important for the company board to make sure that the procurement department has the right kind of specialists [Ciesielski 2006, p. 110]. The fabrics they purchase have already been selected by the designers on the basis of their knowledge of textiles and ideas gained at international fairs or from the representatives of textiles producers who do the rounds presenting the samples of available products. On these occasions, prices and financial terms of deliveries are negotiated (whether the advance payment should cover part or the full amount of the delivery, whether the payment will be required on delivery or several or more weeks later). In the negotiations, the clothing company is represented by its procurement staff, who use their knowledge and experience to optimise the costs of deliveries [Mead, Andrews 2011, pp. 184–193]. Polish manufacturers of clothing use fabrics made in the European Union (for high-end products) or in Asian countries (all other products). This geographical division of suppliers is mainly based on the quality, wearability and prices of fabrics. Most contracts for fabrics are concluded under the pressure of time because high quality fabrics are not manufactured until an order is placed. Depending on the type of raw materials and the particular method of manufacturing, an order may take as long as three months to be completed. The numbers of garments that will be made for each prototype included in the seasonal collection must therefore be calculated before the manufacturing subprocess is planned. More details on procurement strategies [Wojciechowski 2002, pp. 173–180; Cole, Bardi, Langley 2002, p. 150] and the powers and responsibilities of the procurement staff can be found in the pertinent literature [Muhlemann, Oakland, Lockyer 1992, pp. 516–524; Pająk 2007, pp. 203–215].

The manufacturing plan is prepared after the technical and technological aspects of manufacturing have been agreed upon. Manufacturing planning is an undertaking that aims to streamline the course of manufacturing operations. The term 'undertaking' denotes an organised and purposeful human activity that must be carried out within a fixed period with the use of a predetermined amount of human resources, technical means, energy, funds and information. It is a sequence of interrelated actions performed in an established order; an action cannot start unless the preceding ones have been completed, although some actions can be carried out at the same time [Jędrzejczak, Kukuła, Skrzypek, Walkosz 2004, p. 180]. This definition of an organisational plan implies that information from many sources is needed to prepare it. As regards clothing companies, the types of information they need to set up the manufacturing subprocess are the following:

- human resources (where, when and how many workers with specific skills will be needed),
- equipment and machines (how many and what types of machines must be available in work areas at particular times),
- fabrics and supplies (the type and optimal quantities of fabrics or semi-finished goods that workers must be supplied with at particular times).

The labour and technological demands set out in the manufacturing plan differ in specificity depending on the company size. In organisations that **outsource** [Trocki 2006, p. 34] the manufacturing of their products to external providers, the main purpose of a manufacturing plan is to ensure the coordination between:

- the dates when fabrics should be delivered to the company and then shipped to the service provider,

- the technological capabilities of the service provider and the technological demands of manufacturing,
- the date when manufacturing should end and the date when finished products must be shipped to the buyer.

Polish clothing industry started providing garment assembly services to companies in Western Europe and the US in the 1970s. In 1998, with the Polish market becoming part of the Single European Market, clothing accounted for 93 % of the total export of the domestic textile and clothing sector [Garczyński 2003]. Most clothing was exported under apparel assembly services. The transition period that started in Poland in the late 1980s radically changed the business environment of Polish companies and today the services are offered much less frequently. Foreign companies still use Polish producers to make products targeted at high-end customers because they offer high quality of workmanship and charge relatively low prices, which gives them advantage over their competitors. Big and medium-sized companies in Poland have become clients themselves and use Asian producers to deliver mass-produced goods. Small runs of garments for the high-end market are made in-house or through local producers. A clothing company choosing to manufacture garments in-house must decide about the most appropriate system of manufacturing (an assembly line, an assembly line with sections, sections with synchronised work teams, a flow system or an arrhythmic system) [Więźlak, Elmrych-Bocheńska, Zieliński 2009, pp. 132–137]. A manufacturing plan must also indicate the number of garments per order, whether some of the garments can be made simultaneously, etc. Its purpose is to reduce the manufacturing time to the necessary minimum and to ensure that the quality of the products will meet the demands of the target market segment.

2.3. Product manufacturing and quality assessment

The manufacturing subprocess consists of fabric cutting and the assembly of cut components. The technological aspects of these two tasks are explained in the technical and technological documentation and the organisational aspects in the manufacturing plan. The key operations within the first task are the following:

- fabric spreading,
- placing the marker on the layup,
- fabric cutting (using computer-controlled systems, stationary cutters, portable oscillating knives, die cutters),
- the application of adhesive interlinings to the cut components to stiffen or reinforce them,

- numbering the cut components and the evaluation of their quality,
- the bundling of patterns into units for sewing teams.

The critical operation in this sequence is fabric cutting because it determines the output of cut components. A steady flow of work to the cutting machine can be ensured by one of two methods. The first of them involves the spreading of additional fabric layups, but then the amount of work in progress is increased. In the other method, fabric layups are created dynamically on at least two tables. When the operation is well synchronised, there is no risk that the amount of work in progress might increase, but the cutting room must be sufficiently large for this approach to be used. The best productivity and coordination of tasks in the cutting room can be obtained, though, when automated solutions are used. This leads to the conclusion that the organisation of the first stage of product manufacturing is mainly determined by the stock of machines the company has.

In the second stage of the manufacturing subprocess, the work team is formed according to the technical and technological documentation and test garments are made. Whether and how many test garments will be necessary is decided between the technologist and the work team manager. The need for preparing test garments usually arises when the product is new or the technological operations it involves are particularly difficult. Cut patterns are joined by stitching, adhesive bonding and thermal bonding. It is estimated that the stitched joints account for around 70–80 % of all joints in a garment (in the clothing industry, stitched joints are made with the use of all-purpose sewing machines, semi-automated machines and automated sewing machines; garment complexity causes, however, the situation whereby the latter can only be used to perform some selected stitching operations or to stitch together simple products such as tablecloths or towels). The remaining over 20 % of joints is made with the use of adhesives [Więźlak, Elmrych-Bocheńska, Zieliński 2009, p. 323]. Depending on the technology used, adhesive joints are divided into glued, thermal bonded and welded. In the clothing industry, glue bonding is the most common. The operation is performed by a fusing machine that heats a glue-coated element on one side until the glue melts and then applies mechanical pressure to form a bond. Adhesive bonding significantly reduces the amount of time necessary to make a garment, so technologists constantly seek new uses for this method.

The thermal processing of garments is used during the assembly stage as well as afterwards. In the case of the high-end garments, the method is used particularly frequently because it can improve their appearance and correct minor flaws in workmanship. The thermal processing machines can:

- give shape to garments (by applying temperature, mechanical pressure and steam),
- improve products by pleating, applying images transferred from paper, permanent pressing, etc.,
- steam garments to correct minor flaws in workmanship or to refresh clothing that spent a long time in shipment (e.g. in boxes transported from Asia),
- press stitches between assembly operations, which will be inaccessible after the lining is set in,
- perform the final pressing (this process is decisive for the quality of garments, so companies make substantial investments in specialist equipment and machines).

The quality of stitched and adhesive joints and of thermal processing is very important for the final appearance of a garment, so companies establish specific quality standards for them. During the whole process of manufacture, trained members of the staff make random quality checks, as well as help to solve problems as they arise. All small-run garments made for the high-end market are inspected for quality before shipment. The quality of mass-produced garments is evaluated on the basis of their samples, the size of which is prescribed by in-house standards (garment quality is discussed at greater length in section 3).

2.4. Sale and customer service

The subprocess of distribution consists of activities that the company undertakes to deliver its products to the final consumer [Kotler, Armstrong, Saunders, Wong 2002, p. 142]. Most clothing companies in Poland do this through their sales departments. The sales department of a manufacturing company is an organisational solution that allows customers to conduct wholesale trade without intermediaries [Armstrong, Kotler 2011,p. 518]. The design and structure of the department are covered more widely in the literature on this subject [Kotler, Keller 2011, pp. 529–601]. A valuable Polish contribution to this field is the monograph edited by M. Ciesielski [2006, pp. 128–149]. In this chapter, the distribution subprocess is not discussed in detail, as it lies outside the scope of the production cycle model for seasonal products.

The above descriptions of the production process are based on the author's findings and her 17-year-long experience as a manager in the clothing industry. They seem to be specific enough to enable the construction of a production process cycle model for seasonal products (section 5), in which time is the central parameter. In section 3, the critical role of time in managing the production of this type of products will be demonstrated.

Part II. The role of time and of exogenous and endogenous factors in the production of seasonal products

3. Time – a key parameter in the production of seasonal products

Managing the time variable is a crucial factor allowing companies to optimise the production process. Limited availability of time is the strongest motivator today; it offers opportunities to improve performance, but in some cases, it can be an expression of formalisation [Komorowski 2011, p. 334]. The time pressure involved in designing and marketing a product is of strategic importance for the competitive position of a company and its revenues [Morgan, Levitt, Malek 2010, p. 180]. Because each production process is a function of time, the literature recognises time as one of the three aspects of operations management (in addition to goal contents and the absolute or relative dimension of a goal) [Banaszyk, Urbanowska-Sojkin, Witczak 2004, pp. 303–304]. The results of the author's research into the clothing industry confirm that this is actually the case. In the case of her research, the contents of the goal of operations management were the production of seasonal products and the dimension was defined by:

- the garment prototype selected for production,
- order size,
- the expected garment quality,
- productivity as a ratio between inputs used in the production process and its output,
- the order completion date.

The list shows that time is not only one of the parameters used in operations management, but also an integral element of the goal dimension. Because of its importance, its role in the production of seasonal products will be discussed in more detail.

The term 'prototype' was already defined when the design and prototype construction subprocess was explained. A specific garment prototype indicated by the customer in the order is an obligation for the clothing company to start manufacturing. How long manufacturing will take depends on when fabrics will be delivered and on how much time is needed to develop technical and technological documentation indicating the labour intensity of the selected manufacturing technology. Labour intensity is determined by the type of fabrics to be used, the complexity of garment construction and the degree to which manufacturing can be automated. The amount of time necessary to complete an order is therefore directly determined by the characteristics of the ordered garment.

It is obvious that **the size of the order** (a sum of orders for particular prototypes) must affect the duration of production. This duration is basically determined by the number of garments to be made for each prototype, but only in companies that complete orders using their own resources because then the maximum number of the same-design products that can be made is limited by the order completion date, which naturally limits the length of manufacturing. The minimum size of an order depends on the break-even-point, i.e. a point at which the company's profits on sales are zero [Froeb, McCann 2012, p. 70]. In the case of companies that decide to manufacture their products through external service providers, the maximum order size is not limited by the duration of the manufacturing subprocess, but by the seasonality of apparel sales, causing the necessity to end its manufacturing by a fixed date. The order size is, therefore, another factor influencing the length of the manufacturing subprocess.

Still another factor is the **expected product quality**, which must be consistent with what the target customers expect. When products are required to meet more stringent quality standards, better materials must be used and the precision of manufacturing must be given more attention. Because garments are largely made by humans operating machines, the expectation of higher quality must naturally prolong the manufacturing subprocess. This prolongation can only partly be reduced by improving the human-to-machine labour ratio. Both buyers and clothing manufacturers must be aware of the consequences of unreasonably high quality expectations. Expectations of higher quality increase manufacturing costs and thereby the price of the product. Only high-end customers consider the price of a garment to be secondary to its quality. The expected product quality is defined in line with the buyer's expectations in the technical and technological documentation (providing workmanship standards, accuracy tolerances, etc.) and its physical exemplification is the prototype. The prototype has a dual role: 1) it shows what quality characteristics the product should have and 2) serves as a benchmark for mass-produced garments. To sum up, the expectations of high quality increase the amount of time needed to manufacture a garment.

Another element of the goal dimension is **productivity.** Its costs are expressed through the normal depreciation of production factors (arising from the organisation and technology of manufacturing) and economic (income generating) depreciation of these factors [Stabryła 2000, p. 326]. The first part of this definition clearly points to productivity being related to the length of manufacturing. This subject will be elaborated on in section 6, which deals with the construction of the production management model for seasonal products. At this point, let us only formulate a hypothesis that the duration of manufacture is determined by productivity and manufacturing techniques used.

The order completion date depends on when the manufacturing subprocess started and on the durations of individual tasks on the critical path [Rangaswamy, Lilien 1997, pp. 177–184]. That this element of the goal dimension is correlated with time (which distinguishes it from the elements presented above) does not have to be proved because the order completion date is clearly expressed in units of time. The only comment that should be made here is that the date depends on when earlier subprocesses ended.

The critical role of time as a parameter in the production of seasonal products does not need a special proof either. The range of clothing products available on the market changes with seasons. A season lasts three months, but only global players (e.g. the Spanish group Inditex, which has in its portfolio brands such as Zara, Bershka, Stradivarius, Massimo Dutti, etc.) work at this frequency, delivering fabrics and supplies to their contractors every three months and receiving finished garments every week to sell them through their chains of shops [O'Shea 2008, p. 152]. Most clothing companies try to economise by launching two seasonal collections a year: one for the spring-summer season (early February) and one for the autumn-winter season (early September). Regardless of whether two or four collections are marketed, the selling period for clothing is always shorter than for other consumer products, which is by no means related to their becoming unattractive. Krzos [2004, p. 258] stresses that time is important throughout the production process, arguing that time minimisation has many aspects because this function occurs in many areas. Morgan, Levitt and Malek analyse time in the context of sales [Morgan, Levitt, Malek 2010, pp. 70–71]. In Byrne [2013], the importance of time in company management is highlighted already in the introduction to his book. In the scheduling of the production of seasonal goods, time plays a central role, too, and the critical moment is the start date for the sales subprocess. All the other subprocesses must be coordinated with the date, as will be demonstrated after the construction of the production cycle model for seasonal products in section 5.

4. Changes in the factors determining the production of seasonal products

Anyone managing a company in the 21st century must accept the fact that economic realities are changeable and complex, and that human resources, capital and technical means must be effectively and skilfully combined within manufacturing processes. The awareness of these requirements allows flexible reactions to changes as they occur [Łukasiński 2014, p. 37]. In business terms, a **change** is a modification to the way an organisation has acted so far in the „hard" sphere (structures and processes, etc.) and in the „soft" sphere (attitudes and behaviours) [Fisk 2014, p. 241]. Kotler and Caslione [2009, p. 89] indicate the main causes of changes and explain how organisations (including enterprises) can adapt their behaviour in different areas of the business model (resources, clients, partners, etc.). Brilman [2002, p. 288] presents the characteristics of a process-centred enterprise, focusing on the management of improvements and changes. Prahalad and Krishnan [2010,pp. 186–188] view all changes as tendencies that will determine the character of the relations between consumers and firms and between firms, as well as the direction of the evolution of cooperation among firms. These tendencies include the convergence of communications technologies, easy access to computational technologies and tools and experiments with new platforms enabling cooperation. All this implies that organisations are surrounded by closer and more distant circles of changes, which differ in terms of the strength of their impact [Komorowski 2011, p. 65]. The works mentioned allow concluding that when conditions are changing and archetypes are not available, managers must make decisions and solve problems based on their knowledge, experience and intuition. The steady development of management science should make it easier for them.

There are two types of changes that can alter the course of production: planned and unplanned. A **planned change** is the most effective when the people in charge of it show personal commitment to convincing others that a change is needed, explain what it should be like and how it can be achieved [Foster, Kaplan 2001, p. 279]. A planned change may become necessary because a new event has occurred in the environment of the organisation, such as the lowering of barriers restricting trade and international cooperation. Another reason may be the company's decision to redefine its strategy (Morgan, Levitt and Malek [2010, p. 25] have formulated six imperatives for redefining a strategy). Failing to keep pace with changes may have far-reaching consequences. For instance, Pascale [1990, p. 11] mentions 143 companies that were dropped from Fortune's list of 500 largest organisations as a result. At the other end of the spectrum, there is the international success of Benetton, a recognised Italian clothing company. One of its sources was Benetton's realisation that consumers in different regions have different tastes and preferences [Vignali 1999, pp. 48–52]. As a result of Benetton's approach, the branches of transnational corporations were given a greater strategic role, which increased their contribution to regional development [Kuemmerle 1999, pp. 1–24]. Benetton is not thought to be a particularly fashionable brand of clothing, but it has its own distinctive style. Consumers know that even though the style remains the same year by year, colours reflect the latest trends [Vignali 1998, pp. 149–161].

When planned and unplanned changes are extensive and multidirectional, they exert strong influence on all institutions, including enterprises. It is therefore worth asking what causes changes in enterprises and where they arise. The question has been answered by Osterwalder and Pigneur [Osterwalder, Pigneur 2012, p. 214], who point to the impacts of market and industry forces, and to major macroeconomic trends and developments that create the possibility of delineating "a design space" where new ideas can be formulated. It was one of such design spaces that the author used to create her Production Process Control Tree, a method for investigating production changes, which will be presented in section 7.

Fisk [2014, p. 241] views change management as a process whose aim is to ensure efficient operation of a company. Until recently, the process concentrated on quality and firms' performance, but now, according to Fisk, stronger emphasis is given to external changes induced by forces that organisations cannot control. While doing her research, the author of this chapter could observe irregularities in production processes whose source was external, i.e. **unplanned changes**. An extreme example of unforeseen external changes affecting companies is the surprising result of Polish parliamentary elections (4 June 1989), which led to the establishment of a new political system that laid foundations for a new economic reality [Grandys 2007]. The new situation enabled productivity increases, improved the competitiveness of the entire economy and opened up the path to socially and economically sustainable development [Commission of the European Communities 2002, p. 4]. An exciting and challenging time came for textile producers, when the oldest manufacturing industry in the world became one of the fastest developing industries [Henderson 1996, p. 95]. With changing environment in which companies had operated so far, it became necessary to expand the knowledge of production management, also by research conducted by scientific institutions [Kotler, Caslione 2009]. As a result, new management methods are developed or the existing ones are improved with changes in the market and products made for it. Companies also gain new knowledge through intra and inter-industry diffusions [Chen 1996, p. 186], which transform management systems and organisational structures. All the authors mentioned agree that changes also play an important role in company management.

Changes in the production of seasonal products must be analysed in terms of their causes, which may be internal or external to the company. If changes in the production process are the strengths of the company or opportunities, they will become an engine of its growth [Nogalski, Rutka, Wójcik-Karpacz 2007, p. 132]. As observed by the author, planned and unplanned changes may be caused by many factors. The first category of changes and their sources will not be discussed so as not to deviate from the main aim of this chapter. It will be simply assumed that such changes may affect the course of production too. The presentation will focus on unplanned changes, such as belated deliveries of fabrics and other supplies, their unsatisfactory quality, as well as machine and equipment breakdowns. It is just this group of changes that inspired the author to create a method with which they can be investigated and dealt with to mitigate their negative impacts on production (the main objective of the work). In this research, unplanned changes are divided by their source into exogenous (external) changes and endogenous (internal) changes. External changes are independent, meaning that companies cannot control their sources. Internal changes are variations in factors controlled by companies. This subject area will be analysed in the next subsections.

4.1. Exogenous changes in the factors determining the production process

According to available studies, exogenous factors influence the way an organisation acts, but also how it analyses its environment [Hough, White 2004, pp. 781–783]. Grant [2011, p. 86] proposes classifying external impacts by their source into political, economic, social, technological, etc. Factors such as general economic trends, changing demographic structures and social or political trends decide what opportunities or threats a company may face in the future. What is the most important, however, is how these general factors can influence the setting of a company (its suppliers, competitors and customers).

The author has identified many external factors that can variegate the production of seasonal goods (including clothing). One of them is the already mentioned political transition in Poland after 1989, and its far-reaching consequences for the country's economy. Other changes that have had a major influence on the Polish textile and clothing industry are:

- Poland's accession into the World Trade Organisation (WTO) and integration with the European Union;
- China's accession into the World Trade Organisation.

While Poland's accession into the WTO in 1995 and then the country's integration with EU in 2004 were planned changes, the circumstances that enabled these acts (the change of the political system) were not. The changes were so radical and their impact on Polish economy was so strong that they cannot be omitted from this discussion. The primary consequence of these changes was Poland's adoption of the whole *acquis communautaire* resulting from the Treaty [Leonard 2002, p. 314]. This led to increased competition and induced changes in industry because of the so-called industrial policy that Molle [2001, p. 305] defines as a set of measures developed by the government to stimulate the growth of manufacturing firms and to facilitate their structural adjustments towards new conditions in global competition. As regards the Polish textile and clothing industry, the policy imposed the compliance with the provisions of the 1994 GATT, which abolished the restrictions of the Multi-Fibre Arrangement of 1974 protecting the European textiles market. The Agreement on Textiles and Clothing [Porozumienie WTO 2004] that was signed instead during the Uruguay Round removed protective clauses in international trade in textiles and clothing (from early January 2005). All its signatories agreed to introduce measures to make textile markets more accessible, to respect fair trading policies and not to discriminate against imports on the grounds of their origin. As Poland became a EU member on 1 May 2004, the country agreed to implement the external customs tariff and other measures protecting its market in line with the pertinent EU laws. The customs duty rates on clothing provided in the Single Customs Tariff were lower than those in Poland before the integration: the average bound rates for textiles and clothing were 7.9 % in the EU and 13.1 % in Poland [Kaczurba, Kawecka-Wyrzykowska 2002, pp. 108–109]. The necessary reduction in customs duty rates and the obligation to respect EU laws made Polish producers change their business orientation.

The liberalisation of international trade had both positive and negative consequences for the Polish economy. The changes it brought about (from the perspective of companies the changes were external) will not be discussed in greater detail but only mentioned to keep the chapter on track.

- The restrictions which the Polish government imposed on the citizens of the Commonwealth of Independent States (CIS) in January 1998 reduced the export of Polish clothing to these countries. Statistics show a decline from USD 114.6 m in 1997 to USD 97 m in 1999 [Wysokińska 2001].
- The crisis in Asia in 1998 depreciated some Far East currencies, reducing the prices of clothing made in this part of the world. As a result of an inflow of inexpensive clothing to EU markets, the demand for apparel exported from Poland decreased.
- Polish exports of clothing became less competitive after the government increased fiscal burden on companies' wage funds [Urbaniak, Żelazo 2001].
- Substantial imports of second-hand clothing flowed into the Polish market. It is estimated that in 1998 their volume accounted for 90 % of the production capacity of the domestic industry.

This concentration of negative changes threw Polish clothing industry into a crisis and made it reduce its output. Many companies had to file for bankruptcy; others initiated costly and laborious restructuring processes that only some of them completed successfully. Interestingly, in the same economic reality new clothing companies started to be formed. One of them is the Gdańsk-based company LPP SA, established in the early 1990s. Over the years, it has grown to become the largest Polish producer and exporter of clothing. In the middle of 2014, LPP distributed its brands through a chain of 1,488 shops. After the first six months of 2015, the company's net profits amounted to PLN 154.2, being 10 % greater than a year before [www.lppsa.com].

Another exogenous event that significantly affected production and trade in clothing in Poland and other European countries was China's accession into the World Trade Organisation in 2001. After a transitional period during which the Agreement on Textiles and Clothing, concluded in Marrakesh on 15 April 1994, was still in force, China started trading with other WTO members on equal terms. With the clauses protecting trade in textiles and clothing becoming ineffective in the early 2005, the volume of imports from China expanded rapidly. Some contemporary forecasts predicted a decline of the clothing industry in Europe. The low-priced Chinese clothing became less appealing to European customers after they discovered that its quality was below their standards (garments turned out to have limited resistance to pilling, maintenance processes caused deformations, colour fastness was poor, etc.). Moreover, the business conditions in China changed seriously in the last years. The yuan-to-US-dollar exchange rate decreased between 2006 and 2008 by around 26 %. The Chinese government decided to gradually withdraw tax exemptions available to local producers to cut the country's high export surplus [Informator 2008, pp. 42–44]. All these developments increased prices of Chinese clothing and thereby reduced its import to Europe. Of significance is also the agreement that the European Commission and the Chinese Ministry of Trade signed on 9 October 2007. The agreement established a bilateral system for monitoring Chinese exports to EU Member States, which became operational on 1 January 2008. The annual increase allowed for eight categories of products was set at the level of 8–12 % (t-shirts, sweaters, men's trousers, blouses, dresses, bras, bedclothes, linen yarn). Under the agreement, a Chinese producer must apply for an export licence in China and after it has been granted, the producer must seek an import licence in any of the Member States (a double-checking system) [Commission Regulation 18.10.2007]. If the provisions of the agreement were to be breached, the EU may, on a motion from any Member State, introduce measures protecting its market. The agreement contributed to an increase in the production of clothing in European countries such as the UK, Italy and Poland. China started losing its position as the provider of garment assembly services in favour of other Asian countries that do not have any privileges in trade with EU.

The exogenous changes presented above had a significant effect on the production of seasonal goods, including clothing investigated by the author. How strong the effect was is shown in Table 1, which presents the statistics on production and foreign trade in clothing in Poland.

Tab. 1. Production and foreign trade in clothing in Poland (PLN million)

Year	**1995**	**2010**	**2011**	**2012**	**2013**
Total production of clothing	6,648.8	9,210.9	9,591.1	9,539.1	9,712.9
Exports	5,466.5	13,484.1	14,906.1	15,323.3	16,332.4
Imports	6,877.6	13,459.2	14,876.8	14,397.9	14,868.6
The size of the Polish clothing market	8,059.9	9,186.0	9,562.4	8,613.7	8,248.4

Source: calculated by the author on the basis of *Rocznik Statystycznego Przemysłu 1996 i 2014* (p. 81, 403, 408, 412, 416) and *Rocznik Statystycznego Handlu Zagranicznego 1996 i 2014* (p. 47, 54), Wydawnictwo GUS, Warszawa 1996 and 2014.

Of the four columns in Table 1, three contain data spanning the period of 2010–2013 [*Rocznik 2014*] and one shows data on 1995 [*Rocznik 1996*], and was added to illustrate the decrease in production and foreign trade in clothing, mainly caused by exogenous changes. Let us note that the 1995 values are not the lowest the clothing industry recorded after the economic transition started in 1989 because in 1992 the production of clothing was estimated at a total of PLN 3091.1 m.[*Rocznik 1995*] Even so, 1995 was selected as a benchmark for the years 2010–2013 because this year marks the end of turbulent times in the Polish economy. After 2010, the average total production of clothing in Poland was approx. PLN 9500.0 m, so it was greater by 143 % compared with 1995.

Polish customers can buy clothing made in the country as well as imported clothing. Fashion houses from Western Europe offer short-run garments to high-end customers, while mass-produced clothing is delivered to other segments of the market and exported. This explains why the 2012 value of clothing made in the country was PLN 9.5 bn., but exports amounted to PLN 15.3bn. How the values of exports and imports were arrived at must be clarified at this point. For a long time, the Polish Central Statistical Office (GUS) did not separately account for the export and import of clothing and garment assembly services rendered by foreign providers, so the data after 2010 were calculated by adding these two values (for instance, after the 2012 value of clothing exports (PLN 11,880.9 m) was added to the value of garment assembly services (PLN 3,442.6 m), a total value of PLN 15,323.3 m was obtained. Similarly, the 2012 value of clothing imports (PLN 12,631.0 m) plus garment assembly services (PLN 1,776.9 m) produced a total value of PLN 14,397.9 m). In this way, the export and import values after 2010 could be compared with the 1995 data. Clothing exports increased by around PLN 10,860 m (299 %), with most of the exported products (87 %) being sold in developed countries [Grandys, Grandys 2014]. The expansion of Polish producers into international markets was made possible by their knowledge of intercultural negotiations [Chmielecki 2012], market surveys, risk assessment skills and the use of sophisticated marketing tools, which allowed them to gain competitive advantages [Seliga 2012].

The data on imports in Table 1 show similar trends. Their value increased between 2010–2013 and 1995 by approx. PLN 7,990 m, i.e. 216 %. As mentioned above, some imported clothing is also exported from the country. A company that is engaged in both these activities is LPP SA, the largest clothing company in Poland, which outsources its production to Asian countries. Around 1/3 of its receipts comes from sales in the CEE countries (Central and Eastern Europe). The company was planning to open five shops in Germany in the autumn of 2014 to gain a foothold for its further expansion into Western European markets. The conclusion that can be drawn from the above data is that the first response to exogenous changes was the concentration of business activities on the domestic market, and export became necessary only after the market got saturated. The figures in the last line of Table 1 show the size of the domestic market for clothing, which was calculated by subtracting exports from the total production of clothing and adding imports. The resulting value of approx. PLN 8,900bn after 2010 indicates that after 1995 the market expanded by 110 %, as the wealth of Polish society increased.

In the early 1990s, the presented exogenous changes affecting the production of seasonal goods were the main reason for many companies to file for bankruptcy, but for the restructured companies they became growth opportunities. This situation can be summed up by what R. Love of Hewlett-Packard's said, i.e. that changes are so fast these days that reacting to them is a source of competitive advantages for those companies that can actively capitalise on them.

4.2. *Endogenous changes in factors determining the production process*

According to Borowiecki [2010, pp. 409--410], internal factors are related to the actions an organisation takes, its financial situation, material resources, intellectual capital, organisational structure, strategy of development, management methods, entrepreneurialism and ability to innovate and quality of products and services. The list Borowiecki has created is comprehensive and all its items are explained in detail, so discussing them at length would be superfluous considering the purpose of this chapter. It is worth noting, however, that the list shows, in fact, the endogenous sources of possible changes. In the next part of the chapter, the focus will be given to these factors from the list that the author observed during her research. The most frequent endogenous changes will be formed into four groups, following the earlier division of the production process.

The main endogenous changes causing variations in **the garment design and prototype construction subprocess** are delays resulting from:

- limited availability of design information,
- the designer lacking in ideas, belated selection or delivery of fabrics for the prototypes,
- funding not being available in the necessary amounts (to finance market surveys, to buy fabrics, etc.) when it should be available according to the design work schedule.

To be creative, the designer needs three main types of information (for a detailed presentation of their sources, see above): style and colour trends for the new season, the results of surveys of the target clothing market and the knowledge of garment construction rules and manufacturing technologies. Customers' expectations must also be known for a seasonal collection to be created, and fashion trends must be promoted by the media, which have a role in forming the expectations. But even if all necessary design information is available, there is no guarantee that the design work will be completed as scheduled. The speed of designers' work may be reduced by factors that they cannot control, as well as by inefficiencies in the organisation of work or poor discipline. If funding is not available when needed, a seasonal collection may not be ready on time, or substitute materials must be used that will make garments less attractive for the buyers.

If the garment design and prototype construction subprocess is affected by endogenous changes, its tasks must by adjusted accordingly. The available options are the following:

- rather than designing a seasonal collection in-house, a company may decide to use the services of a design firm, e.g. the MMC (the first letters of the designers'

surnames: Majer, Michalak and Czudak), which can design garments meeting the specific needs of the client and guarantees that the designs will be ready on time,
- a company may purchase ready-made designs from individual artists and compose them into a seasonal collection.

The downside of the other option is that it is quite unlikely for the designs to be able to meet all of the company's criteria (its technical and technological capacity may not be fully exploited, etc.). The optimal solution is one that fulfils the design criteria and accommodates a delay, thus enabling the garment design and prototype construction subprocess to end on time. Both presented options increase the costs of the seasonal collection, so the profitability of the whole production process must be analysed. Adopting a solution without an in-depth analysis of its impacts may have far-reaching consequences. A problem that a company choosing the other option may face is the limited number of the providers of clothing design services in Poland. The complexity of the situation means that the choice must be made at the company board level.

Endogenous changes affecting **procurement planning** can also disturb production, sometimes to the extent where its timely completion is at risk. A good illustration of the intricacy of procurement planning is the fact that around 40 items are needed to make an overcoat. Before the manufacturing subprocess can start, all items necessary to make a seasonal collection must be available. Problems may arise due to:

- limited access to information necessary to plan the procurement of fabrics and supplies,
- delayed delivery of fabrics and supplies,
- inefficient organisation of work or poor discipline among staff.

To do their job, a procurement specialist must be in touch with the producers of textiles. First communications can be initiated electronically, but then personal meetings are necessary, since otherwise the physical properties of the available fabrics cannot be evaluated. The best opportunity for such meetings is industry fairs (domestic and international), where many producers come at the same time to promote their products. Their stalls are visited by procurement specialists and designers, who screen fabrics and gather information about the terms of transactions (prices, lead times, minimum orders for patterned or unicolour fabrics, the terms of payment, etc.). Most producers offer samples of fabrics that clothing companies can test for physical properties and patterns in-house, and decide whether they are suitable for the designed garments. The members of staff who are involved in the preparation of the seasonal collection must have unrestricted access to fabrics. Attempts at minimising the costs of business trips, limitations on telephone calls or the use of company cars, etc. may cause delays in production. It is also important to remember that good relations between the producer of clothing and the producer of textiles provide grounds for the effective negotiation of contracts and optimal claim handling procedures.

On the basis of the contract for the delivery of fabrics, their producer can start manufacturing them in amounts and colours required by the client. This procedure applies to fabrics that will be made into garments for the high-end customer and that have high unit costs. It may take as long as three months for the fabrics to be ready, depending on the type of raw materials, the manufacturing technology, expected quality, etc. In other words, the date when the fabrics can be delivered to the clothing company depends on when the contract was signed and on its terms. For instance, some producers of textiles want the customer to make an advance payment or to pay the full value of the contract upfront. Protracted negotiations, a contract that is signed too late, failure to make payments on dates indicated in the contract or to meet other contractual obligations may delay the delivery of fabrics. In some cases, shipments are delayed due to the inefficiency of the textiles producer. One of the responsibilities of the procurement specialist is therefore to investigate the commercial integrity of the supplier (whether they deliver fabrics of the requested quality, whether deliveries arrive on time, etc.).

There are two types of fabrics that clothing companies use. One is readily-available on the market (shirt fabrics, clothing fabrics, fleece, etc.) and the other is classified as articles of fashion. The problem with the other type of fabrics is that they practically cannot be replaced with different materials. This means that changes in dates of their delivery provide a reason for the clothing company to go back on the contract (this involves the payment of contractual fines to its customers). Alternatively, if the delay is relatively insignificant, the company may decide to put off the manufacturing start date. A seasonal collection being sold later than agreed with its buyers also involves the payment of contractual fines, but their amount can be offset against the fines the supplier of fabrics will have to pay. In some cases, it is better to put off the sale of a seasonal collection instead of selling the part of it that has been completed. The best approach, however, is to take all possible precautions to protect the production of seasonal goods (particularly clothing) against the consequences of belated deliveries of fabrics and supplies.

Other important endogenous factors that can cause variations in the **manufacturing planning subprocess** (involving the determination of the technical, technological and organisational aspects of manufacturing) are the following:

- the preceding tasks were completed later than planned or the information necessary to prepare the plan is incomplete;
- a great number of garment sizes in the order, fabric patterns of the kind that needs special attention to ensure pattern consistency, etc. resulting in a situation whereby planning takes longer than planned;
- the company not having a computerised system which facilitates manufacturing planning,
- inefficient organisation of work or poor discipline of staff.

The manufacturing plan is created on the basis of information delivered by various units in the organisation. The design department initiates planning works by providing patterns for grading and the prototype demonstrating how the garment should be made. The production control department prepares a schedule of manufacturing, which indicates what must be done and when, and which work team will be involved. The schedule is prepared in cooperation with the procurement department, which is responsible for working out the materials delivery timetable. The maintenance department must make sure that all necessary machines and equipment will be in working order and available where and when needed. The sales department sets the dates when the manufacture of the seasonal collection must end. The manager in charge of manufacturing planning must be a competent person, capable of coordinating information coming from many sources and of ensuring that it is properly used to streamline the preparation of the manufacturing plan. The process is a good illustration of the importance of internal problems (e.g. units receiving belated or incomplete information) as a source of changes in manufacturing planning.

The rhythm of manufacturing planning is usually disturbed by belated deliveries of fabrics and supplies, their insufficient quality and the resulting claims (which may result in the materials' being returned to the supplier). The inspectors who control fabric quality measure also its width because markers are prepared for the actual width of fabric (a roll of fabric is measured at its beginning, mid-point and end; patterns are arranged with the use of the lowest of the three values). Markers are made for the fabric that has been put into a warehouse after passing quality tests. Some causes of unplanned changes can be a particularly large number of garment sizes or fabric patterns, which makes it necessary to ensure consistency between pattern layouts, etc., as all these factors extend the preparation of the necessary documentation beyond the scheduled date. Their impacts can be eliminated by working longer hours or by using computerised systems that can substantially increase the speed of work and propose alternative solutions for the manufacturing plan (e.g. different arrangements of patterns for choosing the one that causes the least waste of fabric).

An important part of the presented subprocess is operational planning. Operational plans have the lowest status, but they determine the timely completion of the tasks they cover. The most frequent causes of changes in the plans are incomplete information coming from the following units in the organisation:

- the sales department (in charge of preparing the list of garment prototypes approved for manufacture, the number of garments to be made by size and colour and the dates for shipping the finished garments to customers),
- the procurement department (providing the dates when fabrics will be delivered),
- the technological department (in charge of defining materials consumption standards and processing times per unit product),
- production control department (keeping track of the production capacity of the in-house work teams and the external work teams providing garment assembly services).

A review of the literature and the author's own observations allow defining operational planning as a process of distributing tasks among work teams on the basis of the economic, organisational and technical characteristics of the tasks. The planning process sometimes requires a compromise between the need to provide the company's own work teams with work and trying to reduce costs by outsourcing manufacturing services to external providers. The choice must be made by the company board, which must consider the advantages and disadvantages of the available options. The most radical change takes place when a company decides to stop to manufacture clothing with the use of its own resources. The advantage of this decision is that the production potential can be increased without making additional investments or reduced without paying the cost of redundancies. The downside is that the quality of products is usually lower then (because of limited control over manufacturing, communications problems with the service provider and transport conditions affecting the finished goods, which are frequently shipped between continents).

There are many endogenous factors the changes in which are likely to influence the **manufacturing subprocess**. The manager must therefore ensure the balance between the demands of technological operations, the skills of individual workers and the availability of machines and equipment. The length of manufacturing can be reduced by standardising the working methods (by workers' specialisation in particular operations) and by ensuring a steady flow of work between workers. This topic is covered more widely in the literature on this subject [Więźlak,

Elmrych-Bocheńska, Zieliński 2009, pp. 133–138,379–390]. Unplanned changes in the manufacturing subprocess usually arise from:

- machines and equipment breakdowns,
- an irregular flow of work between workers,
- the work team members' frequent absences on workdays.

A machine breakdown is by its nature an unplanned change that makes a work station unproductive for a period necessary to replace the machine. If the broken machine is the only one of its kind the consequences may be serious, and include the necessity to use an alternative method of work until it is repaired (a broken plotter causes the necessity to make markers manually, etc.).

An irregular flow of work between workers may have many causes, including inefficient organisation of work in units providing inputs for the manufacturing subprocess, fabric flaws, incomplete job orders (insufficient amounts of fabrics and supplies, inefficient warehouse manager), etc. The only way to make up for idle times that usually occur then is to work longer hours after their causes have been removed.

Workers missing workdays make their team less productive, disturb the pace of work and see those workers who come to work being less efficient in their jobs because they have to cover for their colleagues. An incomplete work team is a reason for tasks' not being done on time. The operational plan must respond to such cases, for instance by transferring some jobs to another team inside or outside the company.

It follows from the above analysis that changing endogenous and exogenous factors alter the course of the manufacturing subprocess, increasing the risk that the seasonal collection will be delivered to the market later than planned. The consequence of this is a shorter selling period and a financial loss of the company. In the worst-case scenario, the company may even go bankrupt. The finding inspired the author to build a production cycle model for seasonal goods. The model was a stepping stone leading to the creation of a production management model that served as a basis for developing a method for analysing changes in the production process and eliminating or mitigating their negative impacts. In this way, one of the cognitive gaps in production management theory has been plugged.

Part III. A production cycle model, a production management model and a method for investigating changes in the production process

5. Constructing the production cycle model for seasonal goods

The product lifecycle curve that T. Levitt published in *Harvard Business Review* in 1965 has been permanently introduced to economic sciences. One of those who have appreciated its significance is Drucker [2004, p. 144], for whom it is one of the best known and sustainable models developed within the management theory. The lifecycle model is an ideal and therefore abstract construct that can reflect real-life phenomena to some degree [Kall, Sojkin, Szymaczak 2003, p. 146]. According to some studies, versatile lifecycle models that could be applied to any product do not exist [Kotler 2003, p. 146], but it is possible to create lifecycle models for particular groups of products, a proof of which is a life cycle curve for articles of fashion (Graph 1).

Graph. 1. Kotler's lifecycle curve for the articles of fashion

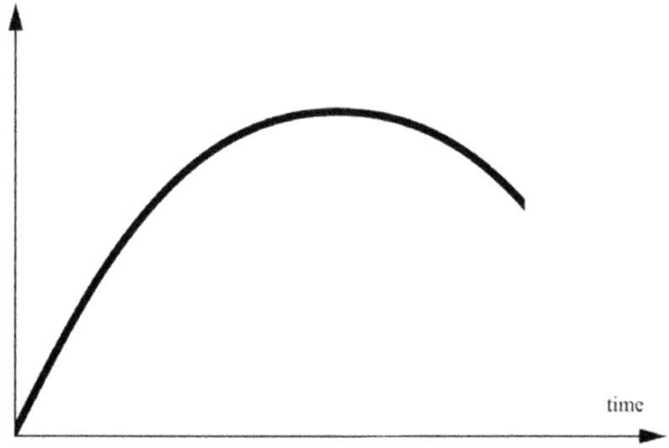

Source: developed by the author on the basis of Ph. Kotler, *Marketing Management,* Prentice Hall, New York 2003. p. 328.

The presentation of the garment design subprocess in subsection 2.1 makes it clear that apparel also belongs to the category of articles of fashion. The author of the chapter endorses the views of the above authors, but a comment must be made at this point that the modelling of any process is determined by the assumptions made and the factors that may disturb its course (see section 4).

The creation of the production cycle model was inspired by Grant [2011, p. 337], who stated that if a product has a lifecycle on the market, then there must exist lifecycles for the pre-sale (production) subprocesses. Accordingly, Graph 1 was supplemented by the subprocesses preceding the sale of a seasonal collection of clothing. The definition of a seasonal collection can be found in subsection 2.1, where it is described as a set of garment prototypes consistent in terms of style and colour that the producer offers to wholesalers and retailers, who sell it on the market with changing seasons and fashion trends.

The modelling methods offered by management theory are the following: analytical, graphic or grapho-analytical [Waters 2001, p. 140]. This means that the theory approves the use of the graphic method in modelling. According to Waszczyk and Szczerbicki [2003, p. 166], the purpose of modelling is to approximate a certain reality and the model's deviations from it should not be viewed as falsifications but rather as an omission of some events taking place in the economic reality. Leśkiewicz and Leśkiewicz [1999] criticise this approach as an internally incoherent acceptance of unrealistic assumptions and strong accentuation of the predictive function of economics. In response, Waszczyk and Szczerbicki state that a reliable description of realities (based on the good knowledge of the object of research) increases the probability that the constructed model will have good prognostic properties. The author of this chapter endorses this opinion and will present arguments in favour of it in the next part of the argument.

The production cycle model for seasonal goods presented in Graph 2 is constructed with the use of real-time measurements that the author made in the years 1989–2005. Such a long period of research and industrial practice points to their accuracy and provides solid grounds for accepting the model as sufficiently reflecting the real circumstances of production. The curves in the graph represent the temporal distribution of workloads related to tasks constituting particular subprocesses. The way the subprocesses are presented (section 2) and the model description (in this section) show that the author has good knowledge of the object of research, sufficient for inference purposes. On the basis of what Waszczyk and Szczerbicki say about the predictive values of models created in this way, the proposed model can be accepted as fully reliable.

Graph 2. The production cycle model for seasonal goods

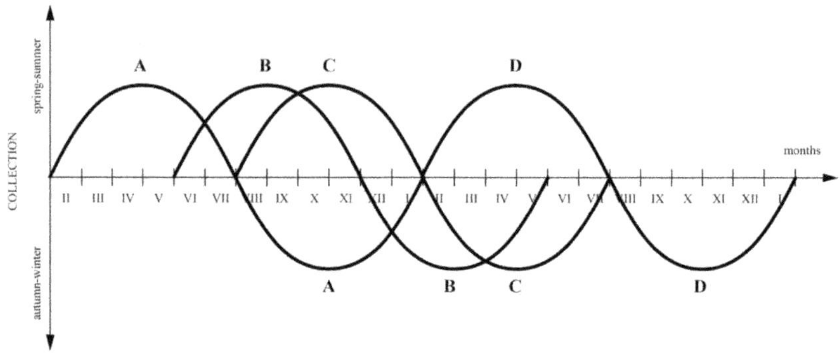

Source: E. Grandys, *Rodzaj kreowanego produktu a struktura organizacyjna przedsiębiorstwa odzieżowego*, in: *Przedsiębiorstwa sektora tekstylnego – teraźniejszość i przyszłość,* S. Lachiewicz ed., Wyd. Politechnika Łódzka 2006, p. 143.

The division of the production process in section 2 provided a basis for constructing a **production cycle model for seasonal goods** which consists of the following subprocesses:

- garment design and prototype construction (curve A),
- manufacturing planning (curve B),
- manufacturing and product quality assessment (curve C),
- sale and customer service (curve D).

The backbone of the model is time axis *x* with empirically established points where particular subprocesses start and end. Each of the four curves shows that the intensity of work on a seasonal collection first increases and then falls. The points where the curves start are shifted against each other by a period of time determined in the course of empirical research, i.e.:

- four months (curves A and B),
- two months (curves B and C),
- six months (curves C and D).

Time axis *x* clearly divides activities involved in the preparation of two seasonal collections. The curves above and below it represent the subprocesses carried out to prepare the spring-summer collection and the autumn-winter collection respectively. Each of the four subprocesses lasts 6 months, so if they were executed consecutively, a total of 24 months would be necessary to complete them and the company's working capital would be tied up for as long. The production cycle must therefore be reduced, i.e. the curves on the time axis must be rearranged (for the role of time as a critical production parameter, see section 3). Research shows that some tasks constituting subprocesses A and B can be performed at the same time, so the whole production process can be reduced by two months. If some tasks within subprocesses B and C are also performed simultaneously, another four months can be deducted from the production process. Consequently, the production cycle for the analysed group of products lasts 18 months (the model created confirms this fact). Theoretically, the sales subprocess (curve D) should not start before the entire seasonal collection is ready (curve C). In business practice, however, its delivery to the market is sometimes divided into two parts: primary and supplementary. This approach is used, for instance, when spring comes early or when summer is very short. By putting a new collection on the market ahead of other producers, a company may gain a competitive advantage. The production cycle model for seasonal goods also shows that the spring-summer collection and the autumn-winter collection are prepared at an interval of six months. This means that the teams preparing them must repeat tasks constituting particular subprocesses with the same frequency.

The research proves that the production cycle for seasonal goods can be reduced (by 6 months for clothing) **and that it must not end later than scheduled because its end date is related to the coming of new seasons**.

To sum up, it can be stated that the production cycle model for seasonal goods is a simplified representation of the process investigated. Its usefulness was verified empirically during industrial research that the author conducted for a period of over 17 years. According to Sudoł, such a long period of research and thorough knowledge of its object provide grounds for accepting the results of modelling [Sudoł 2007, p. 71]. The constructed model consists of curves that:

- represent the four subprocesses within the production of seasonal goods (described in section 2),
- are cyclical and shifted against each other by intervals determined during the empirical research,
- show the interval between the start of production and the withdrawal of products from the market (for seasonal products, its value is deterministic) and between the subprocesses,
- indicate that the total time of three subprocesses (garment design and prototype construction, manufacturing planning and manufacturing) is relatively long compared with the sales and customer service subprocess, which may span three or six months, depending on whether four or two seasonal collections are prepared,

- show that the point in time when curve D can start depends on the timely completion of the preceding subprocesses: if they take longer than planned there is a risk that the collection will be put on the market with a delay. Given that the end date of the production cycle is deterministic, the collection may find fewer buyers on the market or none at all.

Inductive methods that are used in empirical research to draw general conclusions are the main building block used by management sciences [Sudoł 2007, p. 69]. This allows for the acceptance of the presented results of modelling as being of scientific value as well.

6. The production management model

6.1. Introduction

The production management model for seasonal goods will be constructed in the framework of graph theory. Graph theory is an element of mathematical sciences that helps, *inter alia*, find the shortest routes connecting points by means of network or tree diagrams. For that reason, graph theory has found many applications in management theory. A review of the relevant literature shows that graph theory has already been used:

- to build models of organisations as networks of events (a single entry-single exit directed graph),
- to support decision-making on the basis of a tree graph (a single entry-multiple exit directed graph),
- to design product or service delivery flows (Ambler's sequence diagram) [Muhlemann, Oakland, Lockyer 2001, pp. 187–192].

The proposed production management model will represent the production process for clothing. **It is completely different from those known so far in that it is formed as a directed graph with many entries and a single exit** because the production of clothing uses inputs from many sources. The results of activities arising from these inputs are integrated along the way until the final point is reached, where the finished product is delivered. **The process is represented by an inverse tree** that has not yet been used in production management theory. An inverse tree is a simple, acyclical, coherent and directed graph with p vertices and $p-1$ edges, where each pair of vertices can be connected with the use of only one edge. There are two reasons why an inverse tree has been selected instead of a network: a network has only one entry and although it is useful for planning purposes, its suitability as a means of controlling a running production process is limited. This contrasts with the requirement that the model should be flexible and capable of handling dynamic changes in exogenous and endogenous factors presented in section 4.

The process of modelling consists of the following stages:

- setting the goal (the goal of this research is to construct a production management model for seasonal goods allowing for the deterministic duration of the production cycle),
- the determination of activities leading to the goal (scheduling activities constituting the production process),
- the formulation of assumptions (finding the start and end points for each activity),
- constructing the model (as an inverse tree).

Before the modelling can start, the complex production processes must be divided into subprocesses that will be modelled on an individual basis. The appropriate procedure is presented in section 2, where four subprocesses are discussed. The subprocesses will be reintegrated in the last stage of modelling. A model created in this way allows for investigating the impact of changes in endogenous and exogenous factors (section 4) on the production process.

6.2. Scheduling activities constituting the production of seasonal goods

The sequence of activities constituting the production process arises from the organisation of the company, its technical and technological capabilities and the type of products it manufactures. If necessary, the structure of activities can be decomposed into their elements [Waters 2001, p. 486].· The resulting blueprint of activities performed over a period of time is called a **schedule**. The problem of scheduling is widely covered in the literature on management theory [Durlik 2007, pp. 207–210; Burchard-Korol, Furman 2007,95–100; Pająk 2007, pp. 232–244] so it will not be discussed here beyond what is necessary to briefly present the workloads involved in particular stages of the production of seasonal goods.

The production management model constructed in this section focuses on the activities that are likely to change the duration of production. Finding which activities they would be was more difficult than it might appear because direct observations showed that production was disturbed by changes occurring in external as well as internal factors. The decisions that are made in response to the changes determine the further course of action.

Graph 3. An algorithm for designing a seasonal collection.

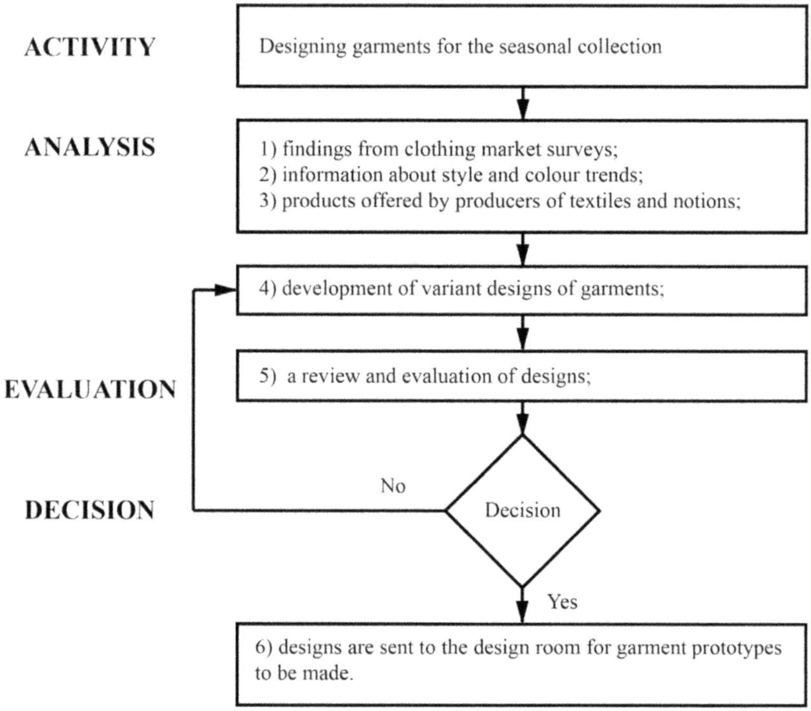

Source: developed by the author.

Which route will be used to get to the next stage of the production process is determined by whether a given activity is evaluated positively or negatively. The approach is enabled by analysing production activities by means of Altshuller's algorithm of inventive problem solving. In this research, the algorithm is used to verify activities and to determine which activity should be performed next. Creating a sequence of activities is a prerequisite to building the production management model for seasonal goods. Given that particular subprocesses are described in section 4, Altshuller's algorithm will be used to investigate activities allowing the next sequence of activities to be started.

The scheduling of the production process should start by dividing it into parts that will be modelled on an individual basis. Let us consider the creative input of the designer shown in Graph 3. Activities starting at vertices 1, 2 and 3 are initiated by the primary sources of information and in practice are carried out simultaneously. The proposed garment designs are evaluated by a design commission authorised by the company board. If the commission approves the designs, the process goes to the activity initiated at vertex 6. Otherwise, the activity starting at vertex 4 must be performed. Additional designs are produced until their number is deemed sufficient. Their number is usually greater than the number of prototypes that will be produced because the next evaluation of the prototypes will reduce their number.

Graph 4. An algorithm for the provision of materials for the design room

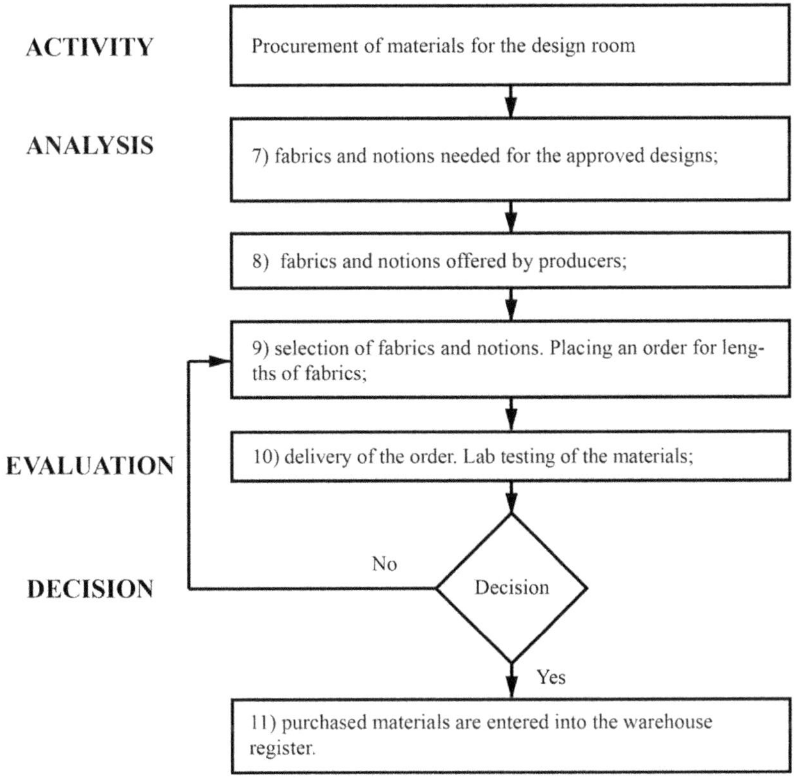

Source: developed by the author.

Before constructing the prototypes for the seasonal collection, the availability of necessary lengths of fabric must be ensured. If such availability is ascertained, and if the metrology lab confirms that their quality is adequate, the process goes to the activity starting at vertex 11 (the warehouse receives the fabric and enters it into the register). Otherwise, the process must return to vertex 9. The algorithm for the provision of fabrics for the design room is shown in Graph 4.

6.3. Constructing the production management model for seasonal goods

The next algorithm (Graph 5) shows the main activities as a result of which the master patterns are made, the garment prototype is prepared and the short version of the technical and technological documentation that allows estimating the costs of manufacturing of particular prototypes and calculating their prices is drawn up. An approved prototype opens the way to starting the next activity initiated by vertex 22 (choosing the composition of the seasonal collection). If the prototype is rejected, then the process goes back to the activity starting at vertex 12 (pattern making and the next tasks). This can be avoided when the number of approved prototypes is sufficient to create a seasonal collection (designers and constructors usually prepare more prototypes not to extend the garment design and prototype construction subprocess if some of the least attractive prototypes were rejected). The most important task in this subprocess is the evaluation of prototypes' aesthetics, functionality and prices (between vertices 21 and 22). The high-end garments are not evaluated for their price, but the aesthetics criteria they must satisfy are much more stringent than in the case of other classes of apparel. Garment functionality is always analysed, regardless of the target market segment. A seasonal collection consists of approved garment prototypes. Once complete, the collection is presented to external clients and internal clients (i.e. the company's own shops) to establish volumes of production by prototype. The next sequences of activities will not be discussed to ensure clarity of the argument, so the next step is the construction of a production management model as an inverse tree.

Graph. 5. The algorithm for making garment prototypes constituting a seasonal collection.

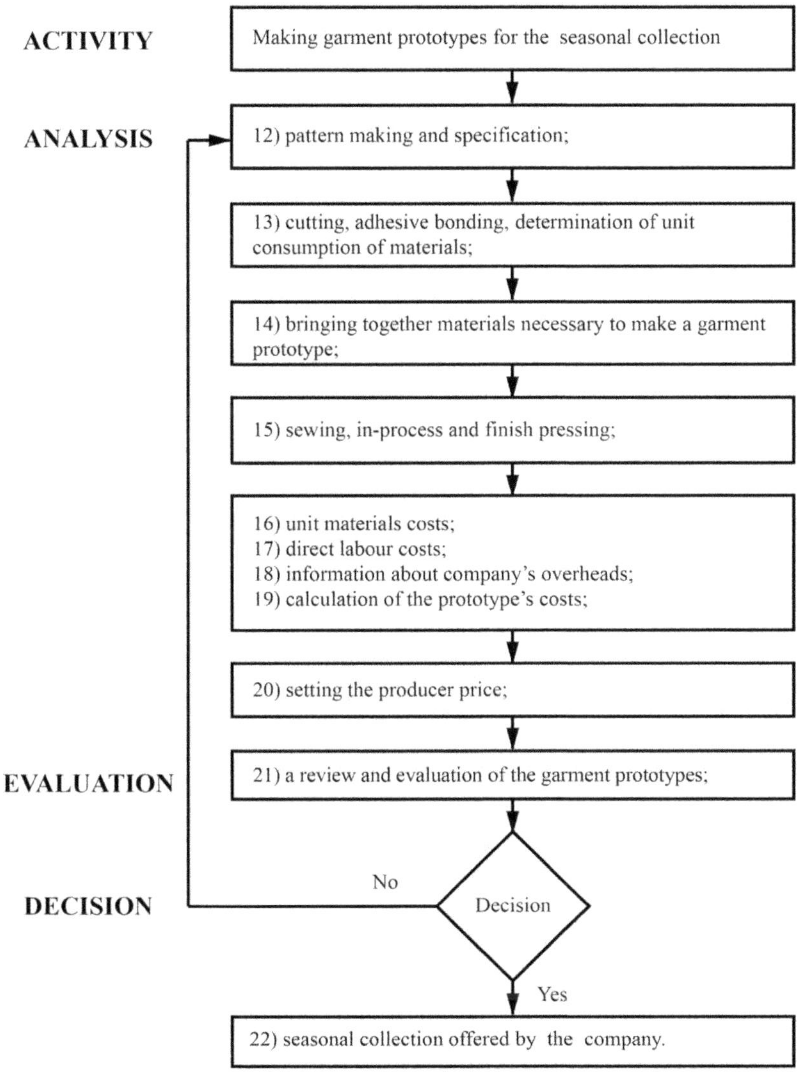

Source: developed by the author.

Management theory has made use of graphs before. The type of a graph that will be used to construct a production management model is an inverse tree. The reason why this graph was chosen for the purposes of developing a new method is that a review of the literature on graph theory showed that for some authors trees are a special case of networks of relationships [Wilson 2000, p. 170]. In the context of Hammer's study, this generalisation seems unjustified [Hammer 1999, p. 18]. Hammer questions the universal applicability of networks, arguing that the two types of graphs are evidently different. According to Hammer, there are three products that arise from the completion of an order: delivered goods, satisfied customer and paid invoice, meaning that the operational handling of orders requires something more than the simple manipulation of stocks and shipments. Hammer recognises this view as revolutionary and the results of the author's own research confirm that it is really so.

The proposed model starts at vertices where information or fabrics are entered into the production process. In terms of the graph theory, they are called leaves. Leaves initiate branches that consist of many events (vertices) and activities for executing them (edges). The lengths of the edges are not indicative of the amount of time necessary to perform particular activities; they were selected to ensure the transparency of the model. On the other hand, the sequences of events in the model are consistent with industrial practice. The branches of the tree will be connected together at the successive stages of the modelling process to form the root of the tree (the finished product), which is the final event.

In constructing the production model for seasonal products as an inverse tree, the following assumptions were used:

- the time when each elementary activity in the production process starts depends on external factors (the date when information, fabrics, etc. are received) and internal factors (the natural sequence of production activities),
- the duration of each elementary activity is a deterministic value expressed in concrete units (hours, days, etc.); a deterministic duration is the expected (the most probable) duration of an activity established during research.

A question may arise of whether the other assumption is not overly simplistic and therefore results in the construction of an unrealistic model. It must be remembered, however, that the duration of activities in the production of seasonal goods allows little room for deviations on account of external factors, e.g. changing seasons.

The requirements that must be met in constructing a production management model as an inverse tree are the following:

- each elementary activity of the production process must be represented by an edge, with a label attached to it to indicate its duration.

- each intermediate state in the production process must be assigned one vertex/node (the literature treats the terms as equivalent) of the tree, in which all edges representing activities that directly precede it end. The same vertex is the starting point for the next edge (activity).
- vertices denoting the initial states of the sequences of activities are the leaves of the tree.
- the vertex representing the final state of the production process is the root of the tree.
- because the graph is a root-directed tree, the chronologically later stages of production must be closer to the root (the finished product) than the initial ones.
- each vertex u of the tree must be assigned a pair of numbers $p(u)$ and $q(u)$, denoting, respectively, the earliest and latest time for an activity originating from this vertex to start.

The terms used in the last requirement must be defined. The **earliest time when the activity represented by an edge originating from vertex *u* can start, $p(u)$**, is the moment when state u occurs, under the assumption that all activities preceding it were completed on time. Similarly, **the latest time when the activity denoted by an edge coming from vertex *u* can start**, $q(u)$, is the moment when state u occurs, under the assumption that all activities following it will be performed on time.

For the sake of simplifying notations and expressions, a state in the production process represented by a vertex of the tree (e.g. vertex u) will be considered identical with that vertex and so the term 'state u' will be used. Likewise, an activity in the production process extending from vertex u to vertex v will be considered identical with the edge $u-v$ and so it will be called 'activity $u-v$'. Its duration will be denoted as $t(\mathrm{u}-v)$. Let us consider two cases of trees (graphs 6 and 7) before we proceed to the construction of the model.

Graph 6. A tree with robust vertices

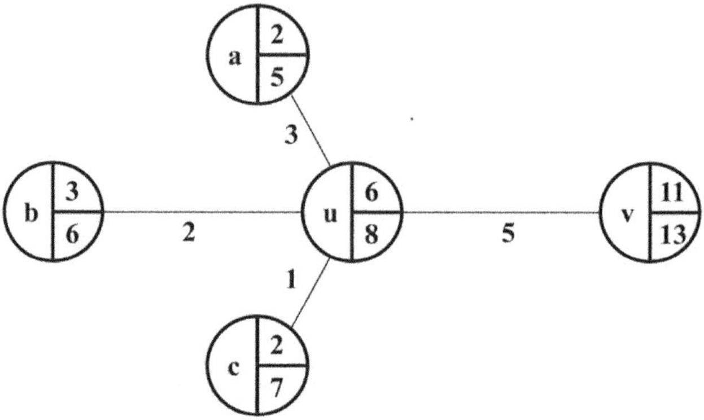

Source: developed by the author.

The parameters of the vertices in Graph 6 are the following:

$p(a) = 2$, $q(a) = 5$,
$p(b) = 3$, $q(b) = 6$,
$p(c) = 2$, $q(c) = 7$,
$p(u) = 6$, $q(u) = 8$,
$p(v) = 11$, $q(v) = 13$

and the duration of the activities is denoted as

$t(a–u) = 3$, $t(b–u) = 2$, $t(c–u) = 1$, $t(u–v) = 5$.

Therefore, for each vertex of the tree, there is an inequality:

$$p(u) \leq q(u) \quad (1)$$

Let us analyse the two possibilities individually. For $p(u) < q(u)$, state u has a time reserve that can be used to accommodate a delay in the sequence of activities preceding this state. The delay may not be greater than $q(u) - p(u)$. The production completion date will not be affected by it if the next activities are performed on schedule. In the second case, i.e. $p(u) = q(u)$, any delay in the sequence of activities preceding state u may push the production completion date forward. These relationships must be known to calculate time reserve $r(u)$ for state u. The reserve is the difference between the latest and earliest points in time for starting an activity:

$$r(u) = q(u) - p(u) \tag{2}$$

for $r(u) = 0$, state u will be considered a sensitive state,
for $r(u) > 0$, state u will be considered a robust state.

All vertices in Graph 6 are robust.
Graph 7 is a case of a tree that has both sensitive and robust vertices.

Graph 7. A tree with sensitive and robust vertices

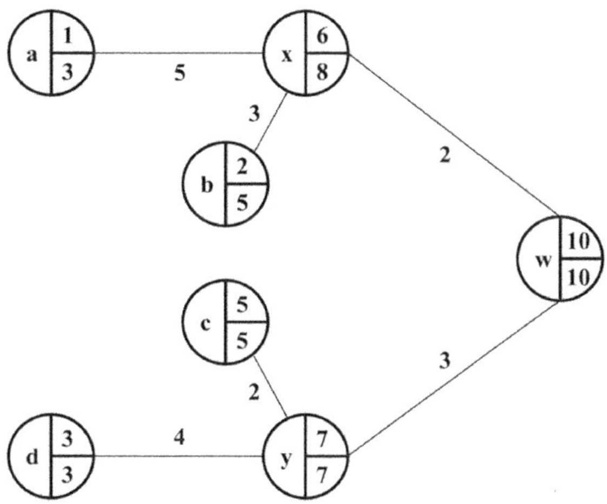

Source: developed by the author.

The sensitive vertices are *c, d, y* and *w* and the robust ones are *a, b* and *x*. Any delay in the sequence of activities *c-y-w* or *d-y-w* postpones the time of reaching state *w*. The available time reserve is $r(x) = 8–6 = 2$, so activity *x-w* can be safely delayed by two units of time. Similarly, activity *a-x* can be delayed by $r(a) = 3–1 = 2$ without the whole production process falling behind schedule if activity *x-w* is performed as planned and activity *a-x* starts at the earliest possible time $p(a)$. Under the same assumption, activity *b-x* can run late by $r(b) = 5–2 = 3$ units of time

Using the selected elements of graph theory, we can start **constructing a production management model** for seasonal products (clothing). According to the modelling approach adopted, the complex production processes will be divided into segments and will be modelled individually. Graph 8 explains the garment design and prototype construction subprocess.

Graph 8. The production management model – the garment design and prototype construction subprocess (the numbers correspond to vertices initiating activities).

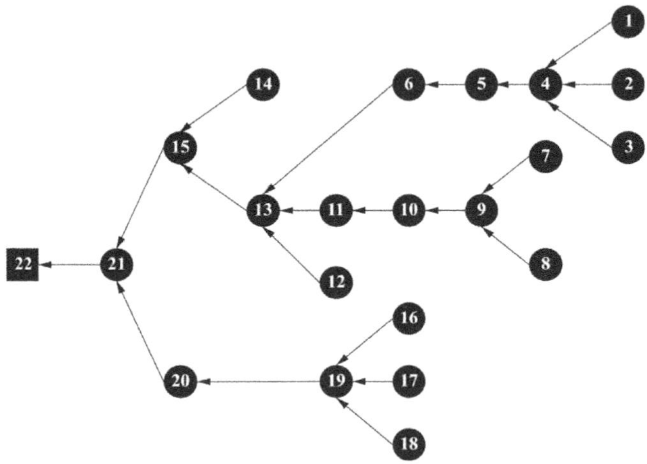

Source: developed by the author.

The segment of the tree presented above has been constructed on the basis of the schedules of activities illustrated in graphs 3, 4 and 5. The sequences of activities are leaves (vertices) 1, 2 and 3, related to the compilation of information necessary to design the seasonal collection. The next leaves, 7 and 8, initiate activities resulting in the procurement of fabrics for the design room, and leaf 14 stands for the purchase of notions for the prototype. The third group of leaves, 16, 17 and 18, initiate activities aimed at the preparation of the short version of the documentation, which allows the garment manufacturing costs to be estimated. The last activity in the tree is edge 21–22, i.e. the evaluation of the aesthetics of garment prototypes against their manufacturing costs performed by the design commission, which ultimately leads to the formation of the seasonal collection.

Graph 9. The production management model – the subprocesses of manufacturing planning, manufacturing and product quality assessment, sales and institutional customer service

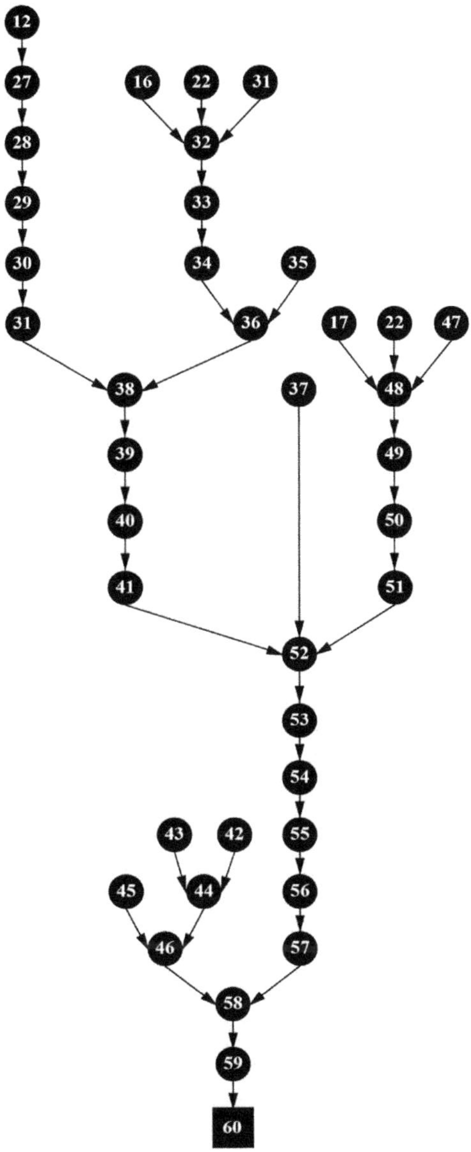

Source: developed by the author.

The same approach was used to model the next segments of the tree, which were connected to form the production management model for seasonal goods presented in Graph 9. The model is not very detailed, but it is sufficient to explain the method used to construct it. To make sure that the model is clear and understandable, the preceding subprocess (garment design and prototype construction) has been omitted from it. In Graph 9, the starting points are vertices 23–31 and 38–41, where the technical and technological preparations for manufacturing begin. The procurement of materials for manufacturing is denoted by activities originating from vertices 32–37. The operational planning activities are initiated by vertices 47 through 50. In vertex 52, the branches of the model are integrated, so the vertex is the state preceding the manufacturing of the product (activities coming from vertices 52–59). Vertices 53–57 are the cutting room activities and vertex 58 is where the patterns and notions are integrated. A more complex model, i.e. with a greater number of branches, would be less transparent. The presented model is based on the results of the author's own research and elements of graph theory that were used to the extent necessary to construct a management model for the production of seasonal products.

Let us note that the construction of a production management model whose elementary activities are not deterministic (i.e. described by a random variable) invites further research.

6.4. Sensitive routes and the method for finding them in the production management model

We proposed that the notion of a critical path used in network theory should be replaced with the notion of a **sensitive route**, which is more appropriate in the tree graph context. From the production management perspective, it is very important to know which route is sensitive because it indicates which activities deserve special attention. If their durations extend beyond what has been scheduled for them, then the production process may not end on time. The information about the duration of activities can be obtained by constructing a production management model and each time the model has been verified in the context of unplanned exogenous and endogenous changes affecting the course of production.

For the purposes of our production management model (Graph 9), an assumption is made that the production end date indicated in the schedule and the actual date should be the same. This means that between the initial event (the leaf) and the final event (the root) there is always at least one sensitive route. The number of sensitive routes may be greater than one because, at least theoretically, every route between the initial state and the end state may be sensitive. The number of sensitive routes indicates the susceptibility of the process to exogenous and endogenous changes that may extend its duration. A sensitive route is one consisting of activities for which time reserves are not available, so if any of them runs into delay, the whole production process is prolonged. Process robustness to unplanned changes and the number of sensitive routes must be analysed after the production management model is constructed. The length of the production process can be optimised by means of scenario-based planning.

To find out which route is sensitive, the sequence of activities for which time reserves are not available must be identified (using an approach analogous to the critical path method (CPM)). Let us assume that the production management model we consider has been constructed as shown in subsection 6.3. Its uppermost vertex w is the final event (the root of the tree). Among the states that directly precede vertex w (its children), there is state u without a time reserve: $r(u) = 0$. A different situation (where all preceding states have time reserves) would be inconsistent with the modelling assumptions. Hence, we have the following equality:

$$p(w) = q(w) \tag{3}$$

i.e. $r(w) = 0$

where: $p(w)$ – the earliest time for starting an activity,
$q(w)$ – the latest time for starting an activity,
$r(w)$ – time reserve for state w (the root of the tree).

The same procedure is repeated for state u and the states that come directly before it. One of them is state v without a time reserve, i.e. $r(v) = 0$. We proceed in the same way until a state without a time reserve is one of the leaves a (an initial state of the production process). By using this approach, a sensitive route starting at a and ending at w is created. Each state on this route is sensitive, including the initial state a. In seeking the sensitive route, we may establish that among states directly preceding state u there is more than one sensitive state. Then the model will have more sensitive leaves (initial states) and sensitive routes that will be equal in number.

6.5. *An indicator of production robustness to unplanned changes*

The seeking of a sensitive route involves the calculation of the production robustness indicator (PRI) (see Formula 4). Let us assume that a production management model has n initial states (leaves), of which k states are sensitive. This means that k must be within the range $1 \leq k \leq n$. The PRI can therefore be calculated as:

$$\mathrm{PRI} = \frac{n-k}{n} = 1 - \frac{k}{n} \tag{4}$$

where: n – the total number of initial states (leaves),
k – the number of sensitive states.

For $k = n$ and $k = 1$, the PRI takes extreme values, which define its range, i.e.:

$$< 0;\ 1 - \frac{1}{n} >$$

If all routes in the production management model are sensitive, then $k = n$ and PRI = 0. When there is only one sensitive route, $k = 1$ and PRI ≈ 1. The PRI allows evaluating the constructed model. For PRI = 0, the risk that unplanned changes will protract the production process is substantial. It is important to remember that all sensitive routes and the PRI values must be determined both at the model designing stage and each time the model has been verified.

Example: let us calculate the PRI value for the model in Graph. 8. The model has 10 leaves, two of which are sensitive: vertex 2 – the dates when guidelines developed by fashion creators are obtained (premiere vision shows in Paris and Milano) – and vertex 3 – the start of international and domestic fairs where samples of fabrics and notions are ordered for prototype garments to create the seasonal collection. Therefore, the PRI for subprocess A is = 0.8, so the subprocess is correctly designed. There is no guarantee, however, that it will be correctly performed. As a means of monitoring its course and possible variations, the author has developed a method called the Production Process Control Tree (PPCT).

7. The Production Process Control Tree – a method for monitoring process changes

7.1. Introduction

The need to plan production and to oversee its course necessitates the creation of operational algorithms or the selection of appropriate algorithms from among the existing ones. In both cases, the aim is to optimise the production process using the selected criteria. The results of the author's research show that the key parameter in the production of seasonal goods is the duration of production activities. This parameter can be disturbed by unplanned changes (see sections 3 and 4). To eliminate or reduce this risk, a method was developed from the production management model constructed in subsection 6.4. The model shows the type and sequence of activities making up the production process. Each activity has a label indicating its direction and the number of time units necessary to perform it. Activities form the branches of the tree that converge to finally create the root of the tree. Because of the assumptions made, the tree is directed towards its root.

The amount of information contained in the production management model for seasonal products is sufficient to achieve the primary goal of the research, i.e. to create a method for investigating unplanned changes in the production process that enables:

- active control of the production process to make sure that it is completed on time,
- verification of the management model when unplanned changes jeopardise the timely completion of production.

7.2. The Production Process Control Tree Method (PPCT)

The literature provides an exhaustive answer to the question about how firms should develop considering changes in their environment. Osrewalder and Pigneur [2012, p. 214] point to the influence of the market and industry forces and to major macro-economic trends and factors that enable "a design space" in which new ideas such as the Production Process Control Tree (PPCT), a new method for investigating changes in the production process, can be developed. Before presenting the method in more detail, let us notice that a delay in state u may have one of two causes:

- one of the states directly or indirectly preceding state u (e.g. state a) occurred later than the time $p(a)$,
- one of the activities preceding state u, e.g. a-u, took longer to be completed than the planned time $t(a-u)$.

A delay in the occurrence of state u may, but does not have to, cause the production process to end later than planned. A delay will take place when state u is a sensitive state on a sensitive route connecting it with the root of the tree. If state u is sensitive but the route is not sensitive, a delay may be accommodated by time reserves available after state u. The tree in the PPCT method is a structure that continuously takes account of variations in the scheduled durations of activities. It also provides a range of options to the process manager who should:

- take action when a change in the duration of an activity may cause production not to end as planned,
- refrain from action when, notwithstanding changes in activity durations, production will end on time (but then the production management model must be adjusted to account for these changes).

In both cases, the method has the same purpose, i.e. to signal that the production process may not end as scheduled and to enable the necessary countermeasures.

To monitor for changes that might unexpectedly affect production, one must know the way of calculating $p(a)$ and $q(a)$, which, respectively, denote the earliest and the latest starting times for state a by means of a recursive method (recursion allows infinite structures of objects to be determined using a finite number of instructions). The duration of an activity can be determined by:

- a deterministic method, stating that because activities within the production process follow fixed rules arising from the most common method of production used in the company, they are precise in indicating the length of the production process;
- a probabilistic method, according to which the durations of activities obtained from an empirical method are not absolutely reliable because the available data are not reliable either.

Let us assume now that the tree graph consists of events and activities with deterministic durations and that times when the initial states of the sequences of activities should occur are known. Using the same symbols as above, let us denote the duration of the activity running from state a to state b as $t(a–b)$ and the earliest time for state u to occur as $p(u)$. Let us now propose a method for calculating $p(u)$, i.e. the earliest moment when state u (which is not a leaf of the tree) can start. Its children are the vertices that directly precede it, i.e. $a_{1, \ldots,} a_k$ (for a tree directed towards the root). Then:

$$p(u) = \max \{p(a_i) + t(a_i – u) \text{ for } i = 1, \ldots, k\} \tag{5}$$

where: $p(u)$ – the earliest time for starting activity originating from vertex u,
$p(a_i)$ – the earliest time for starting activity originating from vertex a_i,
$t(a_i – u)$ – the time for performing activity connecting vertices a_i and u.

Formula 5 allows for calculating $p(u)$, i.e. the earliest times for starting activities directly succeeding the leaves. Next, the recursive method is used to arrive at the earliest times when other vertices of the tree can start (see Mead and Andrews [2011, p. 582]). Finally, the moment $p(w)$ ending the production process is found and compared with T, i.e. the end date of the production process indicated in the schedule. If the condition $p(w) \leq T$ is not met, the production management model must be revised.

The latest moment for state a to occur, $q(a)$, is equally important. It is particularly significant for the root of the tree, which, according to the assumptions, must meet the following equality:

$$p(w) = T = q(w) \tag{6}$$

where: $p(w)$ – the earliest time for starting activity originating from vertex w (the root of the tree),
$q(w)$ – the latest time for starting activity originating from vertex w (the root of the tree),
T – the production completion date indicated in the schedule.

According to Formula 6, the root of the tree is a sensitive vertex (no time reserves are available). If equality 6 is not met, then a dummy state w' must be introduced. The earliest time when an activity originating from this state can be initiated is the same as T, so the following condition is met:

$$p(w') = T \text{ and } t(w{-}w') = T - p(w)$$

where: $p(w')$ – the earliest time for starting activity originating from a dummy vertex w',
$p(w)$ – the earliest time for starting activity originating from vertex w (the root of the tree),
T – the production completion date indicated in the schedule,
$t(w{-}w')$ – the amount of time by which the production completion date will change.

By transforming Formula 2, time $q(u)$ for state u can be determined. Assuming that state a directly precedes state u (in a tree directed towards the root), time $q(a)$ can be derived from the following equation:

$$q(a) = q(u) - t(a{-}u) \tag{7}$$

where: $q(a)$ – the latest time for starting activity originating from vertex a directly preceding vertex u,
$q(u)$ – the latest time for starting activity originating from vertex u,
$t(a{-}u)$ – the duration of the activity taking place between vertices a and u.

The numerical value on the right-hand side of Formula 7 is exact because there is only one edge running from a to u. This means that there is no need to use either the minimum operator or the maximum operator. The recursive determination of $p(a)$ and $q(a)$, i.e. the earliest and latest times when state a can occur, was used in the PPCT method to investigate changes in production.

7.3. Using the PPCT method to investigate production changes

The production management model was built as an inverse tree graph by using the procedure explained in subsection 6.3. For each vertex of the tree, the earliest and the latest times when activities can start (respectively $p(u)$ and $q(u)$) were determined, under the assumption that $p(u) \leq q(u)$. It was also assumed that state w ends the production process and that the earliest and latest times for starting the state are the same, i.e. $p(w) = q(w)$. Production is monitored on an on-going basis. All changes and variations from the data contained in the production management model should entail appropriate adjustments to it. If an activity extends beyond its time limit (due to unexpected exogenous or endogenous changes), then the production process may, but does not have to, end later than planned. If the risk of delay is real, an appropriate warning message must be generated.

The PPCT method consists in ongoing comparisons (in real time) between the schedule and the actual durations of each activity making up the production process. If activity $a–x$ is carried out in time $t'(a–x)$ longer than the planned time $t(a–x)$ by n units, then:

$$t'(a-x) = t(a-x) + n \tag{8}$$

Let us assume now that the route between state x and the root of the tree w passes through intermediate states $y_1, y_2, \ldots, y_k$, so it can be written down as $x–y_1 – y_2–\ldots– y_k–w$. For the purposes of our discussion, let us also assume that the activities before state a were completed on schedule and that activity $a–x$ started at time $p(a)$. In this case, one of three situations defining the amount of intervention from the process manager may occur:

$$1° \; p(a) + t(a-x) + n \leq p(x) \tag{9}$$

$$2° \; p(x) < p(a) + t(a-x) + n \leq q(x) \tag{10}$$

$$3° \; q(x) < p(a) + t(a-x) + n \tag{11}$$

where: $p(a)$ – the earliest time for starting activity originating from vertex a that comes before state x,

$p(x)$ – the earliest time for starting activity originating from vertex x,
$q(x)$ – the latest time for starting activity originating from vertex x,
$t(a–x)$ – the planned duration of the activity taking place between vertices a and u,
n – the number of units by which activity $a–x$ is longer than planned.

The PPCT method offers procedures for handling each of the three defined cases.

1. When the situation obtains as described by Formula 9, there is no risk that production will end later than scheduled. Although activity $a–x$ is longer by n units (due to a delay), the time planned for it $t(a–x)$ plus the amount of the delay n still allow state y_1 to start on time. Therefore, the production management model needs no adjustments. The only change that is required is to replace time $t(a–x)$ by $t'(a–x) = t(a–x) + n$. Likewise, the manager does not have to be informed that a delay has occurred and no action on his or her part is required.
2. Formula 10 describes a situation that does not carry a direct risk to the production process. Because the delay is n units, the total time of the activity is $t(a–x) + n$, so it is smaller than the time reserve $r(x) = q(x) – p(x)$ available to state x. Activity $a–x$ will end no later than at time $q(x)$, representing the latest moment when activity $x–y_1$ should start. In this case, the production model must be adjusted as follows:
   1) Time $t(a–x)$ must be replaced by $t'(a–x) = t(a–x) + n$.
   2) For each state on the route $x–y_1 – y_2–...– y_k–w$, a new time of its earliest occurrence must be determined by using Formula 5, which also needs obvious transformations (state u must be replaced by the appropriate vertex and a_i by the preceding vertices).

The manager must be informed about a delay and the changes made to the model, but intervention is not necessary.

The following comments seem relevant at this point:

- it is not correct to think that the computation of new times $p(x)$, $p(y_1)$, $p(y_2)$, ..., $p(y_k)$ is of no practical significance because unplanned changes may turn robust states into sensitive ones and this will influence the structure of the production process.
- times $q(x)$, $q(y_1)$, $q(y_2)$, ..., $q(y_k)$ are the same because they determine the timely completion of the production process on day $T = p(w) = q(w)$, which remains unchanged, and the planned durations of particular activities.

3. In the situation described by Formula 11, the production process will be completed later than planned because state x starts later than its time reserve $r(x)$ allows. The model must be adjusted as follows.
   1) time $t(a\text{-}x)$ must be replaced by $t'(a–x) = t(a–x) + n$.
   2) for each state on the $x – y_1 – y_2 – ... – y_k –$ w route, new times $p(x)$, $p(y_1)$, $p(y_2)$, ..., $p(y_k)$, p(w) must be calculated by using Formula 5 (the symbols must be changed as above),

3) the end date T for the production process must be replaced by $T' = p(w)$ and the assumption must be made that $q(w) = p(w)$, where $p(w)$ is the new end date of the production process calculated in step 2 above.
4) for the new times calculated in steps 2 and 3, the latest times for starting the next production activities must be determined. Their durations are the same.

The production manager must be advised of the fact that the above transformations changed the production management model. The manager must analyse the new model and make decisions based on what has been established. For instance, the manager may propose technical, technological or organisational improvements shortening the sequence of activities $x - y_1 - y_2 - \dots - y_k - w$. If they reduce time $t(yi\text{–}y_{i+1})$ by m units, transformations 1–4 must be repeated, but time $t(yi\text{–}y_{i+1})$ in step 1 must be replaced with $t(yi\text{–}y_{i+1}) - m$. Because the changes entail additional costs without guaranteeing that the delay will be eliminated (it may be considerably reduced, though), the competent staff must decide which option should be implemented. If after intervention the duration of the sensitive route in the new production management model allows ending production as originally planned, then further work is based on this model; otherwise, the competent body may decide to terminate production (having assessed the potential losses) or sell products later than planned (then the delay-caused losses such as price reductions, additional promotions, etc. must be estimated).

Seasonal goods must be sold over a determined period of time that unexpected endogenous and exogenous changes in production may reduce or even make unavailable (depending on the delay). The PPCT method proposed by the author provides information ahead of time that a delay may take place. Prompt decisions and actions can eliminate (sometimes at additional costs) or mitigate its impacts (by minimising losses). Such decisions are made under the pressure of time, though. Many authors indicate, therefore, that because of the stressful circumstances most of them are made instinctively and that it is only afterwards that they are consciously interpreted and rationalised [Weick 2001, Gladwell 2005]. Given that such decisions bear measurable consequences for production processes, it is important for managers to have in their minds a possibly rich resource of information that the PPCT method can provide. Production managers should also have the traits of transformational leaders, meaning that they should be able to introduce changes and implement their visions also by winning the emotional commitment of the teams of workers [Sułkowski 2010, p. 108]. The concept of leadership is an important part of management theory, but this field of research is different from that explored in this chapter.

Conclusion

The goals of the chapter have been attained by combining resources offered by management science and graph theory. Firstly, a production management model for seasonal goods was constructed as an inverse tree graph (section 6). This dynamic model allows for analysing production as it runs. In the next step, a procedure for finding the model's sensitive route (determining the duration of production) was developed as well as an indicator showing how robust the original or verified model of production is to the occurring changes. The production management model for seasonal goods served as a basis for creating a method called the Production Process Control Tree to investigate unplanned changes in production (section 7). The method allows monitoring production for changes on an ongoing basis, as well as providing early information that variations are possible. This functionality is particularly valuable because variations may extend the production of seasonal products that have a determined selling period beyond the planned date. Another advantage of the method is that it allows for modifying the production management model in such a way as to eliminate or minimise the negative impacts of irregularities, and thus to reduce the losses a company might incur. The intermediate objective of constructing the production cycle model has been attained as well. The model shows (section 5) that the investigated production process has a deterministic duration. A question that is worth raising is whether the production management method proposed by the author will be adopted by business practice. Asking this question is justified, as it has been observed that although the global resources of knowledge are expanding, their efficient use is prevented by increasing organisational barriers [Bednarek 2007, p. 47].

The development of management methods is driven by institutionalisation, validation and internationalisation. Their nature is conventional, meaning that they are based on consensus [Berger, Luckmann 1966]. Therefore, will management theory accept the production management model and the PPCT method put forward by the author as its paradigm? Management sciences have many levels of theorisation arranged by the degree of generalisation [Hambrick 2007]. Theorisation may be used to build or test theories [Colquitt, Zapata-Phelan 2007] but regardless of its level, concepts must always be defined within the framework of commonly recognised cognitive assumptions. This chapter seems to meet this requirement.

It must be admitted, however, that building theories is a special challenge for applied sciences, not only because of an interdisciplinary field and scope of research, but also due to limitations affecting methodological and epistemological reflection [Koźmiński 2006]. Sułkowski [2010, p. 95] argues that while the aim of management science is to derive coherent and logical theories from evidence, the theories themselves may be founded on different paradigms. Consequently, resources of scientific knowledge are expanding, but within particular paradigms. Incommensurability frequently hinders the transfers of knowledge between particular paradigms and schools. The resources of knowledge expand with advances in management theory, but the knowledge is not fully coherent. The opinions of the authors mentioned above seem to provide grounds for an affirmative answer to the question about whether the proposed method for investigating unplanned changes in the production process for seasonal goods (PPCT) may aspire to become a paradigm of management theory.

Science has three levels of theories: macro, meso and micro. Micro theories focus on individual cases and their aim is to explain the sense of the processes they investigate [Sułkowski 2010, p. 97]. The method put forward by the author meets at least the conditions of a micro theory of management, as it promotes organisational order that does not exist by itself, but is constantly sustained, redefined and modified by researchers and scientists. This conclusion should not sound controversial to researchers, regardless of whether they advocate revolutionary changes of paradigms or base their scientific activity on the classical organisation and management theory.

Bibliography

Adair C., Murray B. (2002), *Radykalna reorganizacja firmy*, Wydawnictwo Naukowe PWN, Warszawa.

Armstrong G., Kotler Ph. (2011), *Marketing. An Introduction*, Prentice Hall International Inc.

Bednarek M. (2007), *Doskonalenie systemów zarządzania*, Wydawnictwo Difin, Warszawa.

Banaszyk P., Urbanowska-Sojkin E., Witczak H. (2004), *Zarządzanie strategiczne przedsiębiorstwem*, Polskie Wydawnictwo Ekonomiczne, Warszawa.

Berger P.L., Luckmann T. (1996), *The Social Construction of Reality. A Treatise in the Sociology of Knowledge*, Doubleday, Garden City.

Bitkowska A. (2013), *Zarządzanie procesowe we współczesnych organizacjach*, Wydawnictwo Difin, Warszawa.

Borowiecki R. (2010), *Przedsiębiorstwo w obliczu wyzwań współczesnej gospodarki*, Wydawnictwo Uniwersytetu Ekonomicznego w Krakowie, Kraków.

Brilaman J. (2002), *Nowoczesne koncepcje I metody zarządzania*, Polskie Wydawnictwo Ekonomiczne, Warszawa.

Burchard-Korol D., Furman J. (2007), *Zarządzanie produkcją i usługami*, Wydawnictwo Politechniki Śląskiej, Gliwice.

Byrne A. (2013), *The Lean Turnaround* (*Lean Management*), Wyd. Lean Enterprise Institute Poland, Wrocław.

Chen E.K. (1996), *Transnational Corporations and Technology Transfer to Developing Countries*, in: UNTCTAD *Transnational Corporations and World Development*, London.

Chmielecki M. (2012), *Zarządzanie negocjacjami w organizacji – wymiar międzykulturowy*, „Zeszyty Naukowe Wyższej Szkoły Bankowości we Wrocławiu", no. 30.

Ciesielski M. (ed.) (2006), *Logistyka w biznesie*, Polskie Wydawnictwo Ekonomiczne, Warszawa.

Cole J.L., Bardi E.J., Langley C.J. (2002), *Zarządzanie logistyczne*, Polskie Wydawnictwo Ekonomiczne, Warszawa.

Colquitt J.A., Zapata-Phelan C.P. (2007), *Trends in Theory Building and Theory Testing: A Five-Decade Study of the Academy of Management Journal*, "Academy of Management Journal", No. 50.

Commission Regulation (EC) on common rules for imports of certain textile products from third countries, No 1217/2007, 18 October 2007.

Commission Regulation (EC) No. 330/2009, 22 April 2009.

Co nowego w Chinach (2008), „Informator" – biuletyn *Gdynia Cottons Association*, no. 2.

Council and the European Parliament, Commission of the European Communities, Brussels, 21.5.2002, p. 4.

Davenport T.H. (1993), *Reed Radical Innovation and Continuous Improvement? Integrate Process Reengineering and TQM*, "Planning Review", Vol. 21, No. 3.

Different Routes to Product Innovation Performance (2007), "Journal of Marketing", January, Vol. 71.

Drucker P.F. (2004), *Natchnienie i fart*, Wydawnictwo Studio Emka, Warszawa.

Durlik I. (2007), *Inżynieria zarządzania. Strategia i projektowanie procesów produkcyjnych*, Agencja Wydawnicza Placet, Warszawa.

Düssel M. (2010), *Handbuch Marketingpraxis* (*Marketing w praktyce*), Wydawnictwo BC.edu, Warszawa.

Engelhardt J. (ed.) (2014), *Zarządzanie przedsiębiorstwem*, Wydawca CeDeWu Sp. z o.o., Warszawa.

Fisk P. (2014), *Business Genius* (*Geniusz biznesu*), wyd. II, Oficyna Wolters Kluwer business, Warszawa.

Foster R., Kaplan S. (2001), *Creative Destruction*, McKinsey & McKinsey Company.

Froeb L.M., McCann B.T. (2012), *Managerial Economics* (*Ekonomia menedżerska*), Polskie Wydawnictwo Ekonomiczne, Warszawa.

Garczyński J. (2003), *Tekstylia i odzież w Unii Europejskiej*, „Rynek Mody", no. 5.

Gladwell M. (2005), *Blink: The Power of Thinking Without Thinking*, Time Werner Book Group, New York.

Godziszeski B., Haffer M., Stankiewicz M.J., Sudoł S. (2011), *Przedsiębiorstwo, teoria i praktyka zarządzania*, Polskie Wydawnictwo Ekonomiczne, Warszawa.

Grajewski P., Nogalski B. (2004), *Potencjalne źródła niesprawności w organizacji procesowej*, in: *Podejście procesowe w zarządzaniu*, (ed.) M. Romanowska, M. Trocki, Wydawnictwo Szkoły Głównej Handlowej, Warszawa.

Grandys E. (2006), *Rodzaj kreowanego produktu a struktura organizacyjna przedsiębiorstwa odzieżowego*, in: S. Lachiewicz (ed.), *Przedsiębiorstwa sektora tekstylnego – teraźniejszość i przyszłość*, Wydawnictwo Politechniki Łódzkiej, Łódź.

Grandys E. (2007), *Impact of External Determinants on the Functioning of Polish Clothing Manufacturers*, "Fibres & Textiles in Eastern Europe", Vol. 15, No. 3(62).

Grandys E. (2008), *Barriers to knowledge absorption conditioning development of the polish clothing industry*, "Fibres & Textiles in Eastern Europe", Vol. 16, No. 1(66).

Grandys E., Grandys A. (2008), *Outsourcing – An Innovation Tool in Clothing Companies*, "Fibres & Textiles in Eastern Europe", Vol. 16, No. 5(70).

Grandys E., Grandys A. (2014), *Polish foreign trade in clothing products*, "Fibres & Textiles in Eastern Europe", Vol. 22, No.6(108).

Grant R.M. (2011)., *Contemporary Strategy Analysis* (*Współczesna analiza strategii*), Oficyna Wolters Kluwer business, Warszawa.

Grunberg Th. (2003), *A Review of Improvement Methods In Manufacturing Operations*, "Work Study", Vol. 52, No. 2.

Hambrick D.C. (2007), *The Field of Management's Devotion to Theory: Too Much of a Good Thing?*, "Academy of Management Journal", No. 50.

Hammer M. Champy J. (1994), *Reengineering the Corporation – Manifesto for Business Revolution*, Nicolas Brealey Publishing, London.

Hammer M. (1999), *Reinżynieria i jej następstwa*, Wydawnictwo Naukowe PWN, Warszawa.

Hammer M., Stanton S. (2003), *Jak naprawdę funkcjonuje firma zarządzana procesowo?*, "Harvard Business Review Polska", lipiec 2003.

Henderson G.W. (1996)., *Industrial Commentary, Innovation in the Global Textile Industry*, "J. Text. Inst.", 87 Part, No.2.

Horvath & Partner (Hrsg.) (2005), *Prozessmanagement umsetzen,* Schaeffer-Poeschel Verlag, Stuttgart.

Hough J.R., White M.A. (2004), *Scanning actions and environmental dynamism: Gathering Information for strategic decision-making*, "Management Decision", No. 6.

Jędrzejczak Z., Kukuła K., Skrzypek J., Walkosz A. (2004), *Badania operacyjne w przykładach i zadaniach*, Wydawnictwo Naukowe PWN, Warszawa.

Kaczurba J., Kawecka-Wyrzykowska E. (2002), *Polska w WTO*, Wydawnictwo Instytutu Koniunktur i Cen Handlu Zagranicznego, Warszawa.

Kall J., Sojkin B., Szymczak J., Urbaniak M. (ed.) (2003), *Zarządzanie produktem*, Polskie Wydawnictwo Ekonomiczne., Warszawa.

Komorowski J.P. (2011), *Cele i wartości współczesnego przedsiębiorstwa*, Oficyna Wydawnicza Szkoły Głównej Handlowej, Warszawa.

Kotler Ph., Armstrong G., Saunders J., Wong V. (2002), *Marketing. Podręcznik Europejski*, Polskie Wydawnictwo Ekonomiczne, Warszawa.

Kotler Ph. (2003), *Marketing Management*, Prentice Hall, New York.

Kotler PH., Caslione J.A. (2009), *Chaotics. The Business of Managing and Marketing in the Age of Turbulence*, AMACOM, New York.

Kotler Ph., Keller K.L. (2011), *Marketing Management*, Prentice Hall.

Koźmiński A.K. (2006), koreferat z seminarium: S. Sudoł, *Zarządzanie jako dyscyplina naukowa*, in: *Krytyczna teoria organizacji*, Wydawnictwo Wyższej Szkoły Przedsiębiorczości i Zarządzania, Warszawa.

Krzos G. (2004), *Business Process Reengineering*, in: R. Krupski (ed.), *Metody zarządzania przedsiębiorstwem w przestrzeni marketingowej*, R. Krupski (ed.), Wydawnictwo Akademii Ekonomicznej, Wrocław.

Kuemmerle W. (1999), *The drivers of foreign direct investment into research and development: an empirical investigation*, "Journal of International Business Studies", Vol. 30.

Leonard D. (2002), *Guide to the European Union*, Published by Profile Books ltd, London.

Leśkiewiecz I., Leśkiewicz Z. (1999), *Zarys metodologii ekonomii*, Wydawnictwo Uniwersytetu Szczecińskiego, Szczecin.

Luca de L.M., Atuaehbe-Gima K. (2007), *Market Knowledge and Cross-Functional Collaboration: Examining the Different Routes to Product Innovation Performance*, "Journal of Marketing" January, Vol. 71.

Łukasiński W. (2014), *Zaangażowanie pracownika a jakość funkcjonowania organizacji*, „Ekonomika i Organizacja Przedsiębiorstwa", no. 9(776).

McIvor R. (2006), *Outsourcing*, in: *Business. The Ultimate Resource*, A&C Black Publishers Ltd.

Mead R., Andrews T.G. (2011), *International Management* (*Zarządzanie międzynarodowe*), Oficyna Wolters Kluwer business, Warszawa.

Michalczuk G. (2013), *Zasoby niematerialne jako czynnik wartości przedsiębiorstwa*, Wydawnictwo Uniwersytetu w Białymstoku, Białystok.

Molle W. (2001), *The Ekonomics of European Integration. Theory, Practice 4th, Policy*, Dartmouth Publishing Company Ltd.

Morgan M., Levitt R.E., Malek W. (2010), *Executing Your Strategy. How to Break it Down and Get it Done* (*Skuteczne wdrażanie strategii*), Wydawnictwo Naukowe PWN, Warszawa.

Muhlemann A.P., Oakland J.S., Lockyer K.G. (1992), *Production and Operations Management*, Pitman Publishing, London.

Muhlemann A.P., Oakland J.S., Lockyer K.G. (2001), *Zarządzanie. Produkcja i usługi*, Wydawnictwo Naukowe PWN, Warszawa.

Noga A. (2009), *Teorie przedsiębiorstw*, Polskie Wydawnictwo Ekonomiczne, Warszawa.

Nogalski B., Rutka R., Wójcik-Karpacz A. (2007), *Czynniki dynamizujące rozwój małych przedsiębiorstw*, in: *Kształtowanie konkurencyjności małych i średnich przedsiębiorstw na rynkach Unii Europejskiej*, ed. B. Nogalski, J. Rybicki, Fundacja Rozwoju Uniwersytetu Gdańskiego, Gdańsk.

O'Shea C. (2008), *Asi es Amancio Ortega, El hombre que creo Zara*, La Esfera Los Libros.

Osterwalder A., Pigneur Y. (2012), *Business Model Generation: A Handbook for Visionaries* (*Tworzenie modeli biznesowych; Podręcznik wizjonera*), Wydawnictwo Helion, Gliwice.

Pająk E. (2007), *Zarządzanie produkcją. Produkt, technologia, organizacja*, Wydawnictwo naukowe PWN, Warszawa.

Pascale R. (1990), *Managing on the Edge. How Successful Companies Use Conflict to Stay Ahead*, Viking, London.

Peppers J., Rogers M. (2007), *The Buzz on Customer-Driven Innovations*, "Sales & Marketing Management", Juni 2007.

Porozumienie w sprawie Tekstyliów i Odzieży, załącznik do Porozumienia ustanawiającego WTO z dnia 15.04.1994, art. 7 pkt. 1, DzU. Z 1996 roku no. 9, item 54.

Prahalad C.K., Krishnan M.S. (2010), *The New Age of Innovation* (*Nowa era innowacji*), Wydawnictwo Naukowe PWN, Warszawa.

Rabij M., *Kto nas ubiera*, www.newsweek.pl/wiadomości/biznes.

Rangaswamy A., Lilien G.L (1997)., *Software Tools for New-Product Development*, "Journal of Marketing Research", February 1997, No. 37.

Rappaport A. (1999), *Wartość dla akcjonariuszy. Poradnik menedżera i inwestora*, Wydawnictwo WIG-Press, Warszawa 1999.

Rocznik Statystyczny Przemysłu 1995, Zakład Wydawnictw Statystycznych, Warszawa 1995.

Rocznik Statystyczny Przemysłu 1996, Zakład Wydawnictw Statystycznych, Warszawa 1996.

Rocznik Statystyczny Przemysłu 2014, Zakład Wydawnictw Statystycznych, Warszawa 2014.

Rocznik Statystyczny Handlu Zagranicznego 1996, Zakład Wydawnictw Statystycznych, Warszawa 1996.

Rocznik Statystyczny Handlu Zagranicznego 2014, Zakład Wydawnictw Statystycznych, Warszawa 2014.

Rogut A., Piasecki B. (2007), *Innowacyjność firm włókienniczo-odzieżowych. Poznawanie potrzeb. Przełamywanie barier*, Wydawnictwo „Green", Łódź.

Seliga R. (2012), *Rola marketingu społecznego w koncepcji społecznej odpowiedzialności biznesu*, „Zeszyty Naukowe Uniwersytetu Ekonomicznego we Wrocławiu" no. 260.

Stabryła A. (2000), *Zarządzanie strategiczne w teorii i praktyce*, Wydawnictwo Naukowe PWN, Warszawa.

Sudoł S. (2007), *Nauki o zarządzaniu. Węzłowe problemy i kontrowersje*, Wydawnictwo TNOiK „Dom Organizatora", Toruń.

Sułkowski Ł. (2004), *Status poznawczy zarządzania procesowego* [in:] M. Romanowska, M. Trocki, Wydawnictwo Szkoły Głównej Handlowej, Warszawa.

Sułkowski Ł. (2005), *Epistemologia w naukach o zarządzaniu*, Polskie Wydawnictwo Ekonomiczne, Warszawa.

Sułkowski Ł. (2010), *Ewolucjonizm w zarządzaniu. Menedżerowie Darwina*, Polskie Wydawnictwo Ekonomiczne, Warszawa.

Sułkowski Ł. (2012), *Epistemologia i metodologia zarządzania*, Polskie Wydawnictwo Ekonomiczne, Warszawa.

Szatkowski K. (2008), *Przygotowanie produkcji*, Wydawnictwo naukowe PWN, Warszawa.

Szatkowski K. (2014), *Nowoczesne zarządzania produkcją. Ujęcie procesowe*, Wydawnictwo Naukowe PWN, Warszawa.

Trocki M. (2001), *Outsourcing*, Polskie Wydawnictwo Ekonomiczne, Warszawa.

Tidd J., Bessant J. (2011), *Managing Innovation. Integrating Technological (Zarządzanie innowacjami)*, Oficyna Wolters Kluwer business, Warszawa.

Tidd J., Bodley K. (2002), *The effect of project novelty on the new product development process*, "R&D Management", No. 32(2).

Urbaniak W., Żelazo M. (2001), *Małe i średnie przedsiębiorstwa odzieżowe w procesie integracji z UE*, referat na I Międzynarodową Konferencję Stowarzyszenia Włókienników Polskich „Przemysł włókienniczy w perspektywie integracji z UE", Łódź 29–30.03.2001.

Vignali C. (1998), *Branding and the Marketing Mix Examined in a Benetton Franchise*, "J. Text. Inst., 89 Part 2, No. 2.

Vignali C. (1999), *Benetton's Brand Position Explored and Developed through Nicosia's Consumer-behaviour Model*, "J. Text. Inst.", Part 2, No. 1.

Waszczyk M., Szczerbicki E. (2003), *Metodologiczne aspekty opisowego modelowania w naukach ekonomicznych*, Wydawnictwo Politechniki Gdańskiej, Gdańsk.

Watters D. (2001), *Zarządzanie operacyjne. Towary i usługi*, Wydawnictwo Naukowe PWN, Warszawa.

Weick K.E. (2001), *Managing the Unexpected*, Jossey-Bass, San Francisco.

Więźlak W., Elmrych-Bochenska J., Zieliński J. (2009), *Odzież. Budowa, własności i produkcja*, Wydawnictwo Naukowe Instytutu Technologii i Eksploatacji – PIB, Radom.

Wilson R.J. (2000), *Introduction to Graph Theory (Wprowadzenie do teorii grafów)*, Wydawnictwo Naukowe PWN, Warszawa.

Wojciechowski T. (2007), *Marketingowo-logistyczne zarządzanie przedsiębiorstwem*, Wydawnictwo Difin, Warszawa.

Wysokińska Z. (2001), *Handel towarami tekstylnymi Polski w okresie transformacji systemowej i integracji europejskiej*, materiały na Międzynarodową Konferencję Stowarzyszenia Włókienników Polskich *Przemysł włókienniczy w perspektywie integracji z UE*, Łódź, 29–30.03.2001.

Zahay D., Gryfin A., Fredericks E. (2004), *Sources, Uses and Forms ob. Data in the New Product Development Process*, "Industrial Marketing Management", October 2004.

ec.europa.eu/Eurostat.

www.lppsa.com.

Mariusz Bednarek, Łukasz Bielakowski
University of Social Sciences

Practical Application of Lean Manufacturing – Some Results of Industrial Implementations

Abstract: The chapter describes the use of tools of Lean / Kaizen in Polish enterprises. Case studies of implementations have been presented, for example the use of 5S and TPM in a wood industry enterprise, or a description of the optimisation of the changeover process using the SMED method in the ceramic industry company.

Key words: Lean, KAIZEN, 5S, TPM, SMED

Introduction

One can stand up to their competitors and survive. The motivation to improve has deteriorated in many organisations, as they started to believe that all improvements have already been made. This belief is, however, challenged by the results of studies of production processes and the organisation of enterprises, which point to irregularities and waste as impairing their efficiency and competitiveness. Additionally, enterprises seeking to increase their competitiveness are faced with developments taking place in the contemporary world economy, such as:

- advances in science and technology, particularly in the field of IT,
- uncertainties in the business environment, where new competitors may appear at any time.

As a result, enterprises must:

1. work towards achieving and maintaining a condition allowing them to handle both predictable and unpredictable changes in their environment;
2. keep their customers satisfied regardless of how dynamically the market conditions change;
3. run their operations in a lean and smart manner.

The lean enterprise concept was conceived in Japan, when Eiji Toyota and his associate Taiichi Ohno realised that the mass production of cars was inappropriate for Japan. This realisation materialised as a model of production called the Toyota Production System (TPS) that evolved over time into the concept of Lean Manufacturing implemented on the basis of restructuring projects. A review of completed industrial projects shows, however, that many organisations fail to see that today's rules and requirements of competition should be based on completely different standards than those used several years ago. With a full range of technologies being readily available on the market, it is not only infrastructure that is important today, but also high flexibility and efficiency in the market.

The essential attributes of an efficient and flexible enterprise are readiness to act and the awareness of the necessity to implement changes in organisation and production, which in practice translates into an ongoing process of improvements driven by the key factor of success, i.e. efficient tripartite relations between the enterprise's workforce (internal clients), managers (depending on the structure of ownership) and external clients (who ultimately decide about the enterprise's position in the market).

In an efficient enterprise experiencing major seasonal variations in orders, two things are crucial: (1) the intellectual capital represented by quality-oriented workers that fully understand the importance of good work and (2) the way the enterprise is managed. The preferable approach to management is one based on Lean Manufacturing (LM) that instils in people the awareness of the need to eliminate waste with the practice of ongoing improvement.

1. Lean Manufacturing

Lean Manufacturing is an unceasing search for and the elimination of waste from production and administration processes. Each identified instance of waste is analysed and evaluated to establish the ways of removing its sources or minimising its impacts. Within this process, sites are selected for an intervention of special teams, whose task is to eliminate waste and measure new performance.

An enterprise is an organisation where all levels must cooperate, collaborate and stay in communication with one another, which creates its corporate culture. This is the only way for an organisation to be successful in the market and gain advantages over its competitors. Lean Manufacturing has become a management standard because it combines organisational culture and high quality of management by integrating goals, processes, leaders and teams in the organisation with continuous improvement. This management solution simplifies the organisation's structure and reduces the number of decision-making levels.

An enterprise choosing to implement Lean Manufacturing must be aware of the costs that it will inevitably have to incur to train its workforce, to purchase software and equipment and, in many cases, to acquire the services of external consultants. However, well-designed LM projects are known to bring efficiencies that exceed their costs many times over. It is frequently reported that LM projects reduce inventory levels as well as the frequency of downtimes and machine breakdowns. In some cases, the rate of defective products can be cut by as much as several tens of percent compared with the baseline period. This allows the lead times to be shorter and more deliveries to be made on time. This is a good starting point for an enterprise to increase its competitive advantage and to create a new structure focused on quality.

Lean Manufacturing is strongly related to KAIZEN because both approaches use similar methods and tools. KAIZEN is considered a road that an enterprise must take to become a lean organisation. The Japanese understand the word KAIZEN as a relatively inexpensive process of ongoing improvements in an organisation to which all managers and workers should contribute. According to the philosophy of KAIZEN, our social, professional and private lives should focus on continuous improvement [Imai 2006, p. 39].

KAIZEN holds that the process of improvement has no end, rejects the *status quo* and recommends using the simplest solutions instead of waiting for a perfect solution to be developed. KAIZEN goes beyond a management concept, permeating the culture and many aspects of life in Japan. Unlike the Western-style managers, who expect workers to follow instructions, it is natural for the Japanese managers to allow workers to propose changes to the existing standards and norms. Another important difference between the Western and Japanese styles of management lies in the way managers handle new ideas. In Japan, there is a widespread acceptance of the workers' right to come forward with improvements, in contrast with other countries, where workers' suggestions face scepticism or even reluctance. This attitude is mainly caused by enterprises' emphasis on the results and by the belief that innovations are uncertain and costly. Some firms choose to implement costly changes, though, if they think they are likely to bring immediate improvements. The Japanese managers are more concentrated on processes, which are perceived as a stepping stone to performance. Small changes that frequently come with no cost at all are thought to be a major factor in making better use of organisation's resources. The main purpose of KAIZEN is to make processes more efficient in order to meet the quality, quantity and timeliness standards expected by customers. Even in the best-performing organisations, there are many processes that do not add value, being a waste of resources from the standpoint of KAIZEN. Organisations that can identify MUDA (waste) and take the necessary actions to eliminate it are also very competitive.

The range of methods and tools used to implement KAIZEN/Lean Manufacturing is very wide and includes [Bednarek, Gajewski, Luna Niño 2013]:

- Business process re-engineering – BPR,
- Computer-Integrated Manufacturing – CIM,

- Highly Integrated Enterprise Resource Planning System – ERP,
- Just-in-time system of deliveries – JiT,
- Integrated Material Requirements Planning System – MRP II,
- Group Technology – TG,
- Theories of Constraints – TOC,
- Total Productive Maintenance –TPM,
- Total Quality Management – TQM,
- Single Minute Exchange of Die – SMED.

An enterprise aspiring to become a lean and flexible organisation must, above all, implement the following systems:

- JiT,
- TPM,
- TQM,
- SMED.

For many authors, these four systems are the main buildings blocks of a Lean Enterprise, with which the following lean management paradigms (lean thinking) [Womack, Jones, 1996] can be fulfilled:

1. Management oriented to value added that is generated when a product is being made or a service is being delivered. Value added is determined by the customer, who at some point of time buys a product or a service at a price meeting his or her expectations.
2. Efficient management requiring a value chain consisting of three basic levels to be defined. These are:
   - a product (service) design process and an adequate programme of tests;
   - a production planning and programming process spanning the period between the placement of an order and the delivery of a product (a service) to the customer;
   - a product-manufacturing or service-delivery process;
3. Management set on eliminating all waste that may arise at any of the three levels of the value chain and on ensuring that the elements of the levels are improved on a constant basis.

The need to define a value chain is particularly related to the paradigm requiring all waste to be identified and reduced, which corresponds to the basic objectives of JiT and TPM. The objectives of TQM are met by the paradigm stating that processes in a lean enterprise must be constantly improved.

The criteria of lean organisations are, quite naturally, met by enterprises adhering to the World Class Manufacturing standards. The implementation of JiT, TPM, TQM and SMED can reduce the enterprise's operational expenses, boost productivity and improve product quality and the timeliness of deliveries to the market [McKone, Schroeder et al. 2001], provided that the enterprise has an integrated structure. Integration involves the implementation of information systems and information technologies such as [Wielicki 2000] MRP II (an integrated system for managing productive inputs) and ERP (a highly-integrated resource management system based on MRPII). The ERP systems contain strategic planning modules, production and inventory modules, financial modules and a so-called Executive Information System allowing managers to assess the riskiness of their projects and to function as market players. The implementation of an ERP system is a key to creating an Integrated Enterprise, the concept of which is based on close ties with the micro and macro environment. Integration is not complete, however, until the ERP system and CIM are linked together. Some modules of the two systems, such as production planning or inventory control, have the same purpose. This means that both ERP and CIM contain MRP II modules, but CIM is additionally provided with a number of dedicated solutions, such as computer-aided manufacturing (CAM), computer-aided design (CAD) and computer-aided engineering (CAE). By combining the ERP and CIM systems, the full-scale integration of an enterprise is achieved.

A lean enterprise organises its operations based on work groups or work teams. This type of work organisation is typically associated with the TQM, JiT, TPM and KAIZEN systems, so it can be concluded that total quality management (TQM), a JiT system of deliveries, total productive management (TPM) and the philosophy of continuous improvement (KAIZEN) combined with CIM, MRPII and ERP constitute a set of critical state-of-the art methods necessary to create a lean enterprise. According to the author's hands-on experience gained during the industrial implementations of JiT projects, the success of projects depends on:

- functional management being replaced with process management,
- production plans addressing manufacturing limitations,
- reduced diversity of the parts that an enterprise makes or uses to assemble subassemblies and products,
- fast and efficient changeovers.

Enterprise management focused on processes is the main idea of Reengineering. The basic recommendation of the Theory of Constraints [Goldratt, Cox, 1984] is that manufacturing and management bottlenecks should be considered in planning processes. The theory holds that an enterprise should maximise its profits by adopting a management approach which takes account of the existing constraints while providing space for continuous improvement to operations through the elimination of bottlenecks. The theory is useful in managing the processes that an enterprise has created by redefining its structures according to the principles of Business Process Reengineering (BPR). A reduced range of components and parts used in assembly and manufacturing processes underlies the possibility of standardising processes and equipment, and of increasing production flexibility understood as the enterprise's ability to handle customers' changing requirements regarding groups of similar products. Group Technology, developed by Pietrov [1968] and Mitrofanov [1963], is a method that allows an enterprise to achieve the desired level of flexibility, but also to standardise processes and transform its organisational structure into a network of units executing production and administration processes. SMED was mainly created as a solution allowing faster and more efficient changeovers of machines and equipment. The outcomes of completed projects show that SMED can cut changeover times by as much as several tens of times, but it sometimes may take as long as a dozen of months or so before consistently repeatable results are achieved. The author and the teams he supervised have succeeded in reducing changeover times from 180 to 15 minutes, but the process was gradual and several months of implementation work were necessary to obtain repeatable results.

Enterprises that choose to implement lean methods and tools obtain a range of business benefits. Some of them are presented in Table 1.

Table 1. The business effects of KAIZEN/Lean methods and tools

Method	**Business benefit**
CIM	• The availability of an integrated enterprise management system. • The availability of a highly-automated and flexible system of manufacturing.
JIT ERP	• With JiT principles in place, the enterprise can produce to demand, eliminate all kinds of waste, permanently reduce costs and raise product quality and customers' satisfaction levels. • The mapping of all functional areas according to the MRP II standard and the capturing and integrated storage of all transactions allows the enterprise to integrate and control its costs.

Method	Business benefit
SMED	• With shorter changeover times, smaller batches can be made and variations in demand are handled in shorter time.
TPM	• This pro-active maintenance strategy allows the enterprise to reduce the waste of downtime and of material inputs falling short of the value chain requirements
MRP II	• This combination of business processes into an integrated and centralised system ensures balance between deliveries and demand.
TG	• The creation of very productive production units and the elimination of waste from production processes.
BPR	• The enterprise and its business processes are managed by flat and efficient structures and procedures.
TOC	• Bottlenecks in the enterprise's processes are defined and removed.

Source: developed by the author

In Figure 1 below, the sequence of steps that the author has created and used to implement Lean Manufacturing projects is presented. The actions related to particular steps are explained in more detail below [Bednarek 2013].

Audits are mainly performed to determine the degree to which Lean Manufacturing principles are obeyed in the audited enterprise. In particular, an audit procedure aims:

- to identify and describe wastes and inefficiencies,
- to identify the elements of visual communication,
- to analyse methods and approaches used to solve problems,
- to investigate the ways of delivering material inputs,
- to analyse the layout of workstations and warehouses,
- to analyse the organisation of workstations.

The audits' findings are used to define the scope of tasks to be carried out during the next steps.

In Step 1, the LM implementation process consisting of the following activities is organised:

- training in LM principles for the board of the enterprise and selected managers
- promotion of the Lean project among the workers
- information meetings for the workers and trade unions
- the organisation and training for the Lean Team.

In Steps 2 and 3, the pilot LM project is run. The following activities are performed in relation to the steps:

- the selection of the pilot site
- the selection of the production process to be improved and the identification of wastes and inefficiencies
- the designing of the target indicators of success (expected reductions in waste) and of the ways of measuring them,
- the delivery of training and workshops to the Lean Team and selected workers
- the launching of the implementation process
- the creation and implementation of a suggestions system
- a review of the completed pilot implementation
- an evaluation of the achieved consistent indicators of success.

Steps 2 and 3 usually result in the following improvements:

- better organisation of workstations
- better use of available machines
- the introduction of a pull system based on KANBAN cards, SUPERMARKETS, the necessary redefinition of the layout and organisational structure
- workers' potential and knowledge being put to practice
- the development of Lean culture
- first measurable savings on the processes run in the pilot implementation area.

In Step 4, the Lean Manufacturing project is extended to other areas in the enterprise. The following activities are undertaken to this end:

- the mapping of other production processes in the enterprise
- using the mapping outcomes to establish which activities from Steps 2 and 3 need to be repeated
- training within Industry – TWI
- continued evaluation of whether the implementation brings measurable gains.

Step 4 usually brings the following benefits:

- machines and equipment's generating less waste;
- the culture of Lean disseminated among workers in the rest of the enterprise;
- improvement of the practical skills of implementing Lean tools and methods;
- a Lean Team ready to implement Lean Manufacturing projects unassisted.

In Step 5, the enterprise uses its own potential to measure and improve the implementation work done by monitoring and fine-tuning.

Fig 1. The sequence of steps leading to the implementation of a Lean Manufacturing project.

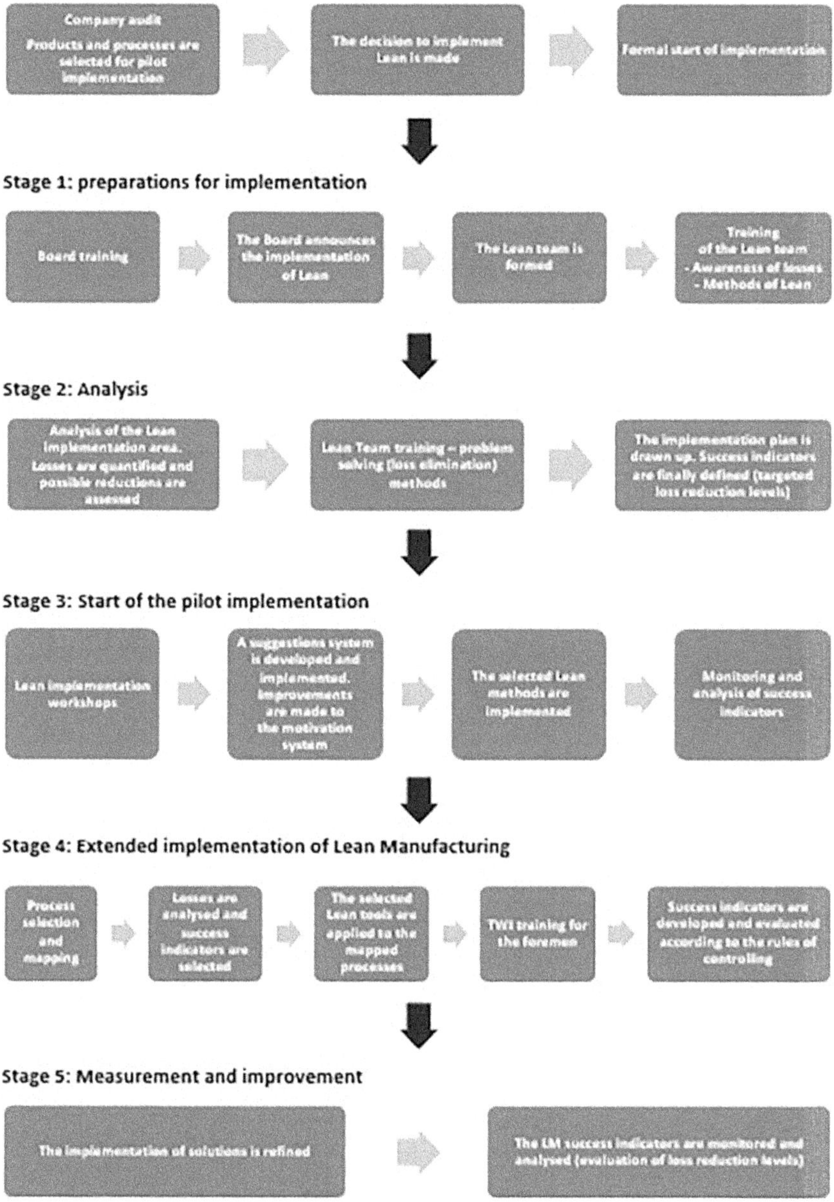

Source: developed by the author

The author has been involved in many projects in which Lean tools and methods were implemented, usually working with the teams of consultants, tertiary students and PhD students. The sections below present several case studies on LM implementations and their results, which have been derived from theses written by students under the author's supervision.

2. The implementation of 5S and TPM [developed on the basis of Bojakowski, 2014]

2.1. Description of the enterprise

The enterprise was a Polish manufacturer of woodwork and aluminium items used in the building industry in Poland and some European countries. Production was based on foreign profile systems characterised by very low heat conductivity parameters, high soundproof quality and security.

The enterprise produced to individual orders, as well as offered services involving the fitting and installation of metal trims and plastering work necessary to carry out complex, large-scale spatial structures at the customers'. It also manufactured elements of door and window systems for two major producers of aluminium structures in Europe.

Within 10 years, the enterprise increased its employment from 6 to 22 workers. Half of them were machine operators or workers providing fitting services. The enterprise had delivered more than 4000 projects to large and prestigious private and institutional customers.

The elements for aluminium structures were produced according to the incoming orders. Production showed seasonal variations because private customers placed smaller orders in summer and winter. In these seasons, the enterprise mainly produced connectors for profiles and replenished its stocks of materials.

The connectors were made with machines such as bench drills, table screwing machines, circular vibrators, band cut off machines, and profile working machines. Based on their age, the machines could be divided into three groups: the equipment used in the locksmith's shop that the enterprise had purchased 30 years earlier when it was starting up; 12-year-old machines acquired in the mid-1990s to cope with the expanding volume of business; and machines that were only several years old.

Figure 2. The organisational structure of the enterprise under consideration

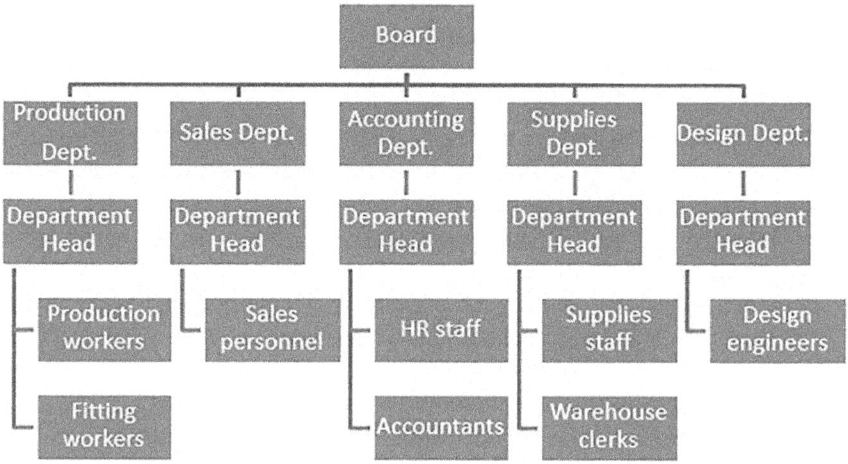

Source: developed by the author [Bojakowski, 2014]

2.2. Identification of wastes and the decision to implement Lean Manufacturing

In 2012, the enterprise decided to implement Lean Manufacturing, partly in response to the expectations of one of its major customers. The implementation processes started with an audit that aimed to identify areas of waste and help decide which Lean Manufacturing tools would eliminate its sources most effectively. The following areas of waste were found in production processes:

1. Quality control was concentrated on identifying and removing defective products rather than trying to establish why they were defective in the first place.
2. The machine operators tended to do their jobs in their own, unique way. Neither workstation arrangement standards nor procedures for the operators to work in a consistent manner and to deliver repeatable results were available. Before they started the production, the operators spent a substantial amount of time setting and adjusting their machines to their individual needs and preferences, in keeping with their ingenuity and comfort.
3. Workstations and machines were dirty and in a poor state of maintenance; the working areas were cluttered with unnecessary items and machine parts that the operators or their colleagues did not use any more, so they only restricted the space within which the personnel moved. To make things worse, scrapped defective products were piling up around the machines. Unnecessary equip-

ment that nobody needed any longer obstructed the efficient arrangement and use of the machines as well as the workers' operations.

4. The operators' tools were in disarray. Each time the personnel reached for a tool they had to check if it was the right one and on many occasions its actual use and size had to be determined (this particularly applied to drills). Workstations did not have special sites for storing the tools and no standards regulated how tools should be stored and organised, so workers had to seek them all over the shop. This increased the risk of mistakes' being made and made work less comfortable. The purpose of maintenance and repairs was to bring the machines and equipment back to working order instead of identifying the underlying cause of a failure. The workers did not identify themselves with the employer and their jobs and had a limited knowledge of the problems related to their work.
5. In many cases, minor machine failures that could be fixed within minutes made the workers unproductive for a whole day. Because machines were maintained and repaired by an external contractor, their operators had little knowledge of how they functioned. The enterprise did not have maintenance personnel dedicated to keeping the machines in working order.

The analysis of wastes resulted in the decision to implement 5S and TPM-Autonomous Maintenance, two major tools in the Lean Manufacturing toolbox. An implementation plan consisting of stages was drawn up (see Diagram 3). First, the managers were trained and then a formal announcement of starting the LM implementation process was made. Following that, the implementation teams were organised and trained in the theoretical fundamentals of 5S and TPM. In the next step, a pilot project was carried out and its outcomes were thoroughly analysed. Lastly, the schedule of the final implementation was developed.

Fig. 3. The sequence of steps leading to the implementation of 5S and TPM in the enterprise

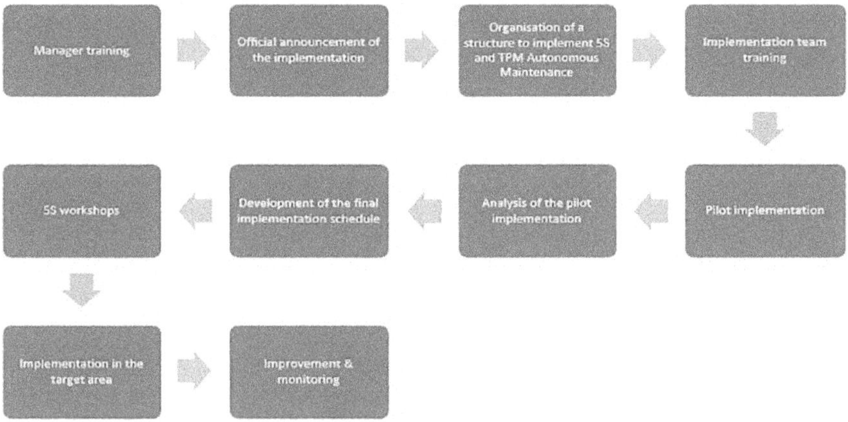

Source: developed by the author [Bojakowski, 2014]

The main elements of the structure that the enterprise created to implement 5S and TPM-Autonomous Maintenance were the following:

- Steering Committee for 5S and TPM – the board of the enterprise
- 5S and TPM Implementation Leader – the manager of the production department
- 5S and TPM Implementation Coordinator – this position was created specifically to coordinate the activities of the two implementation teams and of the support group
- Implementation team #1 – in the profile production dept. A
  - Senior operator
  - Operator
  - Operator
- Implementation team #2 – in the profile production dept. B
  - Senior Operator
  - Operator
  - Operator
- The implementation support team
  - Design engineer
  - Procurement specialist
  - Fitter

2.3. The course of the implementation process

In the table below, the schedule of activities performed in relation to 5S introduced in the first phase of the project is presented.

Fig. 4. The schedule of 5S implementation in the enterprise

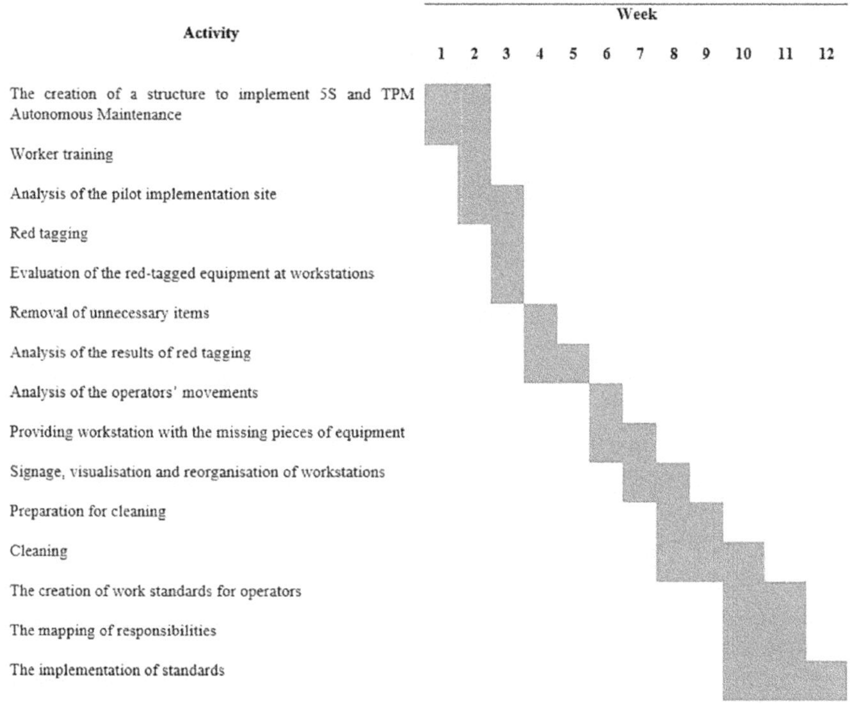

Source: developed by the author [Bojakowski, 2014]

TPM Autonomous Maintenance was introduced following the completion of the pilot implementation of 5S. In the enterprise, the machines were not maintained or inspected on a regular basis (nor were inspection and maintenance procedures available), apart from when they failed or when a seasonal decline in orders allowed them to be serviced. The records of machine failures were not kept. Workstations were cleaned, in a negligent and unstandardised manner, only once a week. As most machine failures were due to human errors and neglect, one of the main goals of the TPM implementation project was to involve the operators. Their maintenance duties usually included regular change of machine fluids, cleaning, visual inspections of their machines and minor repairs. The TMP part of the project was implemented in seven stages (Table 2).

Table 2. The seven stages of TMP-Autonomous Maintenance

Stage	Name	Activities/aims
1.	Cleaning and inspection	Cleaning a machine of dirt, lubrication, tightening the screws, identification of malfunctions.
2.	Elimination of the sources of dirt and hard-to-reach places	Elimination of the sources of dirt and improving the accessibility of all machine parts to facilitate cleaning and lubrication tasks; reducing the cleaning and lubrication times.
3.	Creation of cleaning and lubrication standards	Repeatability of results.
4.	Autonomous Maintenance training for operators	Delivery of training utilising the machine manuals; visual inspections of the machines to find and fix minor malfunctions.
5.	Performance of autonomous inspection of a machine	Development of standard checklists for autonomous inspections. Periodic inspections.
6.	Introduction of visual maintenance management	Standardisation and visual management of all maintenance activities. The newly developed and implemented standards applied to areas such as: • cleaning, lubrication and inspections, • materials flows, • data gathering, • management of tools.
7.	Introduction of Autonomous Management as a permanent solution	Improvement-focused activities as a steady element of daily work routines, keeping the records of average times between machine failures, analysing and using the data to improve the equipment.

Source: developed by the author [Bojakowski, 2014]

The schedule for the implementation of TPM Autonomous Maintenance is presented in Figure 5.

Fig 5. The implementation schedule for TPM-Autonomous Maintenance

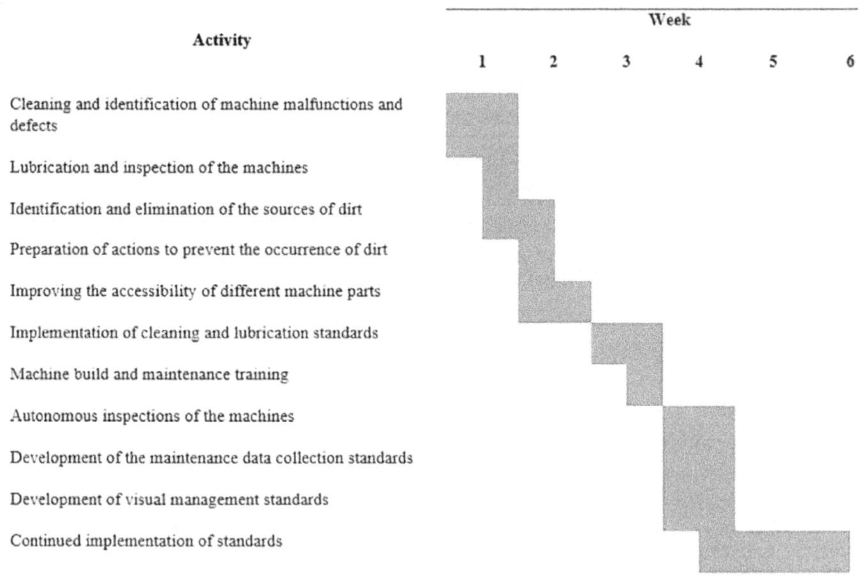

Source: developed by the author [Bojakowski, 2014]

2.4. The effects of implementation

Because of the implementation of 5S and TPM-Autonomous Maintenance:

- the operator work standards were created and problems arising from the operators' inclination to adjust the machines to their individual preferences were eliminated;
- workstations were cleaned up, all unnecessary items were removed;
- better visualisation of the workstations, machines and equipment boosted the enterprise's image in the eyes of customers visiting the facility
- both working conditions and safety improved
- maintenance times decreased by 33 %
- the effective work time fund rose from 20 % to 70 % per workstation.

3. The implementation of SMED [developed on the basis of Romek, 2013]

3.1. Description of the enterprise

The enterprise, owned by an international corporation, was a Polish world leader, in the design, manufacture and sale of specialist refractory ceramic products and industrial control systems. With 650 workers on the payroll, it was the biggest plant the corporation had in the world. Its exports and domestic sales accounted for 64 % and 36 % of total sales, respectively. Products were tailored to the specific demands of installations and processes used in the metal-casting, metallurgical, cement and lime, petrochemical and glass-making industries. The organisational structure of the enterprise is presented in Figure 6.

Fig. 6. The organisational structure of the enterprise.

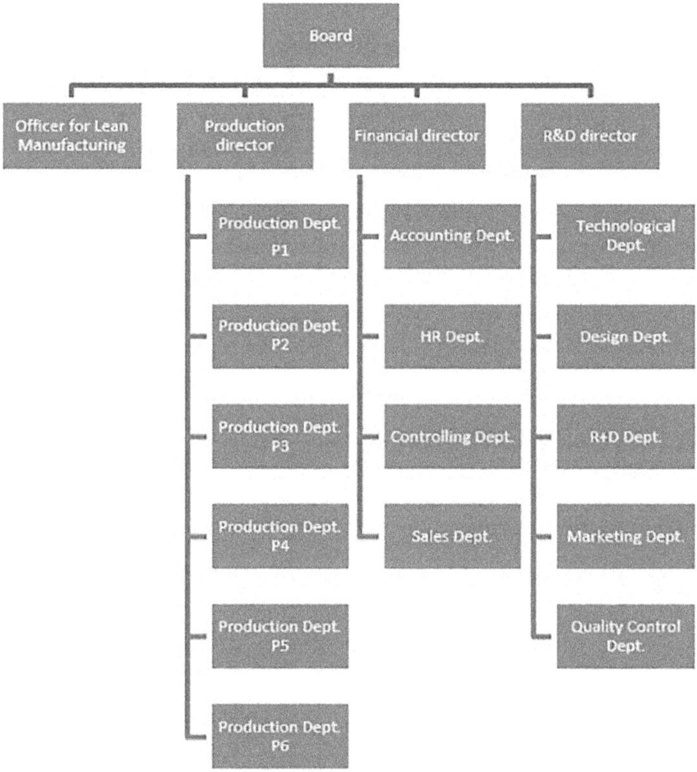

Source: developed by the author [Romek 2013]

Machines used in the enterprise varied in age, but were modernised or replaced with new ones on a regular basis. The Production Dept. P3 was selected as the site of the SMED project; it was where high-alumina products were baked and bonded chemically. One phase of the manufacturing process consisted in the manual or mechanised formation of ceramic mouldings with the use of mainly hydraulic presses with the tonnage of between 1,600 and 2,500 tonnes. In addition to physical and chemical parameters, the final shape of the mouldings is a key determinant of their usability.

3.2. Identification of wastes and the decision to implement Lean Manufacturing

Production Department P3 delivered a wide range of products, but recurrent delays in production schedules (frequently caused by underestimated changeover times) disturbed the timely handling of customers' orders. Because of the lack of appropriate standards, the activities of changeover teams could not be efficiently planned. Long changeover times meant that production plans had to allow for large and uneconomic batches exceeding 10,000 pieces in order to reduce as much as possible the frequency of changeovers during which presses were shut down. Another factor contributing to the necessity of making large batches, and consequently to substantial amounts of work in the process, was the overlapping of customers' orders, which additionally extended the lead times. At the same time, the increasing diversity of orders forced the enterprise to increase the frequency of changeovers so that smaller batches of around 50 pieces could be delivered. With all this in mind, the enterprise's management decided to introduce SMED. Other Lean Manufacturing tools – 5S and TPM Autonomous Maintenance – were already being implemented.

3.3. The course of the implementation process

The table below presents a schedule of activities making up the pilot implementation of SMED in the enterprise.

Fig. 7. The schedule of SMED implementation

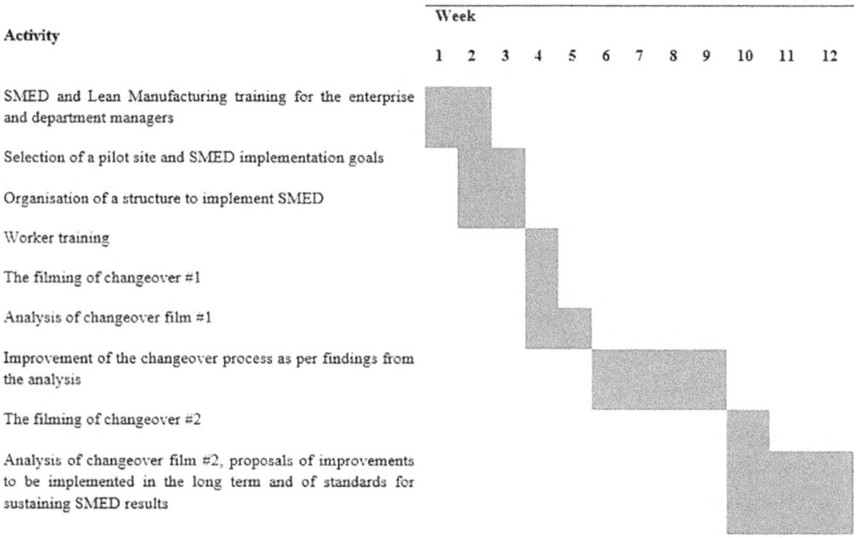

Source: developed by the author [Romek, 2013]

The implementation process started with a training, during which managers were familiarised with SMED principles and advantages. Thereafter, the board of the enterprise named the Laeis 1600 press as the SMED pilot site. The press was one of three identical machines used in the department, so standards created for it would also apply to the other two machines. The longest changeover time recorded for the selected press was 240 minutes. The management wanted to reduce it to around 190 minutes, i.e. by 20 %.

Before SMED was introduced into P3, changeovers were performed on each shift by teams consisting of:

- the machine operator
- two mechanics
- the electrician
- the quality inspector

Teams performed changeovers using their own, non-standard methods, so changeovers varied in duration from 120 to 240 minutes. Even though changeovers were handled in different ways, several operations were common to all of them:

- cleaning of the press
- preparation for disassembly

- disassembly
- mounting of the tools
- centring of the tools
- setting of working dimensions and parameters
- a test run.

The mechanics' duties included the delivery of the moulds to the press by using the gantry crane, the replacement of the used moulds with new ones and setting and regulating the press for work. The electrician checked the moulds for alignments and set the pressure and other working parameters. The test pieces made subsequently by the press operator were assessed by a quality inspector, who approved the changeover process.

The main members of the organisational structure designed to implement SMED in P3 were:

- The Leader: the head of the Production Dept. P3
- Observers
  - o the production foreman
  - o the maintenance manager
  - o the maintenance foreman
  - o the press group leader
  - o the industrial safety and health specialist
  - o the press group leader from another department using the same changeover operations
- The Changeover Team
  - o 2 mechanics
  - o the press operator
  - o the electrician
  - o the quality inspector
- The Facilitator: the Board's Officer for Lean Manufacturing

In the next step, the project team was trained in SMED principles and Lean Manufacturing basics. Its members were also familiarised with the requirements of SMED and the implementation methodology that was to be used during the next stages of the SMED project. They were instructed to perform changeovers at the usual pace (without trying to accelerate or slow down operations), so that the "typical" durations could be recorded.

After training, a changeover was carried out so that its course could be studied. The sequence of tasks performed by the changeover team was the following:

1. the press operator – pre-cleaned the press
2. mechanics 1 and 2 – brought a new mould and dismounted and removed the old mould
3. the press operator – carried out the main cleaning of the press
4. mechanics 1 and 2 – brought and mounted a new mould and adjusted its alignments
5. the electrician – measured the mould alignments and set up the press
6. the quality inspector – measured the test pieces, checked their density and approved the changeover.

The necessary changeover data were recorded with the following tools:

1. An observation sheet on which the sequence and durations of particular tasks was written down,
2. An improvements sheet,
3. A plan of the press site for drawing a spaghetti diagram presenting the workers' movements,
4. A camcorder and a still camera for recording the course of the changeover.

The measurements taken during the changeover are summarised in Table 3 below.

Table 3. Operations recorded during changeover #1 and their times

Operation	**Operator**	**Mechanic 1**	**Mechanic 2**	**Electrician**	**Quality Inspector**
	Duration (min)				
Pre-cleaning of the press	15				
Main cleaning	52				
Waiting		27	39	82	4
Seeking		2			
Extra works		55	50		
Disassembly, assembly and set-up work		103	98	37	
Measurements of test pieces (approval)					33

Source: developed by the author [Romek 2013]

Changeover #1 was completed in 237 minutes. Following its analysis, the SMED team identified the following inefficiencies:

1. Changeover was not prepared. The workers wasted time looking for necessary tools.
2. All tasks were internal (the machine had to be shut down)
3. The workers waited for their turn instead of trying to do their jobs concurrently.
4. The adopted sequence of tasks made the operator clean the press twice and the mechanics made corrections where necessary.
5. The workers were confused because intermediate storage locations or tool storage places were not marked.

To convert internal operations into external ones (the latter are carried out while the machine is running), the SMED team analysed the changeover video and the comments on the monitoring sheets. It was established that in order to make the process more efficient the operator could put on the protective suit before shutting down the machine, prepare tools necessary to clean the press and arrange them on the shadow board by the machine. Providing the mechanics with another shadow board for their tools was also found useful. Another recommendation was that a mould should be delivered before the machine was shut down, when the changeover was already in progress. All electricians' tasks remained internal as before, but the Quality Inspector was requested to prepare for product density calculations beforehand.

A new layout of the press site with designated places for storing the moulds was drawn up. Cleaning standards were created so that the press would not have to be cleaned several times during the changeover. The tasks of particular workers were described as instructions and displayed by the press. The workstation was renovated to make cleaning easy. Other improvements were also proposed, such as the standardisation of the screws and holes, the pre-setting of the basic pressing parameters, the cutting of grooves in mould edges to facilitate their alignment, etc.

After the changeover process was modified and improved as the SMED team recommended, it was rerun in the presence of all members of the SMED team. The new times of the tasks performed during a changeover are presented in Table 4.

Table 4. A comparison of the times measured during changeover #1, target times after the conversion of internal tasks into external ones and the actual times measured during changeover #2

Item	**Opera-tor**	**Mecha-nic**	**Mechanic 2**	**Electrician**	**Quality inspector**	**Total changeover time**
Times recorded during changeover #1 (min)	67	187	187	119	37	237
Target times after the conversion of internal tasks into external ones (min)	40	149	149	91	15	183
Actual times recorded during changeover #2 (min)	39	118	118	47	6	130
Time saved (%)	**40**	**20**	**20**	**24**	**59**	**23**

Source: developed by the author [Romek 2013]

According to the data above, the actual times achieved in the pilot implementation of SMED were better than the company management expected. The modified changeover was completed in 130 minutes, so it was shorter by approximately 46 % compared with the "old" procedure. The analysis of changeover #2 provided an opportunity for defining a range of actions towards sustaining the pilot implementation results. The adopted action plan provided for:

1. the development of changeover standards,
2. the preparation of Gantt graphs showing the sequence of changeover tasks and their times, as well as indicating which tasks could be performed in parallel,
3. the development of a checklist with all tasks necessary to complete a changeover / set up the machine, including the preparation of tools, measurements and logistics
4. the introduction of monitoring and visualisation of changeovers. A board displaying information on performed changeovers such as times, problems

encountered and solutions applied was to be installed by the press. A decision was also made to audit the course of changeovers.
5. monitoring the presses for OEE (overall equipment effectiveness).

3.4. The effects of implementation

The implementation of SMED brought the following benefits to the enterprise:

- the press changeover time decreased from 237 to 130 minutes (by approx. 46 %),
- time inputs from the operator and the mechanics decreased by 42 % and 37 %, respectively,
- time inputs from the electrician and the quality inspector decreased by 52 % and 60 %,
- the total distance the members of the changeover team walked decreased from 1,891 m to 875 m (by 54 %),
- press productivity increased by around 170 additional pieces per shift.

4. The implementation of Kamishibai [developed based on Krajnik, 2014]

4.1. Description of the enterprise

The enterprise presented in this section was established in north-eastern Poland in 1995 to manufacture furniture of honeycomb board (paperboard honeycomb sandwiched between paper liners). Its workforce of more than 1,500 delivered more than 220 different items, mostly lacquered and high-polish beds and unit furniture. Exports, sold mainly to Western European countries (France, the UK, Germany, etc.) and the USA, accounted for almost 97 % of the enterprise's total sales. In 2010, the board of the enterprise decided to implement some elements of Lean Manufacturing. The project started with the implementation of 5S, but it was scattered all around the organisation and failed to reach all areas. As a result, particular departments used 5S in their own way.

Because of its key customer, the enterprise had to proceed with improvements. A new project was set up, in which external consultants were to deliver theoretical training and practical skills workshops on Lean Manufacturing to workers in the selected areas of the company. In the next step, the remaining workers were to be trained by the enterprise's in-house trainers. Administration departments and auxiliary departments backing up production processes were excluded from the project scope.

For over two years, workers were trained in Lean Manufacturing methods and tools, such as 5S, TPM, SMED, standardised work and the identification of waste.

The pace of training was so fast that the workers did not have the time to consolidate their knowledge, nor did it allow the proper planning of improvements. Another shortcoming was that the departments covered by the project and other departments clearly differed in their working methods.

4.2. Identification of wastes and the decision to implement Kamishibai

One of the identified wastes was that the workers did not apply the knowledge of Lean Manufacturing that was imparted to them during the training. The overwhelming curriculum and the high intensity of the training meant that workers had to quickly absorb large chunks of theoretical knowledge. At the same time, there were no plans for verifying or consolidating their knowledge in the post-training period. Consequently, different workers were at different levels of development and this caused problems with making changes in the enterprise.

The high costs of worker training that the enterprise had to incur were accompanied by the cost of the time when workers were in training and were not involved in production. When training sessions were held on Saturdays or after work, workers were entitled to overtime pay. The English-speaking trainers meant that the workers had problems absorbing new information.

The audits that were carried out to assess the amount of Lean Manufacturing knowledge that the workers had retained from the training showed that only every sixth production worker could name the main types of waste in the enterprise and give examples of waste relative to their jobs. It was also found that the workers were not provided with opportunities to consolidate their knowledge or lacked motivation to put it into work (by contributing to a suggestions system, etc.).

To refresh and enhance the workers' knowledge, a system of simple audits utilising the *Kamishibai cards* was designed. Each card had a unique number and contained four simple questions on topics discussed during the training and workshops[1]. Right under the questions, the correct answers were provided for workers' responses to be verified and corrected if they were wrong. The A-side of

---

1 Kamishibai consists in simple audits that assess workers' performance and their use of Lean tools and teach the auditor and the auditee to observe a process and think about how it can be improved. Kamishibai is little known and relatively rarely used not only in Poland, but also in Europe.

the card (with the questions) was green. The red colour of the B-side indicated that the card had already been used during the audit.

The cards were stored in two containers placed by the machine so that the workers could read them at any time. The cards in the first container were placed with the green side up and in the second container with the red side up. Once all cards were used in the audits, they were moved to the second container and turned the green side up. In addition to the cards, a schedule of audits and scoresheets were developed for all workers to view. The scoresheets did not have the names and surnames of individual workers because they presented the scores of departments or of their units. During an audit, the auditor would draw a random card from the container and check the schedule to see which worker's turn it was. An audit did not last longer than 5 minutes and the score was written down on the scoresheet. The numbers of points scored by particular units were reviewed to find out which topics the workers knew best and which needed to be explained more fully. The Kamishibai system is not only inexpensive to implement and run, but it also ensures equal involvement of all workers.

4.3. The course of the implementation process

The implementation of the Kamishibai system in the enterprise was divided into the following stages:

1. First, the results of internal audits assessing the workers' knowledge of Lean Manufacturing were reviewed. A benchmark visit to a company that was a long-time user of Kamishibai allowed the project team to better understand how the system worked and to create their own approach to its implementation. It was decided that the Kamishibai cards (see specimens in Fig. 8) should cover four main problem areas (waste, 5S, standardisation, industrial safety and health (ISH)) and additionally TPM-Autonomous Maintenance and problem-solving methods. Three sites were selected for the pilot run of the Kamishibai audits.

Fig. 8. A specimen of the Kamishibai card

KAMISHIBAI CARD

Card 9 of 15

1. ISH

Are there special places in our factory for fork lifts to park? Are they easy to find?

Special parking places for fork lifts are designated in the production departments and warehouses. / They are marked by a "fork lift" sign on a board or on the floor.

WASTE

What is the waste of overproduction?

Overproduction is the biggest and costliest of all types of waste. It is "production made to stock" in order to utilise free capacity. It consists in making more products than ordered or before they are ordered.

3. 5S

What is the purpose of S4 (standardisation) in the 5S method?

The aim of standardisation is to create procedures enhancing and sustaining S1, S2 and S3.

4. CONTINUOUS IMPROVEMENT

How are defective elements marked in our factory?

With red tags.

Source: developed by the author [Krajnik, 2014]

2. Subsequently, meetings were held with the Managing Director and the top and medium-level management to present the Kamishibai approach and discuss the best ways of implementing it. The schedule of the meetings is shown in Table 5.

Table 5. The schedule of meetings with the management

Week	**6**	**6**	**7**	**8**
Hours	10:00–11:30	14:30–16:00	10:00–11:30	13:15–14:45
Participants	Shift I foremen	Shift II foremen	Shift III foremen	Foremen
	Directors, medium-level managers			
Delivered by	Lean Leader and the team	Lean Leader and the team	Lean Leader and the team	Lean Leader and the team

Source: developed by the author [Krajnik, 2014]

3. In stage 3, a plan for implementing Kamishibai in the pilot sites was drawn up and presented to the sites' foremen and the production manager for discussion. The implementation process was scheduled for 17 weeks. In the table below, the time distribution of particular activities is shown.

Fig 9. The implementation schedule of Kamishibai for the pilot sites

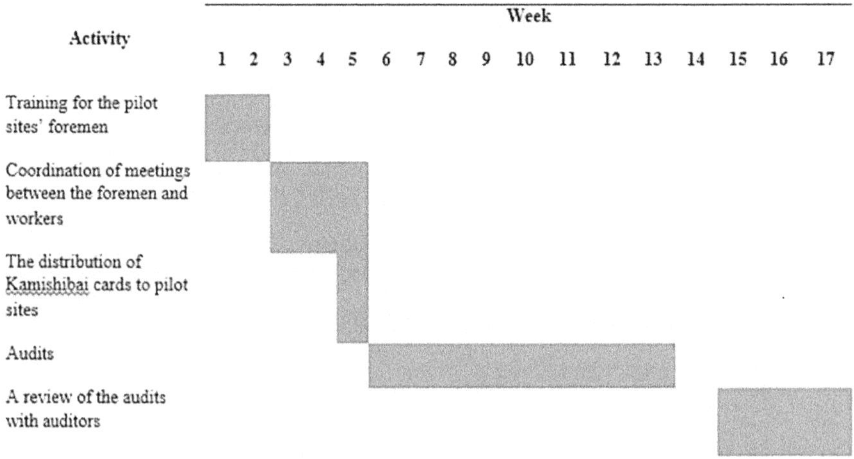

Source: developed by the author [Krajnik 2014]

4. At the next stage, 60-minute information meetings with workers in the pilot sites were held. The meetings were delivered by the sites' foremen, who had been trained in Kamishibai and the methodology of information meetings. This approach was new because in the past all training events and meetings were delivered by senior managers or external consultants.
5. At stage 5, the Kamishibai cards, scorecards and the schedules of audits were delivered to workstations in the pilot sites one week before the audits were to start so as to give workers time to read the cards and ask their foreman for clarification. In total, three sets of fifteen cards each were prepared. Because the questions on the cards did not recur, each worker was expected to read 60 questions on different aspects of Lean Manufacturing. The foremen tried to explain questions that the workers found more difficult to answer. Sixty-five audits were performed. Their results revealed that the workers were the most knowledgeable about industrial safety and hygiene issues, while the 5S questions were the most difficult for them. It was established that the workers gave wrong answers mainly because of lack of measures consolidating their knowledge of Lean Manufacturing.

Figure 10 presents the cycle of Kamishibai audits in the enterprise.

Figure 10. The cycle of Kamishibai audits in a pilot site (first a card is drawn from the container)

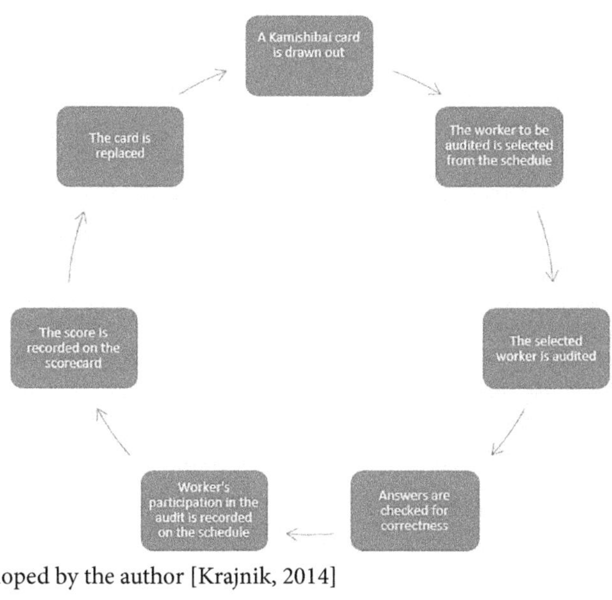

Source: developed by the author [Krajnik, 2014]

The pilot implementation was followed up by an anonymous survey that covered all workers and foremen in the pilot sites. Their answers were analysed to find out how they viewed the Kamishibai method, its effectiveness and the methodology of its implementation. The survey was completed by 93 % of workers, of whom 95 % gave high ratings to activities increasing their awareness of what they knew and to the new working method; 80 % were satisfied that they participated in the pilot implementation. All workers in the enterprise were advised of the survey results. The managers decided that the Kamishibai system should be extended to other areas in the enterprise. It was estimated that the amount of time necessary to implement the system across the enterprise was around 12 months.

4.4. The effects of implementation

The implementation of the Kamishibai method enabled the enterprise:

- to collect data showing how much the workers knew about Lean Manufacturing
- to improve their knowledge of the audit topics from approx. 20 % to 60 %
- to make plans for additional training on particular Lean Manufacturing tools
- to consolidate the knowledge which the workers gained during 2 years of training
- to train the medium-level managers in the delivery of training and information meetings to workers.

Bibliography

Bednarek M., Gajewski M., Luna Niño L.F. (2013), *Continuous Improvement Management – otra vía hacia la empresa lean*, SAN Łódź, UPSLP San Luis Potosi

Bednarek M. (2013), *Lean Manufacturing – results of selected implementation project*, "Journal of Intercultural Management", Vol. 5, No.4

Bojakowski Ł. (2014), *Koncepcja usprawnienia zarządzania produkcją poprzez zastosowanie elementów Total Productive Maintenance (TPM) na przykładzie przedsiębiorstwa produkcyjnego*, a Wydział Inżynierii Produkcji Politechniki Warszawskiej thesis.

Goldratt E., Cox. J. (1984), *The Goal*, Nord River Press,

Imai M. (2006), *Gemba Kaizen*, MT Biznes, Warszawa.

Krajnik M. (2014), *Kamishibai – pilotażowe wdrożenia metody na przykładzie jednego wydziału w przedsiębiorstwie produkcyjnym*, a Wydział Inżynierii Produkcji Politechniki Warszawskiej thesis.

McKone K., Schroeder R. et. al. (2001), *The impact of Total Productivity Maintenance practices on manufacturing performance*, "Journal of Operations Management", Vol. 17.

Mitrofanov S.P. (1963), *The Scientific principle of the organization of group production*, Mashgiz, Moscow –Leningrad

Pietrov V.A. (1968), *Flowline group production planning*, Business Publ. Limited.

Romek A. (2013), *Zastosowanie metody szybkiego przezbrojenia (SMED) na przykładzie prasy hydraulicznej w przedsiębiorstwie wytwarzającym ceramiczne wyroby ogniotrwałe*, a Wydział Inżynierii Produkcji Politechniki Warszawskiej thesis

Wielicki T. (2000), *Ewolucyjny model doskonalenia firmy XXI wieku: od ISO i TQM do organizacji inteligentnej* [in:] W.M. Grudzewski, I.K. Hejduk (ed.), *Przedsiębiorstwo przyszłości*, Difin, Warszawa.

Womack J., Jones D. (1996), *Lean thinking*, Simon and Schuster, New York.

Marcin Lisowski, Mariusz Bednarek
University of Social Sciences

Lean Manufacturing and Logistics Distribution 3.0

Abstract: The importance of logistics distribution has never been greater than today. The magnitude of change in the company environment, driven by digital transformation and modern management solutions and improvement methods (Lean/KAIZEN), has dramatically changed the composition of the market, also setting new rules for the new dot.com normality. Digitalisation presents unique challenges and opportunities in defining new capabilities and competitive advantages in the operation and strategic structure of the business. Big Data and the Internet of Things are becoming the defining paradigms which influence the process of logistics distribution and develop into a key fundament for the third technology evolution.

The convergence of both these trends has changed the data stream that links to the business, where the volume of digital data grows by 50 % [Ross 2016, p. 154] every year. This phenomenon is propelled by the ubiquitous presence of sensor-driven components through which the analogue world gets connected to the on-line network. Companies thus gain new analytical possibilities of obtaining new knowledge from the surrounding infrastructure and of effectively integrating it with the decision process.

This new competitive business landscape is driven by the abundance of the data and proliferation of new technologies that allow data streams to be captured and contextualised into vital business knowledge. This converted information has always been a tool of competition, but it is only today that the cost of generating and transmitting data has been reduced to almost zero. Companies need to implement new solutions for managing the greater volumes, velocity and variety of data to improve their operational capability in order to ensure that the quality of their services measures up to the evolving expectations of all stakeholders and to customer needs.

Key words: Big Data, Internet, E-commerce, logistic, distribution

Introduction [Bednarek 2015]

The implementation practice unifies Lean Manufacturing and Kaizen into a coherent notion of Lean/Kaizen. How Lean and Kaizen differ from each other has been the object of many definitional discussions and debates because they use similar methods, principles and paradigms. In the authors' opinion, resolving this dilemma lies outside the scope of this publication and it is not likely to considerably enhance any aspects of the industrial practice of implementing Lean Manufacturing.

The idea of *kaizen* that has been introduced by Masaaki Imai [1992] can be explained as a continuous improvement of organisational processes through gradual but consistent modifications involving the entire company workforce. *Kaizen* is the antithesis of drastic, one-off measures aimed to radically boost efficiency or productivity or cut costs, which are typical of restructuring initiatives based on the principles of reengineering, etc. The "shock therapies" cost a fortune, disrupt companies' operations and negatively affect both staff and customers, thus amounting to the manifestation of insufficient maturity, opportunism or lack of foresight on the part of the company' managers.

Kaizen is intended for areas where processes adding value, i.e. *gemba*, are carried out. In managing *kaizen*, two main goals are pursued:

- to achieve the repeatability of a task by establishing a performance standard;
- to promote standardisation through training and discipline of work.

The operational basis for *kaizen* is the Kaizen Management System [http://lejecma.vm139.remotion.nl/gfx_content/Kaizen%2520Management], focused on ongoing change management and reduction of waste. The four pillars of the system are:

- Total Flow Management, TFM;
- Total Productive Management, TPM;
- Total Service Management, TSM;
- Total Quality Management, TQM.

TQM is an all-inclusive approach to managing quality issues. TSM consists in the implementation of Lean concepts, mainly 5S and TPM, in offices and service departments. TPM represents a combination of a failure free-production system and initiatives aimed to remove all waste affecting the operation of a company's machinery and equipment. Total Flow Management is a comprehensive concept for overseeing flows taking place within a company (see Fig 1). One of the most prominent authors writing about TFM is E. Coimbra [2009, p. 31].

Table 1. Total Flow Management

TFM – Total Flow Management		
Production line design	Internal logistics flow	External logistics flow
- low-cost automation - standardised work - line supply - line design	- production planning, a pull system - balancing (levelling) - synchronisation - transport, storage	- flow of information - flow of finished products - flow of materials
Supply chain design		

Source: developed by the authors based on [Coimbra, 2009].

The components of TFM [Piasecka-Głuszak 2011, pp. 276–299] include an integrated approach to managing the design of production lines and supply chains and internal and external logistics, including logistics distribution 3.0. TFM is a means of optimising and coordinating deliveries, transport and the storage of materials and intermediate goods provided by suppliers with in-house storage and deliveries to customers.

1. Digital evolution in logistics – the emergence of distribution model 3.0

It is imagined that one of the main roles for the company's logistic operational capabilities is to sustain high competitiveness in the digital market in the midst of dynamic changes driven by new technological developments. The effective integration of company's operational processes with its immediate environment is now a crucial factor defining its strategy. The available literature highlights a variety of logistics functions that allow it to be conceptualised as a scientific discipline. However, there are also coherent elements based on which logistics can be defined as the management of specific functions relating to the movement of goods and storage [Baier, Rutkowski 1995, p. 16], which is central to the ongoing improvement of physical flows from the manufacturer to the final user. The key ingredient of this process is a two-way data stream, with which the optimal cost position of the whole integrated process can be maintained [Gabralski, Rutkowski, Wrzosek 2000, pp. 436–437]. The key concepts on logistics are as follows:

- A physical flow of material final goods and an integrated information stream
- Philosophy emphasising an integrated and systematic nature of the flow
- A field of knowledge that encompasses a complete process and flows of goods and information in the economy

The key elements of these three perspectives reveal two important and parallel flows within logistics. The first one involves physical products and material goods and the other encompasses information, i.e. a stream of data for effective monitoring and refining the elements of the whole logistic process [Skowronek, Wolski 2008, p. 17]. Both flows lie at the core of logistics distribution. Their primary aims are to control and provide effective service to the end user while making constant efforts to optimise the costs [Rutkowski 2005, p. 17]. From this perspective, logistics distribution is a set of rules and processes focused on delivering the final product to the consumer when and where needed, and on ensuring high quality of the service. Its key objective seems to be the role of a link between the production and sales divisions, which is established to eliminate gaps in [Christopher 1996, pp. 151–152]:

- Time – the difference between the actual delivery and customer-expected lead times
- Space – the distance between the customer and the production facility
- Quantity – the difference between the number of products made and the actual demand
- Assortment – the dichotomy between customer needs and expectations and producer capacity
- Information – the amount of information about potential consumers and their product awareness available to the producer.

The moment of change

The foundations of a successful distribution process are information and the company's ability to define and deploy an effective mechanism for storing and analysing the data. According M.E.Porter, we are witnessing the third wave of information technology evolution, which changes the principles of information clustering and analysis [Porter, Heppelmann 2015]. The new form of data exchange leads to a new paradigm of competition, reshapes the business environment and has implications for firms' strategies. The same technology and forces that contribute to the evolution of the logistics distribution structure have also a more direct impact on the structure of information flows. As the velocity, volume and variety of data stream change all along the channel through which it travels, new challenges and opportunities in managing logistic processes arise.

The first wave of information technology appeared before the advent of novel technologies. Hard copies of documents and analyses were exchanged for manual update and first attempts were made to standardise data by introducing computer-based solutions for the automated execution of some business processes [Porter, Millar 1985].

- With the existing solutions being developed into the ERP systems, information was becoming a key element of competitive advantage. Distribution was not planned, nor was it realised that the physical flow handling could be streamlined and some of its costs could be reduced by stronger integration of its key functions [Rushton, Croucher, Baker 2015, pp. 9–10]. The above mechanism can be tagged as logistics distribution 1.0, which is characterised by off-line information processing.
- The second wave of information technology came with the rise of the Internet. Its inexpensive and ubiquitous connections form a new on-line network that allows companies to incorporate more integrated activities into their ecosystems [Porter 2001]. Logistics distribution has earned recognition as a new catalyst for the enhancement of business environment [Porter 2001, p. 9]. The emergence of a popular e-business and electronic channel innovated information flow. Internet allows firms to enter into the second phase of the technology evolution, characterised by the logistics distribution 2.0 and the integration of its key components: e-commerce, intranet and extranet.
- The third wave of information technology is related to the emergence of a product being an integrated element of the stream of information. With the rise of sensor-driven products connected through the cloud solution embedded in the system, it has become possible to store and analyse data in real time with the surrounding environment, by enabling the integration of its own network infrastructure with the digital ecosystem into one data-fuelled information stream. The changed status quo has created new challenges for the companies by reshaping the economy [Porter, Heppelmann 2014]. This is a major leap in technology, influencing the quality and possible uses of information, which becomes now an important asset that companies can use to differentiate themselves in the competitive landscape. It is also a stepping stone towards another stage of evolution – logistics distribution 3.0 – driven by Big Data and the Internet of Things.

Fig. 1. Components of logistics distribution

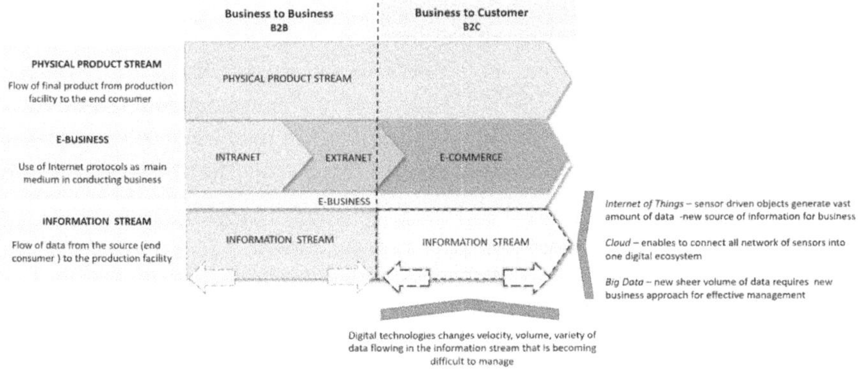

Source: developed by the author.

1.1. Implementation of IoT to support the physical product flow in logistic chain

Today's companies perceive information as a key factor determining their competitiveness in the local market. The ability to capture and analyse data, transferring into information and visualised as an analytical report, becomes a paramount objective for the business decisions. The new information stream is becoming more democratised across all management functions and available to support the decisions of all operational cells. This new process becomes an advantage for companies and can be achieved by providing particular stakeholders with information and the required knowledge. In qualitative terms, information is characterised by [Szymoniak 2015, pp. 11–12]:

- Relativity – adherence to the recipient's expectations;
- Accuracy – correspondence with the recipient's knowledge and capabilities;
- Topicality – updates must take account of the context and the rate at which its current version changes;
- Completeness – information must contain enough data so that it can be converted into the knowledge required by the recipient;
- Cohesion – individual items must be properly arranged, the form and content of information must be consistent with each other and the data must be updated with the focus on the purpose of information;
- Adequacy – the presentation and description of information must be relevant to its content;
- Availability – information must be readily available;

- Credibility – the correctness and reliability of the data must be confirmed;
- Compatibility – information must be consistent with other information.

The flow of information is becoming increasingly complex today. The physical world is gradually merging with the information system where objects embedded with sensors or actuators connected through the wireless technology are slowly integrating into the Internet ecosystem, enabling data transmission in real time. The Internet of Things (IoT) has a unique identity and is becoming part of the digital network. The key focus of IoT is to enhance the capabilities of objects (things) which are traditionally perceived as not associated with the Internet, and to communicate and exchange data between themselves and the surrounding environment. That enhanced connectivity increases the ability of physical products to become part of a new source of knowledge and effectively a new frontier of companies' Business Intelligence.

The IoT is described "as a dynamic global network infrastructure with self-configuring capabilities based on standard and interoperable communication protocols where physical and virtual 'things' have identities, physical attributes, and virtual personalities and use intelligent interface, and are seamlessly integrated into the information network" [Bahga, Madisetti 2014, p. 22]. According to Bagha and Madisetti, the definition of IoT devices addresses some of their key features, characterising them as devices that [Bahga, Madisetti 2014, p. 22–23]:

- can be self-adaptive and can dynamically reconfigure themselves to the surrounding environment, as well as are able to take action relevant to the existing conditions;
- can be self-configured and work together within a network;
- may provide a support to some interoperable communication protocols and communicate with the infrastructure;
- have a unique identity and identifier (IP address or URI) and can be monitored and controlled by the user through the embedded interface;
- are parts of a network, so they can communicate and exchange data with other devices.

Investing in IoT to create a network of physical objects connected via the Internet to communicate with the infrastructure is becoming a paramount activity in the value stream, where the possibility of retrieving data from connected devices to use them in the decision process is considered the biggest gain in the competitive landscape. According to McKinsey, the impact of a sensor-driven information process can be predominantly seen in optimised operations. It is estimated that being able to predict the wearing out of machines can reduce the maintenance cost by almost 25 % [Bughin, Chui, Manyika, 2016]. The clustering of devices into one coherent operating environment can effectively and significantly improve decision-making by creating more accurate and relevant analytical models. Michael Chui, Markus Löffler and Roger Roberts have described the key areas where IoT can generate exceptional results [Chui, Löffler, Roberts 2010, p. 3–5]:

Sensors and actuators embedded into physical products not only monitor and track their behaviour, but also communicate with the infrastructure to report on changes in conditions, thus enhancing the situational awareness. The implementation of the IoT functionality in some factories can effectively elevate productivity from 10 to 20 % and can offer energy savings in the range of 10 to 25 %[McKinsey Global Institute 2015, p. 8].

- Process analysis based on embedded sensors can improve decision-making. This requires the interoperability of the IoT systems in order to capture the value of the system (40 % of the potential value can be unlocked [McKinsey Global Institute 2015, p. 4]) and the ability to utilise vast amounts of data contained in the network (e.g. only 1 % of the data available in a 30,000-sensor-driven oil rig is used to make decisions [McKinsey Global Institute 2015, p. 5]).

1.2. Contemporary models of clustering and analysing information based on the Big Data paradigm

The Peter Drucker's quote that "[y]ou can't manage what you can't measure", repeated by A.McAfee and E.Brynjoslfsson in their Management Revolution article [McAfee, Brynjolfsson 2012], has never been as relevant to management people as it is today. With the big data explosions in the last decade, the need to understand new technology and models is more essential for companies to gain advantage than ever. The Big Data is becoming a basis of competition and a source of firms' growth. According to the McKinsey report, retail companies embracing the big data technology can increase their operating margins by 60 % [McKinsey Global Institute 2011, p. 6].

Decision-making processes heavily rely on providing access to the right information at the right time. The Big Data is another example of the exponential growth in the volume of the data that can be seen as a parallel fulfilment of Moore's Law.[1] The plethora of data in contemporary firms arising from the integration of new technologies is a strong motivator for rethinking their business approach.

---

1 According to the article "Cramming more components onto Integrated Circuit," published in Electronics, the number of transistors on a computer circuit will double approximately every year.

Big Data is usually defined in terms of 5V (Volume, Velocity, Variety, Veracity and Value) that describe the composition and structure of the new data stream. No universal definition of Big Data exists, but following Colin Strong, we can highlight a few elements defining its nature [Strong 2015, pp. 7–8]:

- Huge in volume – it is estimated that 2.5 Exabyte of data were generated each day in 2012 – this figure doubles every 40 months. This rapid growth enables companies to work on a larger set of data that can be now part of one stream [[McAfee, Brynjolfsson 2012].
- High in velocity – created in real time by the ongoing gathering of information from various data endpoints, Big Data allows companies to be more agile in making decisions.
- Diverse in Variety in the structured and unstructured part (noSQL – not only SQL)[2] – Big Data can be sourced from various streams of social media and GPS sensors.
- Exhaustive in scope – in many cases, Big Data captures the entire network information.
- Fine-grained in resolution – Big Data offers an entropic view of the subject.
- Rational in nature – Big Data unlocks a new insight into the subject.
- Flexible – Big Data provides an opportunity to enlarge the scope of the subject analysed.

Fig 2. Big Data grid

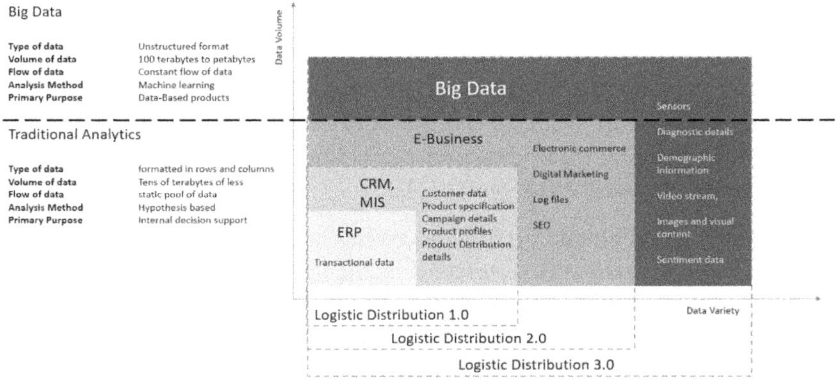

Source: developed by the author based on Davenpoint's [2014, p. 4].

---

2 NoSQL is a data environment that is sometimes referred to as non-relational, as opposed to the SQL-environment data that is a standardised data format.

A debate is still going on about whether the size of the data really matters. In his HBR review, Maxwell Wessel noticed that a more relevant question would be that about the ability to capture the right data rather than their size [Wessel 2016]. M. Wessel suggests that the primary objective should be to determine which decisions contribute to 'waste' in the business so that the legacy system can be appropriately automated to minimise the level of waste.

The continuous flow that Federico Pigni, Gabriele Piccoli and Richard Watson termed the Digital Data Stream (DDS) is a process of "encoding and transmission of data describing a related class of events" [Pigni, Piccoli, Watson 2016, p. 8].

The DDS has the potential to capture and describe six elements of an event known as 5W+H (When, Where, Who, What, Why, How), with a specific event having from one to all elements. The primary objective of the DDS is to identify and eliminate loss and delays by using an element of the event. This is described in the following latency areas [Pigni, Piccoli, Watson 2016, p. 9]:

- *response time latency* delay, which occurs in extracting data from an event
- *capture latency*, the delay that occurs in transforming data into information
- *analysis latency*, the delay that occurs in developing and defining the analytical model
- *decision latency*, which occurs in the decision process.

DDS can help extract value from an event either by the *process-to-accurate* action based on real time data processing, or by *assimilate-to-analyse*, by extracting the information insight through merging multiple data streams and a static data set [Pigni, Piccoli, Watson 2016, p. 10].

Big Data transforms the way we understand and explore the world around us. In the past, a hypothesis could be tested by using a small set of data, but now our understanding develops from the abundance of data [Mayer-Schonerberg, Cuker 2013, p. 71]. There are three classes of values that can be derived from the Big Data stream [Davenport 2014, pp. 22–24]:

- decision improvements: by adding another layer of data (e.g. geographical data, product sentiment), a different inside of the same event can be identified; as Peter Norvig, the Google director, observed, "[w]e don't have a better algorithm. We just have more data" [http://www.forbes.com/sites/scottcleland/2011/10/03/googles-infringenovation-secrets/#6c6fdc26373d];
- cost reduction: the replacement of highly decentralised data siloes with a single platform enables a more consolidated and faster process of complex analysis;

- product and service improvements: these enable a broad array of possible features to be built and define a feedback loop that conceptualises and contextualises data that can be pulled back from the digital ecosystem.

There are a several ways to create value from the Big Data by [McKinsey Global Institute 2011, pp. 4–6]:

- Implementing higher level of transparency by increasing data accessibility to all stakeholders and by exchanging information within the same information flow;
- Implementing on-demand experimentation and improving performance by capturing data in digital form to analyse them across the whole business spectrum;
- Implementing new segmentation models with a view to tailoring services or products to the specific demands of a group of customers;
- Integrating new automated algorithms into the decision process in order to eliminate the possibility of human errors, minimise risks and unearth valuable insight;
- Integrating new innovative business models (e.g. platform-based).

2. Logistics distribution model 3.0 in practice

The new competitive landscape is changing at a faster rate than ever before. The data and the ability to extract knowledge from different datasets become the foundation of a more agile and robust business approach in the digital ecosystem. First the emergence of new, connected products and then their growing number have reshaped the value chain for businesses. Before a product can become 'a smart product', data have to be generated in isolated and fragmented domains inside the company, from procurement to customer service. The deployment of a mechanism for including larger data sets into the process of quantifying all elements of a decision process can, however, be perceived as troublesome. Nevertheless, the coupling of the new source of unstructured data with transactional data and historical product profile patterns enables a much broader spectrum of a new form of analysis. Data analytics allows for unlocking a new, potential value held in the information stream. A 'data lake' connects all individual elements into a single platform for retrieving and feeding the data from various data points into the analytical business intelligence process [Porter, Heppelmann 2015].

Having entered the age of hyperconnectivity described by Rodney Heisterberg and Alah Verma, we are constantly connected to the Internet via a myriad of applications and interfaces. As the business is now becoming part of the network, we are observing a change in the paradigm from the system of records (SOR) – a data management process of storing the data based on the ERP system suit infrastructure – to the system of engagement (SOE), defined as a decentralised real-time interaction process with all stakeholders [Heisterberg, Verma 2014, p. 70–71]. Most companies use the traditional model of business designed as a pipeline structure, which determines a step-by-step process of connecting each business domain in order to deliver value to the consumer. This approach gives this value chain a single-track shape. The availability of a new technology provides companies with an opportunity to create a platform-like structure enabling stronger interaction between the supplier, the distributor and the consumer. The one-way flow of information is replaced by a continuous information flow to generate value [Parker, Van Alstyne, Choudary 2016, p. 6]. Platforms have several features that make them superior to the linear product flow [Parker, Van Alstyne, Choudary 2016, pp. 7–12]:

- platforms utilising the network effect are deployed more rapidly in the market because by eliminating gatekeepers they give access to information when needed. The pipeline model involves a higher risk of information's being blocked at some stage of its flow and therefore of reduced transparency between partners or stakeholders (e.g. 'the bullwhip effect");
- platforms unlock sources of value creation and supply, thus enabling the share of the spare resource capacity between the stakeholders, and harness value contribution across the network;
- platforms use data-based tools to create community feedback loops
- platforms drive firms' evolution from back-office systems such as ERP or CRM to more out-of-office experiments utilising big data and shifting their focus from internal to external activity.

Connected Car

Digitalisation transforms many industries, as the impressive example of the automotive industry shows. For 49 % of respondents in the KPMG industry survey, digitalisation and connectivity was the prevailing trend in this industry [KPMG 2017]. The trend changes relations between the three components of car development – mechanic parts, electrics and software. It is expected that by 2020 the last of them will account for 60 % of R&D [Wedniwski 2015, p. 37]. This emerging shift defines a completely new role of the vehicle manufacturer, who has evolved from the mere maker of vehicles to the mobility services provider. It also enables a higher degree of connectivity between the vehicle and the infrastructure and moves outwards the boundaries of the digital ecosystem. More than 90 %

of executives in the automotive industry agree that connectivity will change the business model and over 80 % of them believe that this transformation will have a direct impact on their business [McKinsey Global Institute 2015, p. 10].

The connected vehicle concept introduced by the OEM (Original Equipment Manufacturer – vehicle manufactures) defines an enhanced communication and the exchange of data between the vehicle and the surrounding infrastructure (V2V – vehicle to vehicle and V2I – vehicle to Infrastructure) via a cloud-based solution. This exchange takes place in real time and delivers much wider and richer customer experience. There is a number of potential features (e.g. on-board diagnostic) that come with Telematics [http://www.telematics.com/ (30.03.2017)] data. The OEM primarily aims to optimise vehicle service and operation within the broader function of VRM (Vehicle Relationship Management), which enables a direct connection with the driver and assists him or her by using the current condition of the vehicle and the historical vehicle data records [McKinsey Global Institute 2014].

The current model of aftermarket distribution is rather static. According to research, the time needed to identify a fault on a vehicle accounts for 70 % of the total time spent on its maintenance [Jhou, Chen 2013, p. 9]. Precise diagnosing and troubleshooting thus becomes the paramount objective of the aftermarket process. The Telematics solution in a car connected via the OBD-II port (retrofit solution) enables direct data transmission from the vehicle directly to OEM. The OBD (on-board diagnostics) enables the provision of functionality such as VDS (Vehicle Diagnostic Server), which can be offered to the driver in the form of augmented service and diagnostics. The full scan of a vehicle can be encoded into a data stream and transferred in real time by using the 3.5G cloud solution [Chen, Wang 2011, pp. 13–16] from OBU (On-Board-unit) to VDS.

With the introduction of this process, the current mechanism of vehicle diagnostics will be replaced by the Big Data solution that derives data streams directly from the vehicle via the VDS system, allows the condition of the vehicle to be assessed without any manual intervention and defines the key issues that may put it off the road. The vehicle diagnostics process can be integrated into the broader platform for handling the aftermarket parts distribution chain, where the fault code is directly assigned to the component of the product. That designed system provides the current model with a new digital solution. The emerging commercial and partnership model based on the V2M/IoT communication protocol enables the integration of remote diagnostics and opens up an opportunity for both B2C and B2B models to be offered via the cloud [Dewey, Ryals 2015]. The list below presents the supply chain participants that can benefit from the new telematics information streams:

- OES (Original Equipment Suppliers) – real-data transmitted directly from the vehicle to the OEM data warehouse server provides ongoing information on how a component of their vehicle functions. This solution effectively improves R&D processes as well as reduces the risk of warranty claims and recalls.
- Parts Distributors – direct information on the vehicle on the road and geolocation allows the product profile in the distribution chain to be improved on the basis of the direct maintenance data fetched from the vehicle.
- Service Centre – operational improvements reduce the amount of time necessary to identify and diagnose the vehicle fault and result in more efficient work schedules.
- Customer – higher mobility, comfort and safety (surveys show that UK residents spend more than 37 million days trying to find a mechanic to fix their car) [http://www.express.co.uk/life-style/cars/707790/British-motorists-lose-37m-days-a-year-finding-mechanic-ClickMechanic-car-repair-market].

Fig. 3. Models of Logistics Distribution

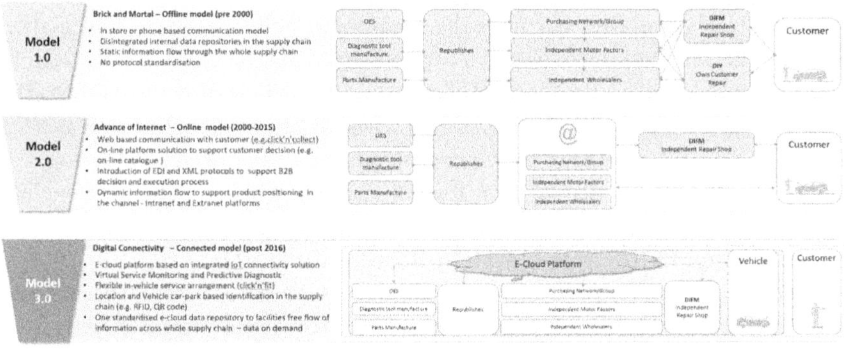

Source: developed by the author.

2.1 Sensor-driven operations as a key factor in the optimisation of internal and external distribution flows

We have already entered into the age of the digital transformation. Its biggest benefit is that we have reached a unique position where we can communicate with the analogue world by using digital means. According to Erik Brynjolfsson and Andrew Mcfree, we are already living in a 'full force' of technology, where computerisation is capable of transforming every aspect of the economy [Brynjolfsson, McAfee 2014, p. 9]. Digitalisation converts all types of information into bits, which are the native language of the machines. In the age of computerisation, "[i]nformation is costly to produce, but cheap to reproduce" [Brynjolfsson, McAfee 2014, pp. 62–63].

The convergence of IoT and Big Data ushers in the 4th industrial revolution. The next wave of digital transformation is expected to bring a surge of data volume and new analytical capabilities and increase connectivity power and communication with the physical world [Baaur, Wee 2015]. What makes this revolution more profound is the fusion of novel technologies and the interaction between physical and digital worlds [Schwab 2016, p. 9]. The ubiquity of digital technology providing a wide range of applications running over the sensor network and data defines a new frontier for business operations, where the management of information has always been a key to excellence [Lamsiti 2015]. This new situation imposes new challenges on companies, which have to improve their models of operation towards a greater agility and robustness and more transparent collaboration within the supply chain. The data-driven business models heavily rely on the harvesting of large data streams and creating new analytical models and data visualisation software to unlock the new 'inside' [Lansiti 2015, p. 59].

In the digital transformation, the development of the network platform hinges on the sensor-embedded systems, the centrepiece of which is the microelectromechanical systems (MEMS) technology based on devices such as sensors and actuators measuring the behaviour of an event. MEMS is an inherent component of the IoT system which enables M2M (Machine-to-Machine) communication in real time [Bauer, Shink 2014, p. 31]. It has already been proved that the MEMS technology is the right solution for mobile devices. By integrating it into other physical products, it becomes possible to feed a small portion of data into the data warehouse and collect data streams across the device network to provide all relevant business domains with new business intelligence analysis capabilities. The MEMS and data feed have already been put into use as infrared sensors, temperature sensors or sensors which detect high-frequency vibrations causing machine failure, diagnose running equipment or control the use of energy. The production of MEMS sensors is predicted to increase exponentially due to their rising popularity in different domains, but also because of a shorter development cycle and greater efficacy of the integration and deployment of this technology in the market [Bauer, Shink 2014, pp. 31–35]. The key drivers of its expansion include [Kellmereit, Obodovski 2013, p. 14]:

- miniaturisation – electronic devices are becoming smaller and more powerful (following Moore's Law), as well as more efficient in the use of electrical power;
- affordability – the cost of components and entire networks is decreasing

- De-wirelisation – wireless is becoming the key feature of analogue and mobile devices as Wi-Fi networks become more common.

Daniel Kellmereit and Daniel Obodovski argue that the M2M network has three major functions [Kellmereit, Obodovski 2013, pp. 30–45]:

- Data acquisition – hardware (mobile chips, sensors, devices and wireless modules, etc.) captures data via various sensors embedded in the network. For instance, the OBD-II device measures the condition of a vehicle and delivers a live data stream. It is estimated that by 2022 there will be 700 m cars with 1.8bn automotive M2M connections (four times as many as in 2015) [Telefonica 2013, p. 13].
- Data transport – the use of wireless networks (Bluetooth, Near-Field Communication (NFC), Wi-Fi and 4G) provides integrated connectivity known as the Connected Device Platform (CDP), which allows data transmission through all nodes across the network, remote access with the nodes and the management of data. Because of the CDP, a data stream can be directly transmitted from the vehicle via the cloud platform to the central database for analysis.
- Data Analysis – described as a wide array of data analytics supporting business functions and decision processes; information is collected from the network of sensors and analysed from the perspective of business requirements. In-between Data Analysis and Data Transport there is the Application Enablement Platform (AEP), which allows building application programming interface (API) to run data from any devices. The interface gives the user access to a device for monitoring or changing its parameters. Data transmitted from the vehicle via the OBD-II contain all diagnostic information and allow the driver's responses to specific conditions to be analysed. This shared pool of knowledge offered by the data stream enhances decision-making on the part of the product distributor (e.g. by helping decode the geolocation of the vehicle and the product profile in the distribution network), the manufacturer (e.g. by measuring the condition of the components) and the customer (e.g. by offering new forms of product support that improve customer service and the comfort of product use).

The centrepiece of a coherent communication and analytical network is cloud computing, which provides on-demand access, analytical capacity and storage that are configurable at a minimum cost and management efforts [Miller 2008, p. 8].

There are three models of cloud computing, namely: Software as a Service (SaaS), which allows a service provider to access an application over the Internet;

Platform as a Service (PaaS), through which a service provider can run or manage applications without having to invest in infrastructure; and Infrastructure as a Service (Iaas), which gives customers access to data processing, storage and analytical capabilities.

2.2 Implementation of a predictive analytical model in internal logistic

The very volume of data streaming through information channels to the company defines new opportunities for developing new analytical models. At the same time, companies are struggling to store and analyse voluminous data to create the desired 'inside'. It is becoming increasingly apparent that Thomas H. Davenport can be right in stating that the problem is not the volume but the variety of data. A survey has shown that being able to analyse a diverse stream of data coming from a new type of sources is becoming a crucial business skill [Davenpoint 2014, p. 177].

The first objective in data analytics is to build principles that will govern the process. The five analytical recommendations that Thomas H. Davenport proposed can be used as a suggestion for defining those fundaments [Davenpoint 2015]:

- identify and frame an analytical problem that needs to be resolved and a decision that needs to be made;
- define and work with the 'quantitative' people, working closely with a group which is defined as 'quant' – people who understand mathematical and analytical aspect of data – teamed up with a management that understands the business, in order to build the context of the problem;
- understand the variegated structure of the data and process, data acquisition, data types and their implications, including both small data (ERP,CRM) and big data that are not structured (e.g. sensors reading, video), fetched from various sources (e.g. IoT embedded products);
- understand the different types of analytics based on three models of analysis [Blum 2015, p. 46]:

Descriptive analysis – the simplest data clustering model for investigating current and past events. This form of analysis, which is sometimes referred to as a 'dashboard' by analogy to the instrument cluster unit in the car, offers straightforward and informative inputs. Simplicity is also its main downside, as it prevents it from generating enough information to solve complex business problems.

Predictive Analytics – i.e. the use of structured as well as unstructured data to "predict value from variables that company doesn't possess but wants to analyse".

The greater volume and broader variety of the data source enable the building of a more reliable analytical model.

Prescriptive Analysis – provides an insight into the 'whats' and 'whys' of different actions; its model is similar to that used in predictive analytics, but its aim is to capture the key determinants of the outcome.

- integrate the external and internal uses of analytics and look beyond the use of analytics as a single-purpose tool for supporting operational decision making in order to also utilise it as a source of knowledge with which new product or services can be created.

The predictive model of analysis is one that businesses desire most because it can be employed to consider various aspects of a specific object to derive a single predictive score. Predictive analytics learns from data to predict the future behaviour of phenomena so that better decisions can be made [Siegel 2013, pp. 26–27]. There is a distinct difference between forecasting and prediction. Unlike a forecasting model that focuses on the macro level, a predictive model can drill into the specifics of an object. It examines and quantifies the behaviour of an individual object and uses the decision tree as a scoring mechanism [Siegel 2013, pp. 109–110].

While companies evaluating the potential of integrating predictive models may pursue different ultimate goals, there are several areas where predictive models can be the most useful for them:

- Predicting demand – this particularly pertains to what Chris Anderson calls "the long tail product"; i.e. a niche product the demand for which is difficult to estimate [Anderson 2009, p. 22]. Companies look for solutions that enable them to build models that more accurately and dynamically quantify product forecast. The need to find a balance between inventory cost and product proximity to the customer creates a challenge in determining the geographical scope of distribution, as well as product profile, geolocation and the segmentation of customers. Historical methods work well on the 'A-B'[3] category products, but are ineffective in an environment where a small signal may bias the output. An integrated model handling different data streams (a Web-based product look-up system) can improve the operational efficiency by optimising product proposition in the local micro sector.
- Improved pricing – the surge of e-commerce websites leads to the establishment of a dynamic pricing mechanism taking account of the promotional

3 ABC categorisation based on a Pareto model, 20 % of the range generates 80 % of the revenue.

sale of a product and seasonal trends. On the basis of the review of the log file information, the product range can be adjusted to the specific customer or product segmentation and the sales funnel can be accordingly modified to match the customer profile. Integrated algorithmic targeting can improve the adequacy of on-line and off-line prices.
- Predictive maintenance – the ability to control and monitor machines in real time allows for the early detecting of potential failures. From the company's operational perspective, it is essential not only to be able to maintain productivity, but also to reinvent the stream of information on vehicle behaviour in the distribution channel.

3. The transformative potential of Logistics Distribution 3.0 in business

Technology is becoming an inherent factor in every company's business strategy. It allows a more collaborative approach and gives all stakeholders a vital role in defining and creating the ultimate value to the customer. This leads to a so-called value constellation, i.e. a sort of a network of correlated activities [Ramirez 1994, p. 54]. The technology propelling the digitalisation shift is becoming an integrated element in the product research and development process. In the McKinsey survey, 80 % of respondents named digital operations as the driver of competitiveness [Nanry, Narayaran, Rassey 2015]. This explains why the deployment of new digital information solution delivering a sustainable data flow is envisioned as a key frontier in the business future.

The solution elevating productivity to a new level will be a stack of new technologies known as SMAC (Social technologies, Mobile technologies, Analytics technologies and Cloud computing), which provide a new stream of data and effectively new knowledge [Frank, Roehrig, Pring 2014, p. 56].

Data and analytical capabilities are becoming essential for all businesses. The focus of Total Productivity Maintenance (TPM), the backbone of the Lean concept, is on waste generated by equipment. Some studies show that over 70 % of companies use the so-called breakdown maintenance [Mayerson 2012, p. 68]. The tools that they use to identify problems (check sheets, scatter diagrams, fishbone diagrams, etc.) could be enhanced through the integration of data sources at the plant level. Sensors integrated into the data-gathering process have a direct and effectively positive influence on the flow of operations. According to Paul Maverson, data analytics is a key trend within Lean Management. It has direct implications for Six Sigma and TQM, where the integration of structured and unstructured data can generate a new value and improve operational processes [Mayerson 2012, p. 182].

Ahmed Bounfour has presented a list of arguments explaining why digital data are key factors influencing Lean Manufacturing today, which are part of a new model called 'acceluction'. In his proposed concept, the value is mainly created by the following factors [Bounfour 2016, p. 80]:

- Digitalisation of space and time,
- Multiple roles that operators play in the production space,
- Dynamic links (transactional and organic),
- The emergence of new technology systems,
- The plasticity of institutional and organisational boundaries.

The key challenge facing companies is to develop new processes for monitoring information flows. Coping with this task in the midst of the digital evolution and ever-changing composition of the data flows is becoming increasingly difficult. If a company wishes to attain competitive advantage, it must *analyse* information from the captured loop *feedback* to concentrate its strategic plans, operations and resources around a common goal [Collis 2016]. This iterative process continuously generates valuable data from which the company can derive the desired knowledge.

The emergence of new technologies has provided companies with the opportunity to integrate the concept of agile supply chain management, which facilitates rapid and continuous response to unexpected changes in customers' demand for goods and services [Rushton, Croucher, Baker 2015, p. 73]. The difference between the Lean and the Agile is that they concentrate, respectively, on reducing waste and making processes fast and nimble. The purpose of the 'agile' approach is to create a responsive operational structure characterised by Rushton, Croucher, Baker [2015, pp. 73–74]:

- Inventory level and profile optimisation;
- Direct deliveries from the manufacturer to ensure minimum delivery times;
- Replenishment orders generated with the data collected via the direct customer interface EPOS (electronic point of sales);
- Highly integrated and transparent supply chain;
- Implementation of the principles of flexible fulfilment.

The foundations of logistics distribution 3.0 described as Big Data and the Internet of Things are becoming the key drivers of digital disruption. The observed cost reduction of the information to almost 'zero' with parallel exponential data volumes growth fuels companies' ability to change their business intelligence models. Given the estimates that the data volume which corporations will handle in 2020 will be 50 times as big as it is today [Frank, Roehrigm Pring, p. 60], it seems essential to consider a new mechanism for distributing data in the information flow, built on the functionality of new technologies. Three change trends can be observed in the world today: physical goods are converted into virtual ones (following the integration of IoT and sensor-driven networks); the content of information is enhanced (as RFID sensors or GPS information is integrated with transactional data); online platforms improving transparency and collaboration among all stakeholders are created [Dobbs, Mayika, Woetzel 2015, pp. 39–40]. As a result, companies face new challenges that make them replace the traditional 'linear' approach operations with the platform-based one and improve their analytical ability and identify new opportunities which can appear on the horizon of the digital transformation.

Bibliography:

Anderson CH. (2009), *The Long Tail*, Business Books.

Bahga A., Madisetti V. (2014), *Internet of Things a hands-on approach.*

Baier F., Rutkowski K. (1995), *Logistyka*, Szkoła Główna Handlowa, Warszawa.

Bauer H., Shink S., Thalmayr F. (2014), *How big data and connected consumer could boost the market for MEMS technology*, McKinsey Semiconductors, no.4.

Baur C., Wee D. (2015), *Manufacturing's next act*, McKinsey, 06.

Bednarek M. (2015), *Zastosowanie Lean Manufacturing w Polsce i w Meksyku. Modele-praktyka-doświadczenia*, Difin,Warszawa.

Blum B., Goldfarb A., Lederman M. (2015), *The path to prescription Closing the gap between the promise and the reality of the big data*, "Rotman Management",10, p. 46.

Bounfour A. (2016), *Digital Futures, Digital Transformation: from Lean production to Acceluction*, Springer.

Brynjolfsson E., McAfee A. (2014), *The Second Machine Age*, W.W. Norton & Company.

Bughin J., Chui M., Manyika J. (2016), *An executive's guide to the Internet of Thing*, McKinsey Quarter, 09.

Christopher M. (1996), *Strategia zarządzania dystrybucją*, wyd. II, Warszawa.

Chui M., Löffler M., Roberts R. (2010), *The Internet of Things,* McKinsey Quarter, 09.

Coimbra E. (2009), *Total Flow Management with Kaizen and Lean Supply Chains*, KAIZEN Institute.

Collis D. (2016), *Lean Strategy*, Harvard Business Review, 03.

Davenpont T.H. (2014), *Big data at Work*, Harvard Business Review.

Davenpoint T.H. (2015), *Essential Principles for Understanding Analytics*, Harvard Business Review, 10.

+++**Dewey R., Leigh-Ann Ryals (2015),** *The AuTomoTive DATA moneTizATion RepoRT 2015–2016*, FC Business Intelligence Ltd, 10.

Dobbs R., Manyika J., Woetzel J. (2015), *No ordinary Disruption*, Public Afairs.

Frank M., Roehrig P., Pring B. (2014), *Code Halos*, John Wiley & Sons.

Gabralski L., Rutkowski I., Wrzosek W. (2000), *Marketing. Punkt zwrotny nowoczesnej firmy*, wyd. II, PWE, Warszawa.

Heisterberg R., Verma A. (2014), *Creating Business Agility*, John Wiley & Sons.

Imai M. (1992), *Kaizen: Tajemnica sukcesu Japonii*, translated by L. Wasilewski, Wydawnictwo ZETOM, Warszawa, based on M. Bednarek, *Doskonalenie systemów zarządzania*, Difin, Warszawa, 2007.

+++**Jheng-Syu Jhou, Shi-Huang Chen (2013),** *The Implementation of OBD-II Vehicle Diagnosis System Integrated with Cloud Computation Technology,* Second International Conference on Robot, Vision and Signal Processing.

Kellmereit D., Obodovski D. (2013), *The Silent Inteligence*, DnD Ventures.

KPMG (2017), *Global Automotive Executive Survey* 2017, 01.

Lansiti M. (2015), *The History and future of operations*, Harvard Business Review, 06.

McAfee A., Brynjolfsson E. (2012), *Big Data: The Management Revolution*, HBR, 10.

Mayerson P. (2012), *Lean Supply chain & Logistic Management*, McGraw Hill.

Mayer-Schonerberg V., Cukir K. (2013), *Big Data, a revolution that will transform how we live, work and think*, John Murray.

McKinsey Global Institute (2015), *Competing for the connected customer – perspectives on the opportunities created by car connectivity and automation*, Advanced Industries, 10.

McKinsey Global Institute (2015), Global Institute, *The Internet of Things: Mapping the Value Beyond the Hype*, 05.

McKinsey Global Institute (2014), *Connected Car, Automotive, value chain unbound*, "Advanced Industries", 10.

McKinsey Global Institute (2011), *Big Data: The Next frontier for innovation, competition, and productivity*, 06.

+++**Miller M. (2008),** *Cloud Computing: Web based application that change the way you work and Collaborate online,*Quer.

Nanry J., Narayanan S., Rassey L. (2015), *Digitizing the Value Chain*, McKinsey Quarterly, 03.

Norman R., Ramirez R. (1994), *Designing Interactive Strategy, from value chain to value constellation*, John Wiley & Sons.

+++**Parker G.G., Marshall W Van, Sangeet A., Choudary P. (2016),** *Platform Revolution*, W.W.Norton & Company.

Parker G.G., Van Alstyne M., Choudary S.P. (2016), *Platform Revolution*, W.W.Norton & Company.

Piasecka-Głuszak A. (2011), *The use of selected tools of TFM in the continuous improvement of business in the internal supply chain*, "International Journal of Management", vol. 31.

Pigni F., *Piccoli G., Watson R. (2016),* *Digital Data Streams: Creating Value from the Real Time flow of Big Data*, „California Management Review", Vol. 58, no. 3.

Porter M.E. (2001), *Strategy and the Internet*, „Harvard Business Review", 04.

Porter M.E., Heppelmann J.E. (2015), *How Smart, Connected Products Are Transforming Companies*, „Harvard Business Review", 10.

Porter M.E., Heppelmann J.E. (2014), *How Smart, Connected Products Are Transforming Competition*, Harvard Business Review, 11.

Porter M.E., Millar V.E. (1985), *How Information Gives You Competitive Advantage*, Harvard Business Review, 06.

Ramirez R.N.R. (1994), *Designing Interactive Strategy, from value chain to value constellation*, John Wiley & Sons, p. 54.

Ross A. (2016), *The Industry of the future*, Simon & Shuster.

Rutkowski K. (2005), *Logistyka dystrybucji*, Wydawnictwo SGH, Warszawa.

Rushton A., Croucher Ph., Baker P. (2015), *The handbook of logistics and distribution management, 5't edition*, Kogan Page.

Siegel E. (2013), Predictive Analytics, Wiley.

Schwab K. (2016), *The Fourth Industrial Revolution World Economy*, Forum.

+++**Shi-Huang Chen, Jhing-Fa Wang (2011),** *The Implementation of Real-time On-line Vehicle Diagnostics and Early Fault Estimation System*, EEE Computer Socety, Fifth International Conference on Genetic and Evolutionary Computing.

Skowronek Cz., Wolski Z.S. (2008), *Logistyka w Przedsiębiorstwie*, Warszawa.

Strong C. (2015), *Humanizing Big Data*, Kogen Page.

Szymoniak A. (2015), *Informatyka dla potrzeb logistyki*, Diffin, Warszawa.

Telefonica (2013), *Connected Car Industry Report.*

Wedniwski S. (2015), *The Mobility Revolution in the Automotive Industry,* Sprinter Verlag.

Wessel M. (2016), *You don't need Big Data – you need the right data,* Harvard Business Review, 03/11.

http://www.forbes.com/sites/scottcleland/2011/10/03/googles-infringenovation-secrets/#6c6fdc26373d site accessed 26.12.2016.

http://www.express.co.uk/life-style/cars/707790/British-motorists-lose-37m-days-a-year-finding-mechanic-ClickMechanic-car-repair-market data freached 21.01.2017.

http://lejecma.vm139.remotion.nl/gfx_content/Kaizen%2520Management (24 Aug. 2015)..

http://www.telematics.com/ (30.03.2017) .

Remigiusz Kozłowski
University of Lodz

Technology Innovation for Logistics Service Providers

Abstract: One of the most important and difficult tasks facing logistics service providers is choosing the appropriate technology. This service industry faces intense competition, meaning service providers need to continuously improve their production efficiency and market effectiveness. This article presents a framework for technology development for logistics service providers as a framework that provides guidance for advanced technology implementation and use.

Key words: technology selection, monitoring technology use, technological innovations

Introduction

The continued increase in labour costs is conducive to investment in technologies which can replace human inputs, be it partially or almost entirely, thus reducing the enterprise's operating outlays.

In all sectors, technological progress has been very dynamic and still tends to accelerate due to intensive globalisation processes, improved innovation commercialisation systems, facilitated information flow, etc. As a result, we now stand at the threshold of an era of automation, and also in the field of logistics. Thus, one of the most important decisions enterprises face is what technology to use to support their operations.

Currently, there is an abundance of public organisations and private enterprises offering such technologies, many of which have been newly developed and commercialised. Thus, given the increasingly broader range of technological solutions available, the question arises as to which to choose with a view to boosting growth while minimising potential problems. Therefore, technology users must apply a professional technology selection when making purchases. The implementation of a wrong technology may cause serious consequences for the company. The scope of poor selection of technology and its effect have been discussed by Kozlowski and Matejun [2015, pp. 46–57]. This included purchasing technologies too advanced for companies and implementing operations with labour not adequately familiar with the new technology. Such considerations have motivated this chapter, which presents a method of selecting the right technologies for enterprises.

The logistics industry is global in nature and often rapidly implements the latest innovative organisational and technical solutions. Logistics involves the technology-dependent movement of goods on a global scale. This entails using recent technologies in the area of the operations-supporting information flow as well as the value-generating logistics operations, i.e. transportation, storage and order picking, including the handling of goods during those processes. In the logistics service provider (LSP) industry, an inadequate choice of technology always leads to lost profits, increased costs and the erosion of competitive position, at times causing business failure.

1. The role of technology and its selection

To maintain or increase their market share, enterprises must produce goods or provide services characterised by parameters enabling effective competition with the offering of their peers. One of the fundamental prerequisites in this respect is to use such technologies which ensure that goods or services meet the customers' requirements while creating a competitive advantage. This issue has been tackled, among others, by Antonelli and Amidei [2011, pp. 11–12], Kaldor [1972, pp. 1237–1255] and Schmookler [1966]. Enterprises must develop or acquire solutions that would allow them to deliver attractive goods and services characterised by:

- desirable functional parameters,
- appropriate safety levels (e.g., by special safeguards or the application of appropriate materials),
- environmental protection,
- acceptable costs of technology use.

As can be seen, it is technology that largely determines what goods or services the enterprise can offer. This situation is schematically presented in Figure 1.

Figure 1. Mechanism determining what goods and services can be produced by an enterprise

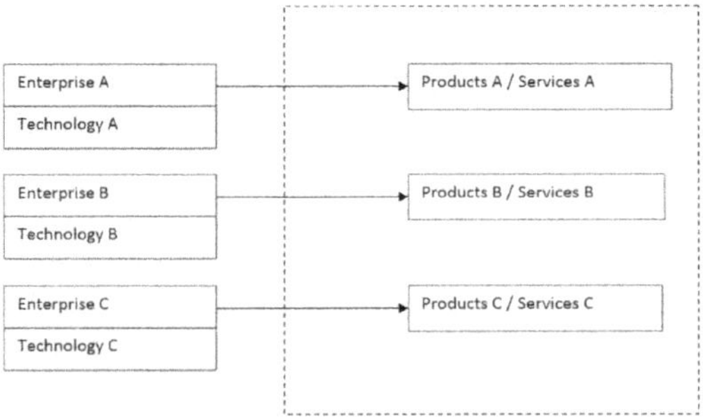

Source: Own elaboration

Of great importance is also the need to formulate technology development strategies (as emphasised by J. Rokita) consistent with the overall strategy of the enterprise [Rokita 2005, p. 217]. In designing such strategies, one must take into account technological progress, which improves the quality of products and the possibilities offered by them, while decreasing manufacturing costs and environmental footprint. These objectives can be attained through **technology management**, which encompasses the selection, installation and implementation of technologies, as well as the monitoring of their further development. An example of technology management in the terrestrial telecommunications sector is given in Kozlowski's elaboration [2007, pp. 272–279].

2. Characterisation of logistics service providers and the technologies they use

LSPs carry out a range of logistics operations. The activities of this fast-developing group of companies constitute what amounts to the bloodstream of any contemporary economy. The main reason for this is an increasing demand for the services offered by LSPs through the outsourcing of logistics functions [Malus 2010, p. 403] in transport, warehouse operations, packaging, labelling, order picking, assembly, etc. Due to that, LSPs can focus on technological innovations concerning their core business (internal and external logistics processes) to enhance their effectiveness [Urbanek 2011, p. 50, Deepen pp. 1–2]. Other factors include the elimination of political barriers limiting international trade exchange (e.g. the fall of the socialist bloc) and rapid technological advancements.

In the near future, LSPs will face the following challenges:

- the need to serve growing (in the foreseeable future) e-commerce – raw materials must be delivered to manufacturers and the finished goods shipped to end consumers via distribution centres (in which goods are labelled, picked and packed),
- ensuring efficient delivery to customers in the face of increasing consumption,
- finding solutions enabling the fulfilment of all orders during periods of high demand (e.g., before Christmas),
- the need to quickly deliver goods from all over the world in an increasingly global economy,
- emphasis on environmental protection.

To meet these challenges, logistics enterprises must be equipped with the right technologies, which can be classified into two groups:

1) production technologies,
2) information technologies.

Production technologies are associated with operations and address aspects comprising their "core business" [Lipsey, Beckar, Carlaw 1998, pp. 30–31]. For LSPs, their core task is likewise the logistics operations they provide as services on the marketplace. The main function of LSPs is providing their customers with transportation, warehousing and handling services of all types of goods, which entails a range of technologies for warehouse and transport operations as well as for process coordination. Examples of technology-based warehousing operations are:

- automated storage racks for efficient order picking [Coyle, Langley, Gibson, Novack, Bardi 2008, p. 507],
- storage equipment (e.g. mobile racks, drive-in rack, etc.) [Tompkins, Smith 1998, pp. 467–477],
- means of internal transport (roller or chain conveyors; cranes; lifts; carrier, lift, and picking trucks, etc.) [Arora, Shinde 2007, pp. 6–8],
- identification and control equipment (e.g. balances, humidity sensors, etc.) [Hompel, Schmidt 2006, pp. 21–22],
- devices for automated product identification (e.g., handheld barcode scanners) [Michael, Michael 2009, pp. 284–285],
- automated stackers [Manzini 2012, p. 166],
- automated sorting systems [Hompel, Schmidt 2006, pp. 127–129],
- radio-frequency identification (RFID) equipment (tags, aerials, gates),
- telecommunications systems (radio terminals, Wi-Fi transceivers, etc.) ensuring communication with warehouse management (WMS) or manufacturing resource planning (MRP) systems.

Recent years have seen an increased use of comprehensive technological solutions in warehousing, such as:

- Pick-to-light – displays show information facilitating the identification of items on racks. This solution is well-suited for a large product assortment and for fast-moving goods. To function properly, it requires reliable information and communications (ITC) solutions, which must be capable of controlling many thousands of indicators and displays at the same time.
- Pick-by-voice – it is based on advanced systems of voice recognition and voice message generation, which guide the picker to the required warehouse locations, improving picking speed and accuracy. Also, this solution relies on very efficient ITC systems, which must generate precise voice messages for workers and flawlessly recognise human speech. In addition, it should be possible to

quickly switch between different languages to meet the needs of individual workers in international environments.

The aforementioned technological solutions for warehouse logistics are being continuously improved, and more innovations (e.g., pick-by-point, pick-by-frame) are continuously being introduced.

In addition, of great importance is the software controlling the warehouse technologies listed above. Warehouse management systems (WMS) are designed to comprehensively manage the processes occurring in warehouses, from stow-away planning and order picking optimisation to conducting quality control of those processes [Van Den Berg 2007, pp. 83–84]. Currently, such systems increasingly often control the tasks performed by humans (e.g., through pick-by-voice) or are entrusted with overall management of SILO-class automated warehouses [website of Schaefer company 2017]. Therefore, modern systems of this type must be able to use object-oriented software or a warehouse control system (WCS) to manage, among others, programmable logic controllers (PLC) [Bolton 2011, pp. 3–16] for machines, in one of the languages specified in the standard IEC 61131–3. A WMS must also be able to work with higher level software such as MRP systems, and thus a WMS is often treated as a module of the latter.

Transportation technologies form another very diverse and numerous group. This sector is extremely varied and can be readily categorised in different ways, for instance into:

- transport of goods,
- transport of people.

Another important classification is by mode of transport:

- road transport,
- railroad transport,
- sea transport,
- inland waterway transport,
- air transport,
- pipeline transport.

Each of these transport modes, except for pipelines, may be used to move both goods and people. These listed fundamental differences within the transport industry indicate a variety of technologies employed in this area. Most specialists responsible for technology management in LSPs work in the road transport segment, which has the largest share in both freight and passenger transportation. Therefore, this chapter discusses primarily the technologies used in that field.

However, both rail and air transport is also considered in the following discussion. Nevertheless, as the operations of road transport companies are becoming increasingly integrated, the knowledge of technologies used in other transport modes is needed, as often, those technologies must be deployed simultaneously in carrying out logistics tasks.

In various sectors, means of road transport are a numerous group in which technologies play a leading role. These include e.g. motor vehicles, semi-trailers and trailers. Public transportation may be divided into within-agglomeration and inter-agglomeration. Also in this case, modern technologies are often used because the expected lifetime of buses is lower than that of trains. In this sector, great advancements have been made in terms of the efficiency of internal combustion engines and the application of ITC technologies with which they are equipped. A considerable proportion of innovations is aimed at improving safety. Currently, it seems that the future of both passenger vehicles and trucks rests with the future implementation of electric motors for propulsion.

Moreover, transport vehicles are equipped with devices supporting drivers in the selection of the optimum route and ensuring safety. Such solutions use ITC based on mobile and satellite telephone networks. Highly advanced technologies are also used in the fleet management departments of road transport companies. An example of such software is a program called "Flota Commandor" [www.softra.pl 2017]. Logistics companies use the services of electronic freight exchanges, such as Trans.eu [www.trans.eu/pl 2017] and TimoCom [www.timocom.pl], which enable cost optimisation both for transport companies and their customers.

Road transport requires many regulations to ensure safety and reduce congestion. However, to attain those objectives, one also needs the following technologies. Intelligent transport systems (ITS) offer forward-looking solutions for the management of the entire transport system [Williams 2008, p. 3]. Their main objectives are transport optimisation to reduce congestion and environmental footprint, increase safety and improve the economic aspect of transport systems. ITS mostly consist of ITC technologies, with the leading role being played by mobile and satellite telecommunication networks. Satellite telecommunication is likely to find wider applications in such systems. Currently, the most widely used solution is the American Global Positioning System (GPS) [Chaplain 2011]. For many years now, the European Union has been developing its own system known as GALILEO, which will offer extensive possibilities to be implemented in transportation, including ITS. Another system used in transport, for example to integrate its different modes, is the Geographical Information System (GIS) [Turkeli, Ariburnu, Vayvay, 2010 p. 16], which is designed to visualise the analysed geographic data, which is critical to logistics.

An important role is also played by technologies gathering data on the movement of vehicles, including smart cameras, vehicle detectors in intelligent signalling systems, automated number plate recognition, vehicle balances and parking slot occupation sensors. Finally, increased automation of vehicular movement has been promoted by, among others, Google and BMW [Kim, Shin 2014, p. 4].

Of great interest are the technologies used in railroad transport. In Poland, the vast majority of locomotives and cars use old technology (according to data from the Railroad Transport Office, the average age of Polish train locomotives is as much as 33 years). Furthermore, the Polish rail infrastructure is obsolete and largely worn out. This translates into low speed limits on many Polish track segments. Recently, the situation has somewhat improved with the launching of regular connections served by state-of-the-art Pendolino trains travelling on modernised tracks and powered by upgraded overhead lines [www.mir.gov.pl, 2017]. The situation may be further improved in 2015 with the commissioning of the new Lodz Fabryczna train station [www.nlf-b2.pl, 2017], and in subsequent years with the construction of tunnels in Lodz [http://wyborcza.pl, 2017]. These developments will significantly shorten travel time between major Polish cities, making trains competitive with car transport. Further improvement in railroad transportation may be expected due to the available funding from the European Union. The railroad sector may also boast the implementation of a smart transport system – the European Rail Transport Management System (ERTMS) [www.ertms.net, 2017]. In inter-agglomeration passenger railroad transport, the focus is primarily on high-speed train connections, which are modern technologies that may compete with the solutions offered by road carriers [http://szybkakolejtak.pl, 2017]. Such a strategy is consistent with the transportation policy of the European Union.

Air transport is characterised by particularly advanced technologies installed both in airplanes and at airports. Moreover, there exist some complicated, but highly reliable air traffic systems, such as Single European Sky ATM Research (SESAR) [www.sesarju.eu, 2017]. Indeed, this transportation sector could not function without information and communication technologies.

3. Principles of technology selection

Technologies may be developed in two ways: [Teegen 1999, pp. 1–22]

1) internally, by an enterprise or group of enterprises,
2) as supplied by external providers.

In-house development of technology is particularly strenuous as then the enterprise has to focus not only on maintaining or expanding its market share, but also on a very difficult process of improving its technology, which requires the employment of highly qualified and creative specialists. Due to these difficulties, enterprises may also consider entering into strategic alliances to access or develop the desired technologies [Carayannis, Alexander 1999, pp. 1–32].

If the enterprise decides to follow the latter variant and wishes to use technologies offered by external providers, then one of the most important and difficult decisions it faces is the **choice of technology** to be implemented, especially given that the range of available options is very extensive. This situation obtains due to the fact that many countries (e.g. the USA, EU states, Japan) have very robust technology development systems ensuring considerable diversity.

The emergence of a multitude of new commercially available technologies is largely attributable to intensified commercialisation efforts of universities, R&D units and enterprises. Importantly, both technology development and commercialisation may be supported by public funds. The latter has been the subject matter of numerous conferences, seminars and fairs, while an increasing number of high-quality educational programs (also in Poland) are offered on the commercialisation and valuation of new technologies, with graduates often representing technology providers and offering their products e.g. to LSPs. Under the circumstances, companies which purchase technologies should also employ specialists who would be able to choose optimum advanced solutions for those entities. Those professionals must make sure that the logistics company does not buy a potentially problematic technology. It should be stressed that once a technological solution is purchased it is very difficult to change it for financial, organisational and technical reasons.

Technology management by LSPs consists of several stages, which can be further subdivided into phases, as shown in Table 1.

Table 1. Stages and phases of technology management [17, 18, 19]

Stages	Phases
1) Technology selection	a) Identification of prospective technology providers and contacting them.
	b) Preparing a report analysing the gathered data on technology providers, their offering and current users of their technologies.
	c) Making a shortlist of technology providers and further negotiations.
	d) Final selection of a provider and a collaboratively developed solution. Conclusion of a detailed contract for the delivery of the technology.

Stages	Phases
2) Technology development	a) Monitoring of the technology development process
	b) Incorporation of improvements arising from technological progress in the course of technology development. Signing of annexes activating the technology delivery contract.
3) Technology installation and implementation	a) Individual modules are installed and implemented in such an order which allows for fast identification and removal of faults (if any).
	b) Training for workers.
	c) Testing of the newly implemented technology.
4) Use of technology and monitoring of its further development	a) Supervision of servicing and fault removal.
	b) Analysis of technological advancement. Staying in contact with the technology provider and the analysis of possible further technology development.
	c) Analysis of offerings of other technology providers, including R&D organisations.

Source: Own elaboration

LSPs can choose between two major technology development pathways. First, they can develop and produce new generations of the technologies they already have, using their own resources. This entails a lower risk in terms of implementation, maintenance, servicing and fault removal. However, it is not always possible to follow this pathway; for instance, the engineers employed by the enterprise may not be able to improve the in-house solution for it to be sufficiently competitive. In such cases, the enterprise should use the services of specialised companies.

For purchasing LSP technology from a third party, a method for selecting the most suitable option is needed. First, the types of companies that are involved in this technology acquisition process should be elaborated on:

- technology provider,
- technology user,
- technology manager.

Technology provider represents an entity which develops and produces technological solutions. Operating in the market, it locates customers for its products, whether directly or through authorised agents. After selling a technology, it implements, and then supports its use. When new, improved versions of the technology are developed, the provider offers upgrades both to existing and new customers.

Technology user is the customer of the technology provider, an entity which cannot develop and produce the technologies it needs for the purposes of its core activity, and so it has to use the solutions offered by technology providers. This implies a complementary interdependency between the provider and the user.

Technology manager is an actor who determines which tasks should be addressed by technologies in the LSP. This implies expertise that should match technological solutions to the needs of the technology used by the enterprise, participate in technology selection and supervise development. Technology managers are employed as third parties either by technology providers or users, or both. In this network triad, they should make sure that the purchased technology contributes to enhancing the LSP customer's competitive advantages.

The first, critical stage of the selection process is the choice of a suitable technology for the LSP. The following **phases of technology provider selection** can be distinguished:

1) Identification of prospective technology providers and contacting them.
2) Preparing a report analysing the gathered data on technology providers, their offering and current users of their technologies.
3) Making a shortlist of technology providers and further negotiations.
4) Final selection of a provider and a collaboratively developed solution complete with the conclusion of a detailed contract for the delivery of the technology.

In the first phase, one has to **identify all prospective technology providers** and request their proposals. It should be noted that the technology provider market is global, with few limitations other than embargos on delivery to countries considered a threat to world peace (in 2014, those included North Korea, Iran and Russia). It is very often the case that the providers of the target technology are based outside Poland, or even outside Europe. Furthermore, the technology market is characterised by the specialisation of its actors.

In the vast majority of cases, the provider needs to customise its technology to the users' needs. The user can typically choose between several different technologies. Once all the offers from competing technology suppliers have been received, they are carefully evaluated, the focus being on technical data. This marks the beginning of the strenuous and time-consuming process of gathering detailed information on the solutions offered by the technology providers, which is founded on long-term business relationships. Figure 2 describes this relationship as expressed through the preceding discussion:

Figure 2. Technology provider – user relations in the initial phase of advanced technology selection

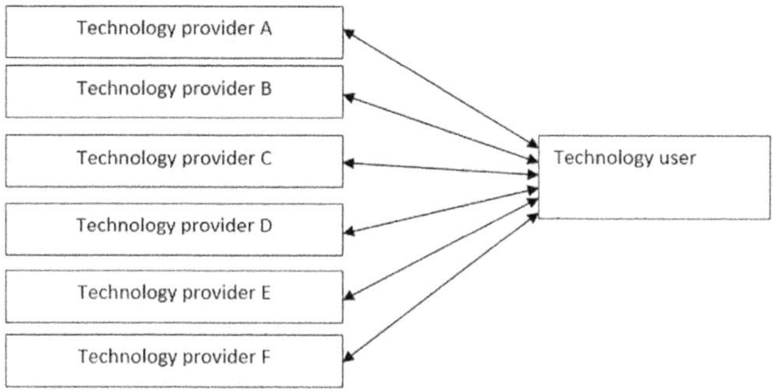

Source: Own elaboration

At the same time, research should involve an exploratory survey of the existing users of the situation-specific actual technologies found on the market. This can provide valuable information about the solutions used by competitors. Efforts may also be made to obtain information about how the target technology performs in practice (although such data should be interpreted with caution). The responsibility to identify technology providers and gather information about them and their products rests with the technology manager of the LSP. The collected data will then be presented in a report for the LSP buyer, which should be submitted to the executive team of this company for a detailed **analysis of information** in terms of:

- characteristics of the providers (experience, technologies implemented, servicing reliability, etc.),
- the target technology (detailed technical data),
- other technologies offered by a given provider (perhaps there is a newer version),
- opinions of the users of the various technologies.

After studying the report, the company's executives, with the collaboration of technology managers, create a shortlist of providers to be considered for further inquiries regarding their technological service offering. This represents another difficult phase, in which a major role is played by technology managers, both those employed by the providers and by the user. This phase leads to the formulation of concrete solutions. Figure three illustrates this logic of technology service provision as an interaction between the LSP and the various competing technology providers discussed in the preceding text:

Figure 3. Provider – user relations in the phase of negotiations with representatives of the short-listed advanced technology providers

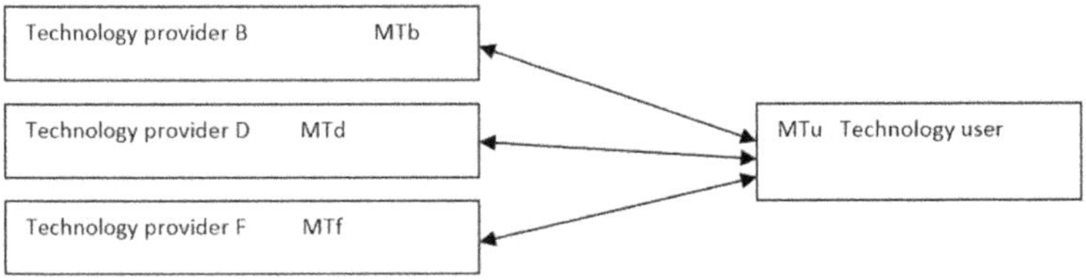

Legend:

MT – technology manager

MTb – technology manager employed by technology provider B

MTu – technology manager employed by technology user

Source: Own elaboration.

Due to this dialogue regarding technology in the procurement process, the user's expectations and the variety of solutions offered, providers are likely to propose – on the basis of this interaction – a wide range of technologies differing in e.g. performance parameters, operator requirements, frequency of servicing as well the costs of purchase and operation. Thus, all technologies on the shortlist should be scrutinised prior to making the final decision. Finally, it is critical to prepare a detailed contract to avoid any future misunderstandings or unnecessary expenses on the part of the technology user, in this case the LSP.

4. Development, implementation and testing of a new technology

The next stage involves the **development of the procured technology** for the logistics company. It is critical for technology managers to be able to monitor this process, which should be reflected in the contract. The technology development process often takes a long time (e.g. over a year) and it may be possible to introduce some improvements to a previously adopted technological design. Such changes may be necessary due to:

- technological advancements that occur after the contract is signed (then modifications should be initiated by the provider),
- changes on the part of the user (then modifications should be initiated by the user).

Good relations between the provider's and the user's technology managers may facilitate changes in the contract and result in a technology that will be better tailored to the user's needs. In addition, the monitoring of the development and production process may allow for early identification of faults on the part of the provider and prevent delays.

Technology development and production is followed by the stage of **technology installation and implementation**. In fact, each technology implementation or modification process meets the criteria of a project which brings about change in the organisation, and thus it can be carried out by using project management tools [Kozlowski 2010, p. 59, Kozlowski R., Matejun M. 2012, pp. 91–101], given that the user's executives have the necessary change management expertise. Implementation should be carefully considered already at the earlier stage of technology selection. Technology managers must decide which of the proposed solutions can be implemented and then estimate their financial, organisational and wider social costs.

Technologies used by LSPs are very often divided into easily manageable modules and then implemented in a sequence ensuring the ease of assembly and facilitating the monitoring of the correct operation of the modules. This makes it possible to quickly identify and remove errors, if any, as well as to precisely programme and calibrate equipment, thus preventing any possible damages due to malfunction. Technology installation and implementation is carried out by the provider's personnel or by its authorised and competent representatives.

Another important phase is the **training of workers** who operate the acquired technology. As a result of this implementation of new solutions, both labour and managers need to develop an adequate level of technological capability [Mikołajczyk 2003, p. 24]. Thus, a careful recruitment and provision of professional training are some of the main prerequisites for achieving success with the newly procured technology. The training programme should address the new tasks to be performed by the workers and be adjusted to their existing knowledge and skills. Too brief, poorly planned or inappropriately executed training programmes may lead to numerous problems throughout the value-creating technology use phase in the supply chain of the LSP.

The installation and implementation of the new technology is followed by a period of **testing.** This is an essential phase that should not be omitted even in the case of severe time restrictions. Testing enables the removal of defects as well as the adjustment of machinery, which has a very significant effect on performance parameters. Such improvements will lead to productivity gains, reduced costs and improved user safety. The user's personnel, and especially technology managers, should participate in this testing.

5. Using and monitoring technology

After launching the improved logistics services rendered by means of the newly procured technology, the technology provider is normally contracted to be responsible for the **servicing and repairs stage.** Such a contract signed by the parties should then regulate the following issues:

- The period of time over which the provider is to service the technology (initially free of charge, and after a specified period of time – for remuneration);
- The duration of the warranty period and provisions for repairs following its expiry. Of great importance is also the provider's reaction time, as it directly affects the length of time during which the user will be unable to use the technology. Furthermore, one should consider the consequences of technology downtime (costs, lost customers, etc.). It is advisable to specify penalties for failure to react according to an agreed schedule.
- The user's technology managers must participate in servicing and fault removal processes to gain experience which can be useful in improving the technology or shifting to a more appropriate one.

Technology managers employed by the user must in these cases monitor the development of the implemented technologies in the areas. This support of technology managers, as discussed, is illustrated in Figure 4.

Figure 4. Scope of technology development monitoring conducted by the user's technology managers

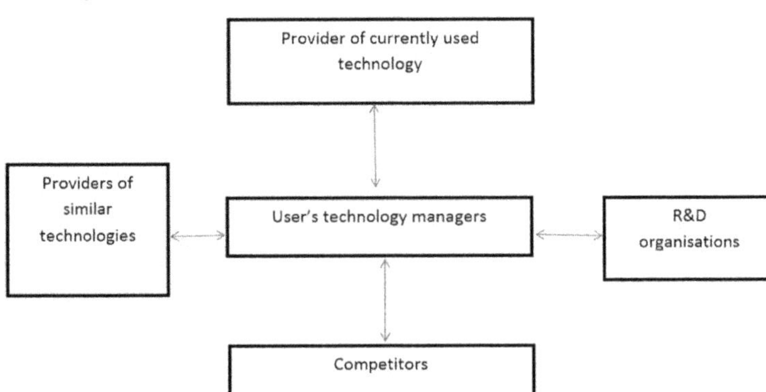

Source: Own elaboration

With this technological advancement, the technology provider, in its capacity as developer, then upgrades the supplied technological solution, with new components offered to the established LSP users. The LSP user then decides whether or not it is profitable to purchase the offered technology upgrades. This decision is influenced by the considerations of the degree to which they need to keep up with the technological progress, in the context of the importance this has to secure their competitiveness in the logistics service market. They should also periodically exchange information with the technology provider concerning:

- new solutions offered,
- problems with the use of the existing technology,
- new technological requirements.

The user's technology managers should also follow the offering of other providers, which may motivate the current technology provider to upgrade its solutions. If the differences in performance and costs are very substantial, the user may decide to change the provider.

The LSP user's technology managers should also carefully investigate signals from its competitors. In business practice, there are ample examples of users developing and improving their own technologies, creating solutions which are superior to those offered by specialised providers. Under such circumstances, if the competitor does not intend to sell its technology, there is very little that the LSP user can do other than work closely with its chosen technology providers to develop an enhanced version of the applied technology to produce competitive logistics services.

Furthermore, new technological solutions may be considered in the context of research and development (R&D) organisations. Most R&D is associated with universities as well as independent R&D institutes. Currently, in the European Union and elsewhere around the world, the rapidly increasing numbers of initiatives also leads to the commercialisation of research [Trzmielak 2013, pp. 116–123]. Barriers in this area have been identified [for more, see Jasiniak, Trippner-Hrabi 2013, pp. 75–103] and solutions have been proposed to facilitate the implementation of new technology in business practice. In Poland, too, considerable funds have been designated for supporting collaboration between enterprises and R&D organisations in creating advanced solutions. These opportunities should not be overlooked by technology managers and company executives.

Summary

Undoubtedly the success of enterprises will be increasingly driven by technology. Globalisation and a wide array of financial and organisational tools supporting the development of new technological solutions and their commercialisation in developed countries leads to rapid economic growth. Thus, it is crucial to ensure an appropriate technology management in industry.

LSPs make use of a great variety of technologies. As logistics is global by nature, a skilful implementation of the usually global technology management is of particular importance in this sector. The most difficult element of this process is technology selection, and this chapter offers an approach to addressing this issue. The adoption of this method will be helpful for technology managers and executives at LSPs in making the right choices to ensure the survival of their firm in an increasingly global, and therefore volatile, logistics service marketplace.

Bibliography

Antonelli C., Amidei F.B. (2011), *The Dynamics of Knowledge Externalities,* Edward Elgar Publishing.

Arora K.C., Shinde V.V. (2007), *Aspects of Materials Handling,* Firewall Media

Bolton W. (2011), *Programmable Logic Controllers,* Elsevier.

Chaplain C. (2011), *Global Positioning System (GPS): Challenges in Sustaining and Upgrading Capabilities Persist,* DIANE Publishing.

Coyle J., Langley C., Gibson B., Novack R., Bardi E. (2008), *Supply Chain Management: A Logistics Perspective,* Cengage Learning.

Deepen J.M. (2007), *Logistics Outsourcing Relationships: Measurement, Antecedents, and Effects of Logistics Outsourcing Performance,* Springer Science & Business Media

Dorf R.C. (ed.) (1999), *The Technology Management Handbook,* CRCPress.

Helpman E. (ed.) (1998), General Purpose Technologies and Economic Growth, MIT Press.

Hompel M., Schmidt T. (2006), *Warehouse Management: Automation and Organisation of Warehouse and Order Picking Systems***,** Springer Science & Business Media.

Hompel M., Schmidt T. (2006), *Warehouse Management: Automation and Organisation of Warehouse and Order Picking Systems,* Springer Science & Business Media.

http://szybkakolejtak.pl/opinie/artykuly/kdp_faq.

http://wyborcza.pl/piatekekstra/1,133659,14675638,W_Lodzi_sie_ciesza__ze_beda_mieli_metro.html.

Jasiniak M., Trippner-Hrabi J. (2013), *Współpraca nauki z biznesem w regionie łódzkim – wyniki badań* (*Cooperation between academia and business in Lodz region: Research results*) [in:] J. Różański (ed.), *Współpraca nauki i biznesu jako* *czynnik wzmacniający innowacyjność regionu łódzkiego* (*Cooperation between academia and business as a factor strengthening Lodz region*), Wydawnictwo Biblioteka, Lodz.

Kaldor N. (1972), *The Irrelevance of Equilibrium Economics*, Economic Journal, Vol. 82, No. 328, December.

Kim J., Shin H. (2014), *Algorithm & SoC Design for Automotive Vision Systems: For Smart Safe Driving System*, Springer

Kleine D. (2013), *Technologies of Choice? ICTs, Development, and the Capabilities Approach*, Massachusetts Institute of Technology.

Kozlowski R., Matejun M. (2015), *The identification of difficulties in using advanced technologies in the implementation of projects*, "International Journal of Business and Management", Vol. III (4)

Kozlowski R., Matejun M. (2012), *Forms of cooperation with the business environment in the process of technology entrepreneurship development*, Volume 2 Number 1/2012 Research in Logistics & Production, Poznan University of Technology.

Kozlowski R. (2010), *Wykorzystanie zaawansowanych technologii w zarządzaniu projektami* (*Use of advanced technologies in project management*), Wydawnictwo Uniwersytetu Łódzkiego, Lodz.

Kozlowski R. (2007), Zarządzanie rozwojem technologii w przedsiębiorstwach telekomunikacji stacjonarnej (*Technology development management in terrestrial telecommunications companies*) [in:] Bogdanienko J., Kuzela M. i Sobczak I. (ed.), *Zarządzanie wiedzą w warunkach globalnej współpracy przedsiębiorstw* (*Knowledge management under conditions of global cooperation of enterprises*), Wydawnictwo A. Marszałek, Toruń.

Manzini R. (2012), Warehousing in the Global Supply Chain: Advanced Models, Tools and Applications for Storage Systems, Springer Science & Business Media.

Michael K., Michael M.G. (2009), *Innovative Automatic Identification and Location-Based Services: From Bar Codes to Chip Implants*, IGI Global.

Mikołajczyk Z. (2003), *Zarządzanie procesem zmian w organizacjach* (*Managing the process of change in organizations*), Wydawnictwo Górnośląskiej Wyższej Szkoły Handlowej im. Wojciecha Korfantego, Katowice.

Reports of the Railroad Transport Office for 2013.

Rokita J. (2005), *Zarządzanie strategiczne. Tworzenie i utrzymanie przewagi konkurencyjnej* (*Strategic management: The creation and maintenance of a competitive advantage*), PWE, Warszawa

Schmookler J. (1966), *Invention and economic growth*, Harvard University Press.

Stabryła A. (ed.) (2010), *Analiza i projektowanie systemów zarządzania przedsiębiorstwem (Analysis and design of enterprise management systems)*, Mifles.pl. Encyklopedia Zarządzania.

Teegen H. (1999), *Valuation of Technology and New Ventures* [in:] Dorf R.C. (ed.), *The Technology Management Handbook*, CRCPress.

Tompkins J.A., Smith J.D. (1998), *The Warehouse Management Handbook*, Tompkins **Press.**

Trzmielak D.M. (2013), *Komercjalizacja wiedzy i technologii - determinanty i strategie (Commercialization of knowledge and technology: Determinants and strategies)*, Wydawnictwo Uniwersytetu Łódzkiego, Lodz.

Urbanek G. (2011), *Kompetencje a wartość przedsiębiorstwa: Zasoby niematerialne w nowej gospodarce (Competence and company value: Intangible resources in the new economy)*, Oficyna a Wolters Kluwer business, Warszawa.

Van Den Berg J.P. (2007), *Integral Warehouse Management*, Management Outlook Publications.

Williams B. (2008), *Intelligent Transport Systems Standards*, Artech House.

www.ertms.net

www.mir.gov.pl/aktualnosci/Transport/Strony/Rekord_predkosci_Pendolino_241113.aspx

www.nlf-b2.pl

www.sesarju.eu

www.softra.pl

www.ssi-schaefer.pl/magazynowanie/regaly-paletowe/system-regalow-paletowych-wysokiego-skladowania/magazyn-samonosny.html

www.timocom.pl

www.trans.eu/pl

Zongwei L. (2010), *Service Science and Logistics Informatics: Innovative Perspectives*, IGI Global.

Łukasz Sułkowski
University of Social Sciences

Dominika Kaczorowska-Spychalska
University of Lodz, Lodz

Social Media in Change Management Process

Abstract: The development of ICT technologies changes the conditions of the functioning of contemporary enterprises, which constantly have to look for new methods and tools as well as ways of implementing them while trying to effectively and successfully compete in the market. What is more, compulsiveness of observed changes results in a situation in which obtained competitive advantage is only temporary. As a result, a management process requires a deeper look inside a multidimensional space of links and relations in which a given enterprise functions. The process of management is increasingly evolving from hierarchical models into solutions where complexity of all things becomes a key issue. In this approach, a change becomes not only an indicator of the presence, but, first and foremost, of the future of every enterprise. The character, depth as well as dynamics of these changes will depend on a range of factors, such as industry in which an enterprise functions, its willingness to implement innovative solutions or a consumer profile and their needs.

Due to their specificity, social media as an inherent element of surrounding reality superbly fit into a process of change management, particularly in a process approach. As a result of mutual interactions of users, they enable the creation of a space in which specific groups of stakeholders, employees and customers, in particular, can combine their experiences, exchange opinions and intensify actions towards the commercialisation of ideas formed that way. Crowdsourcing, crowdfunding or prosuming are only some of a few solutions that allow for increasing the involvement and responsibility of specific groups of stakeholders for implemented changes while making them a crucial element of the whole process. Therefore, opportunities of social media in this area can prove an interesting solution at each stage of change management process for many enterprises. It concerns mainly building an internal and external communication platform thanks to which an enterprise can conduct market research, gain new ideas initiating a process of changes, explain their essence and course, get opinions about them and minimise the risk of failure. Change management is not only an issue of mechanical implementation of innovative technological solutions, but it is also a behavioural modification that influences the way of thinking, attitudes and behaviour of all concerned parties.

Key words: information and communication technologies, competitive advantage, change management process, social media, customer

1. Change as a permanent characteristic feature of management

In human affairs – political, social, economic, or business – it is pointless to try to predict the future. But it is possible – and fruitful – to identify major events that have already happened, irrevocably, and that will have predictable effects in the next decade or two. It is possible, in other words, to identify and prepare for the future that has already happened [Drucker 1997, p. 20]. The power of efficient management lies in understanding that the future is impossible to predict or plan, yet, one can make attempts to read it, to prepare for it and to control it. All actions undertaken by managing people do not guarantee the certainty of the future but they are only an attempt to bring closer what (more or less likely) may happen. The problem is that regardless of conditions in which an enterprise will function in the future, it must create proper resource conditions in order to be able to develop [Urbanowska-Sojkin 2008, p. 13]. What decides the success of the whole economy and individual organisations is a set of factors and accepted solutions. A crucial role is played by the Internet and ICT (*information and communication technologies*), which indicate current directions of actions and jointly determine a strategy of organisation development [Kisielnicki 2013, p. 327]. The specificity of the market, the processes observed in it and entities functioning in new realities are changing and an increasingly greater emphasis is put on management process in democratic terms. ICT technologies enable enterprises to do more by using a smaller volume of resources while increasing their productivity. ICT do not only offer benefits related to productivity at a given moment but they generate them in spite of the passing time [McAfee 2011, p. 16].

Today, the changes in the marketing environment are so momentous that they require a radical strategic and organisational change from virtually all companies. Gone are the days when managers could stick to tried and tested formulas to provide continuous growth and profitability. New industrial structures, rapidly changing technologies and new customer expectations are quickly eroding yesterday's markets, while creating phenomenal new opportunities for those that can move fast and decisively to capitalise on the changing environment [Doyle 2008, p. 11]. Technological revolution caused the situation whereby market reality is determined by three entwining forces: people who want to establish mutual contacts, interactive technologies and online economy. They create a space that enables the absorption of technologies in the business, socio-cultural or behaviour context [Li, Bernoff 2009, p. 28] in every functional area of enterprises. Today, we live in the so-called conversation economy, where enterprises have to conduct a constant dialogue – to keep in touch with communities and to establish multilateral relations constantly [Jurkiewicz, Majewska, Sołtysińska 2012, p. 21]. While evolving, they determine new realities of conducting business activity and philosophy of own market orientation, and at the same time influence the conditions of its implementation. In spite of the fact that the Internet has not generally changed management practices, it definitely strengthened some of its attributes. Therefore, it concerns a degree of intensification of some features, not only their mere existence or kind [Mintzberg 2013, p. 60].

As a result, in a more and more turbulent and hypermedia environment, business models, strategies and procedures require an adaptive approach [Reeves, Deimler, 2013], which is based on various interactions between specific groups of stakeholders and/or a firm. The application of modern technologies gives a new dimension to the relations of enterprises, which in consequence become increasingly active in the hypermedia space as it allows them to achieve tangible benefits [Dobiegała-Korona 2009, p. 95]. It generates new market opportunities that result from a practical adaptation of reasons for reductionism while at the same time it requires a holistic approach. In such an approach, the way a system behaves depends on its elements, yet, this is the system that as a whole determines its behaviour while leading to creating relation capital that ensures a potential competitive advantage.

The purpose of the majority of strategies is to build a permanent competitive advantage through the determination of a beneficial market position and appropriate abilities and competencies to its realisation [Reeves, Deimler 2013]. However, it is hard nowadays to concentrate only on the minimisation of incurred costs or productivity. The environment, including online market space and related individual groups of stakeholders, very often undergo changes of compulsive character, which leads to the exploration of phenomena and market behaviour different than before. As a result, a competitive advantage is temporary, transient and confined to periods of time determined by the dynamics of technological changes, including ICT. This is what actually has become an indicator of a shift from the industrial era to the information era [Mruk 2002, p. 252].

In the heart of the concept of the enterprise of the future, one can find building relations with employees and business partners in order to create new business opportunities through creating new values, better customer service, increased efficiency, improvement of technical competence and building and implementation of new business models [Krawiec 2005, p. 29], including those related to change management. ICT technologies do not offer only benefits related to productivity at a certain moment but they also generate them in spite of passing time [McAfee 2011, p. 16]. This has led to a situation when communication is conducted according to markedly faster and more global rules than before. Specific messages or information can be sent to distant parts of the globe in one moment while increasing efficiency and related benefits [Cole 2004, p. 223].

Therefore, modern management is based on network connections of various relations and non-material competences which condition possibilities of an organisation's survival in the times of volatility and uncertainty. It is the ability to notice a wide context in a specific situation, to understand it in various aspects, to evaluate causes and consequences hidden deeper and often contradictory. It is balancing in a multidimensional space on multiple diverse levels [Mintzberg 2013, p. 226]. Its main purpose is to lead individual groups of stakeholders to higher and higher levels of mutual connections, starting with satisfaction and ephemeral relations, up to partnership and long-time bonds. As a result, a migration can be observed of values from assets typical of relations built in a traditional way to those typical of relations built by using the hypermedia space [Dobiegała-Korona 2009, p. 95].

However, due to the multidimensionality of mutual dependencies, their complexity and dynamics, a special role is given to strategic thinking that distinguishes an ability to meet the requirements of enterprise growth through using opportunities from external and internal conditions of functioning, which determine its strategic potential [Urbanowska-Sojkin 2008, p. 13]. A key role in that process is played by an adopted business model. This is what influences the ability of a given enterprise to achieve and maintain a competitive advantage. Yet, its level depends on numerous factors, including the extent to which an enterprise takes into consideration factors that increase or decrease the attractiveness of a given sector, including the Internet influence [Afuah 2003, p. 117] and related technologies.

The information needs of businesses and of executives are likely to change rapidly. We have concentrated these past years on improving traditional information, which is almost exclusively the information about what goes on inside an organisation. But a winning strategy will require the information about events and conditions outside the institution. Only with this information can a business decide how to allocate its knowledge resources in order to produce the highest yield. Only with such information can a business also prepare for new changes and challenges arising from sudden shifts in the world economy and in the nature and content of knowledge itself [Drucker 1997, p. 20]. The essence of the functioning of modern enterprises consists in the management of knowledge and information and the value of this resource not only does not decrease together with its transfer but it creatively multiplies and develops by new elements, which results from its mere application [Morawski, Niemczyk, Perechuda, Stańczyk-

Hugiet 2010, p. 129]. So, enterprises use acquired skills and specialist knowledge, explore them and configure them again while creating their new value and quality. The strategy becomes a tool of organising the acquired individual and collective knowledge as well as the management of its resources in a conscious way [Probst, Romhardt 2004, p. 65]. In the era of digital economy, a company is increasingly becoming a system of key competencies created in the context of interim relations, processing non-material resources and creating a market. From that perspective, conducting business can to an even greater extent lead to synergy created as a result of combining activities of enterprises, employees and customers [Morawski, Niemczyk, Perechuda, Stańczyk-Hugiet 2010, p. 51]. The knowledge created that way becomes not only an advantage but also a key factor of success. It offers a possibility of synergy and its wider application, it gives the power to identify innovative solutions and unconventional methods of action while making it possible to find, create and provide values for individual groups of stakeholders [Kozielski 2011, p. 27].

The volatility of the environment in which enterprises function nowadays and its unpredictability enforce a constant process of changes both of adaptive and innovative character, which are directed at creating new conditions and trends, whose purpose is to adjust an organisation to an increasingly changing environment, and at the same time to maintain the stability of its functioning [Mintzberg 2013, p. 224]. The character and depth of implemented changes is diverse, can concern various areas and depends on numerous factors related to potential costs, level of risk, knowledge, skills, and the level of involvement of individual groups of stakeholders. However, it requires compatible methods, tools and instruments. As a result, changes observed in external and internal conditions of enterprises' functioning change their factors of building a competitive advantage and force them to look for new conditions of their implementation, rules and models of functioning in the market space. It enables the synergy and symbiosis of observed processes, their exploration, inclusivity and versatility of the current system. In a volatile and competitive environment, management requires not only the ability to show prompt and coordinated reaction to ongoing changes but also the ability to undertake proactive actions while taking into consideration predicted changes or generating changes desired by a specific market entity [Gołębiowski 2001, p. 35]. As a result, management becomes an art concerning self-discovery, wisdom and leadership, which have a practical application [Piotrowski 2013, p. 13]. Subsequently, they accelerate and determine the pace and directions of changes and their absorption.

The evolution of management is, therefore, a constant process of searching for effective solutions to problems arising during attempts related to achieving goals. So, management transformed from the 1.0 model based on a hierarchical approach, in which power belongs to the few, through the 2.0 model, in which lots of additional models and services of scientific status were adopted (e.g. total quality management), towards the 3.0 model, in which the bottom line is the complexity of all things. As a result, all organisations are networks and management concerns primarily people and relations between them, not only departments and profits [Appelo 2011, p. 30].

In such a market space an enterprise must function while adopting a general assumption that change is a constant element of management. A success factor is in that case the ability to constantly redefine areas and ways of running business, the generation and consolidation of changes [Morawski, Niemczyk, Perechuda, Stańczyk-Hugiet 2010, p. 129]. They are generally perceived as a planned modification of a way of functioning, as a reaction to observed or predicted changes in the environment, whose aim is to raise the level of competitiveness [Wendt 201, p. 11]. So, they are not a linear process; instead, they have their dynamics and depend on the context in which an enterprise is at a given moment and on the specificity and complexity of its environment. As a result, a successful management of change is crucial to any organisation in order to survive and succeed in the present, highly competitive and continuously evolving business environment [Todnem 2005, p. 369]. The process of change management does not only concern changes in processes, but it requires a wider approach and constant, permanent business improvements. Building a desired market position in such volatile conditions requires an approach that is directed at a broadly understood innovativeness. A company that will win is the one that will be the first to find a way of using new technologies in a way that will ensure better effects than current solutions do. The biggest winner will be the one that will learn how to create technological brainwaves systematically – one by one [Verganti 2012, p. 123]. In such an approach, a new technology, including ICT, can have a powerful impact on a way of working, obtaining information and creating knowledge, at the same time becoming one of the main factors informing the results achieved by an enterprise. The prerequisite of an efficient implementation of changes is the application of new technologies as a tool of supporting and strengthening new patterns of behaviour [Spector 2015, p. 184]. However, their absorption is based on the specificity of an enterprise, its business maturity, trade, customer profile, its financial potential or know-how resources as well as the openness to new ideas, the ability to acquire new competencies or the flexibility of actions. All of these determine which ICT technologies will be used at which moment of change management and to what extent. In a world in which the ability to change is a key "engine of success", the shift from strategy into capability requires leadership, action planning, the ability to cope with pressure and willingness to learn [Carnall 2007, p. 44]. Everyone knows that the engagement and innovativeness of people are what the company success depends on in that area. Those who develop new products and technologies and their satisfaction, motivation and acceptance of changes condition the achieved results and profits. Therefore, the social media potential seems to be an attractive alternative for many enterprises because social media are above all people. Social media are in effect a massive focus group that can provide intelligence about brand perception, services, competitors and potentially disruptive trends [Masri, Esber, Saraazin, Singer 2015]. They perfectly fit in the concept of process change that is directed at creating context and conditions in which individual groups of stakeholders, employees of all levels and organisation customers in particular undertake a common effort to achieve strategic goals [Spector 2015, p. 52].

2. Social media – the essence and significance in contemporary enterprise

Social media is a group of Internet-based applications that build on the ideological and technological foundations of Web 2.0, and that allow the creation and exchange of User Generated Content. Today, everything is about social media. Some industry gurus claim that if you do not participate in Facebook, YouTube and Second Life, you are not part of cyberspace anymore [Kaplan, Haenlein 2010, p. 61]. Yet, it is obviously not only Facebook or Twitter: social media also include LinkedIn, MySpace, Renren in China, Mixi in Japan, Odnoklassniki in Russia and hundreds of other networks [Shih 2012, p. 31]. Social media generally comprise various types of services, including wiki (social knowledge bases), social networking services, sharing video contents, virtual worlds, sharing information, sharing pictures, games, blogs and discussion fora [Kos-Łabędowicz 2015, p. 101]. They can be divided into two categories. The first one includes social media such as blogs, Twitter, YouTube, Facebook and other websites. The second one comprises corporate social media [Kotler, Kartajaya, Setiawan, 2010, p. 20]. They have different characters, levels of expression and opportunities to adapt to the needs and expectations of enterprises from various sectors and trades. As a result, they influence a way of thinking and perceiving the market reality surrounding enterprises and becomes a catalyst of potential changes. In such a perspective, social media are a specific form of extending senses while shaping the awareness of each enterprise [McLuhan 2004, p. 53]. Traditionally, consumers used the Internet to simply explore the content: they read it, they watched it and they used it to buy products and services. Increasingly, however, consumers are utilising platforms – such as content sharing sites, blogs, social networking and wikis – to create, modify, share and discuss Internet content. This represents the social media phenomenon, which can now significantly impact a firm's reputation, sales and even survival [Kietzmann, Hermkenes, McCarthy, Silvestre 2011, p. 241]. They are a kind of eclectic concept that allows for combining technologies and media while using multimedia formats and numerous platforms to increase global opportunities [Mangold, Faulds 2009, p. 359]. While evolving, they change their form every day. They include text, audio, pictures and video. In each medium, every second. They are like a current in the river – constant, but never the same [Gitomer 2011, p. 15]. Social media are the tool that facilitates socialising, encourage cooperation, interaction and communication through discussions, opinions, comments and the exchange of information with all interested parties [Malita 2010, p. 748]. It is extremely important for a modern man to share things or to do things with others. By belonging to a group, a person not only builds their group identity but also their individual identity [Kasprzycki- Rosikoń, Piątkowski 2013, p. 27]. They are a symptom of the innovativeness of market entities and the openness to processes observed in the environment. They are a result of changes that originally concerned only a platform of communication and nowadays increasingly often determine the realisation of image purposes and the intensification of sales results. They provide a chance to create attitudes and purchasing habits, profiles and needs of consumers and at the same time, they perfectly fit in the area of market and marketing research, including ethnographic research or looking for ideas and their selection. By means of them, one can implement actions in customer service, information actions connected with a company/brand strategy, especially in crisis situations. They also provide an opportunity to enter direct interactions with individual groups of stakeholders, customers in particular, and to create one's own, enterprise-friendly community. The effect of homogenisation observed in the web means that in social groups, communities and organisations there is a common fashion and culture. In spite of a great diversity, a lot of people at the same time start or cease to like the same thing, e.g. a product and its practical or perceptive values, the level of customer service, brand, pricing policy, etc. The wide variety of available online communication options means companies can offer tailored information or send messages that engage consumers by reflecting their special interests and behaviour [Batra, Keller 2016, p. 124]. Social media is about participation. This participation can take the form of simply viewing relevant information that was previously hidden from view. But most often, it takes the form of communicating, collaborating and connecting with anyone, anywhere and anytime [Jue, Marr, Kassotakis, 2010, p. 4]. Social media allow firms to engage in timely and direct end-consumer contact at a relatively low cost and higher levels of efficiency than can be achieved with more traditional tools [Kaplan, Haenlein 2010, p. 67]. So, they make it possible to exceed expectations of individual groups of stakeholders thanks to interpersonal and multilateral relations.

In an era when shifting a customer experience from "average" to "wow" is worth 30–50 % improvements in terms of increased likelihood to recommend a company and make repeated purchases, proactive social media care is critical [Masri, Esber, Sarrazin, Singer 2015]. Then, it seems justified that social media are an inherent part of strategies realised by enterprises, including the area of change management, while ensuring an added value for an enterprise [Żukowski 2016, p. 29]. Thanks to their emergent features, they allow for intensifying the realised processes and multiply the achieved goals while increasing the dynamics of changes, both of adaptive and innovative character. They change what we have already known about running business and about how own brands, products and services or information should be shared with the environment [Joel 2010, p. 12], while generating satisfaction of broadly understood groups of stakeholders.

Social media can be a strategic differentiator in the innovative process, leading to significant reductions in costs or intensifying opportunities to obtain new clients [Dobiegała – Korona 2009, p. 95] and to maintain current ones as well as to create unique key factors of success for a given trade or sector. They are still an evolutionary approach to market space and its present players while creating a new dimension of reality in which the relativity of current relations, the originality of used methods and related instruments and a broadly understood value are the main pillars of management process. However, what still determines the depth, level and extent of their adaptation is the level of maturity towards social media. Diversity of classification in that approach still definitely determines a possibility of effective and efficient strategy of social media. That is why social media are increasingly often perceived through the prism of concrete ventures, tools and technological applications that meet specific business functions and goals [Mazurek 20102, p. 99].

3. Application of social media in the process of change management

The process of change management through a gradual process built on multilateral interactions, by the trial-and-error method, allows for reducing contradictions and to create a new state that is able to meet competitive and human challenges which an enterprise has to face [Kurtyka, Roth 2015, p. 215]. That process rarely unfolds in a sequential way and specific dimensions and perspectives intervene during the creation of a unity based on participation approach. In that process, social media will be a result of clashing of diverse views and numerous interactions while pointing at a transcendent vision of desired solutions and increasing involvement as well as a sense of responsibility for change. As a result, they become an indispensable supplement to a strategy implemented in that area. Nowadays, we live in the times when a customer receives full information about an offer and a company can track their responses, questions and doubts as well as reactions to changes observed in an enterprise [Mazurek – Łopacińska 2003, p. 334]. Moreover, consumers have realised that they have their say, their opinions will not disappear and they can initiate a discussion with the biggest organisations and, what is more, even dictate the terms. A change in the role of the consumer compelled enterprises to engage in interactions leading to building more permanent bonds [Żurek, Brodka – Makara 2016, p. 54].

Common sense tells us that people going through change need in-person interactions with people they trust and a safe space to process what is happening. But because we spend nearly three hours per day on social platforms, and because more than half of employers are already using internal social media, companies also have an opportunity to leverage social media as a change management tool [Clayton 2015]. Their diffusion generally concerns every stage of that process from the beginning, including diagnosis through formulating strategic challenges and goals, formulating a concept and plans of action as well as through the stage of implementation, control and final assessment of the process of changes. Taking into consideration the dynamics and complexity of individual groups of stakeholders as well as the multidimensionality of their environment, the process can proceed in a different way in different companies, depending on their social, cultural or economic context. This conditions a spectrum of potential areas in which social media may turn out to be irreplaceable. They concern first and foremost:

- looking for new, creative solutions concerning specific functional strategies, processes and structures from the point of view of real needs and expectations of people who have contact with them (customers, employees, suppliers, etc.);
- creating a platform of internal communication thanks to which employees can become an integral part of the process of changes, often initiating them;
- formulating a space of free and direct external communication, which allows for explaining the need for implementing changes, their course, consequences, perception and benefits;

- opportunities to gain objective opinions about implemented changes through creating a kind of a platform of users' experience. Thanks to that, an enterprise becomes more reliable and the realised process is more flexible;
- reducing the distance between an enterprise and specific groups of stakeholders, enabling the minimisation of reluctance and potential resistance towards changes;
- minimising the risk of difficult or crisis situations in which an enterprise can be as a result of change management and a possibility to quickly resolve difficulties and problems;
- stimulating the development of individual groups of stakeholders, especially employees and customers, through indicating various areas of activity in the implemented process while increasing their sense of value;

All these areas concern directly a communication process or are related to it. It results from social media features and their specificity, which enables an enterprise to be transparent in the undertaken activity and attributes. Yet, using social media in change management requires the openness of an enterprise, the ability to listen to what is happening around it, the ability to cope with criticism and undertaking activities that will emphasise the efforts of all participants of that process, employees and customers in particular. Undoubtedly, there is a need for the knowledge which, on the one hand, will concern socio-cultural conditions of the conducted communication process as well as the awareness of gathered resources, opportunities and competencies in this area. Values and forms of behaviour certainly depend on the customers and workers' belonging to specific communities and subcultures while conditioning their level of perception of individual social media as well as the forms and contents of messages directed at them. What seems of crucial importance is personality traits of the message recipient that determine the level and degree of sensitivity to sent messages while including an aspect of the selectivity and subjectivity of its assessment. Therefore, an enterprise that wants to use social media in the process of change management must constantly shape their message. As a result, consumers can find what they look for: the realisation of their unsatisfied needs and desires. Obviously, a basic rule for building and deepening bonds with the client is the constant updating and adjusting of a system of communication to their evolving expectations and preferences [Mazurek – Łopacińska 2003, p. 334]. The presence in social media definitely means thinking about clients and employees as long-term partners whom we know, value and trust [Falls, Deckers 2013, p. 267]. As a result, the communicative coordination of new – cooperative and cultural – lifestyle requires new skills and the motivation to cooperate with others through shared intentionality as well as collective intentionality [Tomasello 2015, p. 216].

The emergence of social media has changed the way in which people and business organisations interact via the Internet. That this has implications for business is clear to the managements of businesses, as executives observe the rapid adoption and use of social media by their customers [Yawised, Mashall 2015, p. 14] or workers. It allows for increasing the involvement of each party and build a positive experience connected with an enterprise. What seems necessary in that process is shaping emotional dimension, which requires companies to provide proper stimuli and indications that will show directions to thoughts, emotions and recollections of message recipients while combining their way of life, ideas and values with an enterprise's potential. It will enable the creation of social and business networks in the change management process by means of social media so that they will use contacts established in the offline world and proportionally strengthen them. It enables a search for new ways of using and collecting a value and turn it into cash [Shuen 2009, p. 99] in the hypermedia space that comprises both the traditional and online market.

In the process of change management, social media can prove extremely helpful during the analysis and interpretation of the company's current market position, company image, brand and its products as well as at the stage of testing new ideas and effects of implemented changes. The analysis of information in discussion fora, content websites, corporate or individual blogs and social networks (including own fanpage, if an enterprise or brands created by it have such a page) allow for determining the level of customer satisfaction. A scrupulous analysis of the quantity and contents of posts placed by readers and of materials most frequently sent between users connected with an enterprise or recommendations related to it offers an opportunity to determine the real picture of an enterprise and potential opportunities and directions of its future development, including those related to competitive entities. What is of crucial importance is that these opinions are not declarative but represent real feelings of users which are based on their own subjective experience with an enterprise, its products, services, employees, etc. So, it is not a result of intuitive perception but of the collected information and knowledge. What also seems likely is that social media will increasingly show features related to predictive skills. As a result, the process of their influence will be by far more convincing.

Thanks to that, at the stage of diagnosis, it is possible to identify areas in which a change would be recommended or necessary. Repeated negative opinions should be a signal for an enterprise about critical areas, the duplication of wrong solutions and the need to modify them or reorganise completely. At this stage, social media can also turn out to be helpful in the process of diagnosing opinions about changes that an enterprise plans to implement. Placing this kind of information together with a question about its evaluation or potential ideas to improve it increase trust and the feeling that the recipients are important for an enterprise which respects their opinion. It responds to a human desire of auto expression, interpersonal bonds and a sense of belonging, all of which are particularly useful in the web [Shih 2012, p. 32]. It also reduces the risk of the failure of the process of change implementation, minimises related costs and a possible effect of reluctance, which might result in a great deal of negative comments and actions directed at the company and/or its brand.

Brands that experienced such a situation are e.g. Gap or Polish Airlines LOT, which implemented a change concerning their logo. Unfortunately, the opinion of the public, customers in particular, was not positive. As a result, it caused numerous negative commentaries, fanpages uniting thousands of opponents only within 24 hours or irreverent memes, and, in consequence, the weakening of the company/brand image and its sales results. As a result, both abovementioned companies relatively quickly made a decision to withdraw from the unfortunate changes.

Another way of using the social media potential in the process of change management was applied by IDC Holding a.s, which used them in the process of the rebranding of Horalky wafer biscuits. After monitoring opinions and comments in the social media space, they made a decision to change their name in the Polish market. However, customers and fans were those who decided about its final version, accepted by the enterprise. In comparison, Starbucks, while planning to launch any promotional campaign, first asks for opinions of its customers, also by means of social media, which allows them to collect feedback in a short space time. Heineken, on the occasion of 140th anniversary of the brand, invited Facebook users to design a new bottle from patterns and tools available on the company profile. Citroen invited their fans to design a new look (interior elements, a number of doors, accessories, etc.) and functional elements in Citroen C1 Connection series. In both cases, the winning solution was introduced to the production process.

A very interesting solution is also "The Bank of Ideas" run by BZ WBK, within whose framework bank customers are able to present their ideas for changes that might improve its functioning as well as to comment on proposed solutions. A factor of great importance in that process was the creation of own e-community of customers that is a valuable source of reliable information and ideas for the development of the company, brand, products or services. It currently comprises more than 10,000 users, thanks to whom 780 ideas from people who know the bank and its specificity were implemented. Such an approach enables using the so-called collective wisdom and make decisions based on it while changing the observers into the advocates of change. As a result, social media can help organisations capture the greatest advantages of real-time collaborations, while processes can be redesigned and reconfigured more quickly [Jue, Marr, Kassotakis, 2010, p. 10]. The range and depth of related changes is undoubtedly varied and can concern both operational and strategic aspects, as well as those connected with strategic management.

Creating own community connected with a given enterprise or a brand allows for reaching, by means of social media, a specific group of customers and employees as well. Many companies are just beginning to adopt social media internally. The key to adopting them and making them work as a business tool is to look at entire business processes and work out how they can be supported with social media [Flinders http://www.computerweekly.com/ feature/Social-media-for-communication-inside-the-enterprise]. The process of creating communities of employees within your enterprise and communicating with them by using social media tools (internal social media) is an important element in building and empowering engaged employees [Dalbec http://www.apcoworldwide.com/blog/detail/apcoforum/ 2016/01/25/the-benefits-of-internal-social-media-engaged-employees] and increasing their output. An enterprise that encourages its workers to come up with new ideas can gain a lot. People who have a clear goal focus on achieving it. So, if a culture based on creating values is introduced, new ideas appear. Employees themselves will find ways to look for new solutions [Mruk, Stępień 2014, p. 27]. As a result, both customers and employees of a given enterprise become a factor determining a need for changes, a source of numerous creative solutions in that area; also, they determine its dynamics using the omnipresent social media. A satisfied customer or employee becomes an advocate of a given enterprise and frequently a co-designer who wants to be included in the process of improving company products, services, advertising, etc. [Kotler, Kotler 2013, p. 62]. While wishing to share themselves, they become the initiator of changes and a method of implementing them. Social media definitely contribute to an intensive development of the concept of so-called open innovations, according to which an enterprise should equally focus their attention on internal and external sources of their origin. Thanks to that, the motivation of specific groups of stakeholders to accept and strengthen new behaviour will increase and the implemented changes will have bigger chances to succeed both in a short and long-term perspective [Spector 2015, p. 48].

Great opportunities of social media applications are generated by a stage of testing effects of implemented changes, especially in the area of research and product development. An increasingly bigger number of companies engage customers in social media, which means collecting more and more knowledge and feedback they leave in the network in the context of selected enterprises or products [Sadowski 2013, p. 109]. Individual bloggers eagerly use new products, test them and review them, and while voicing their opinions, they give suggestions. As a result, they become advocates or opponents of a given enterprise and/or its products, encouraging others to buy a product or decidedly discouraging them from buying it. Members of own e-communities are particularly active in that space. Giving a chance to review what is a key issue of the process of changes and holding a discussion about it is a way of generating an added value in the system of change management. It provides benefits for both a consumer and an enterprise. A solution that proved to be perfect is also a corporate blog, thanks to which, especially in the case of highly technologically advanced products, a producer can provide necessary information while increasing the safety of usage or train users appropriately. A good example is Tesla, a producer of so-called connected cars, which belong to the concept of the Internet of Things and are operated by means of an autopilot. The company will start a training for owners of their cars on their own blog as the system is still in the testing phase. Information presented by means of it will discuss all kinds of situations that may occur on the way and the question of how the driver should behave. So, it will comprise specialist information, the results of studies concerning an implemented concept and related changes in the trade as well as information which will show that the enterprise follows the spirit of time, adhering to observed trends and initiating subsequent changes in their market sector. As a result, it has a chance to become an expert that creates new chances and generates factors that can in the future become crucial in the process of building a competitive advantage. At the same time, the producer counts on significant feedback that will not only increase safety but also the ergonomics and attractiveness of a new product. A change implemented then has a chance to be accepted, which will allow an enterprise to achieve related objectives. A corporate blog used that way in the process of change management can also prove useful for employees in the process of the ultimate creation of innovation while engaging them and improving internal communication [Wright 2007, p. 5]. Social media can also influence the process of the diffusion of implemented innovations that are a subject of changes while reducing the time of their acceptance and popularisation. The exchange of opinions with e-community allows for gaining experience connected with a change without a direct contact and prospective recognition of its relative predominance over previous solutions.

Social media enable a real-time with people from the whole world and in a way and time that was not possible before. Fun, controversy and usefulness – these three elements are a key to achieve snowball effects in the context of the enterprise, brand and products in social media [Kasprzycki – Rosikoń, Piątkowski 2013, p. 35]. They definitely improve the process of communication, making it more flexible and coherent, which influences the course of the process of change management. The directness of conducted communication allows for minimising the distance between an enterprise and specific groups of stakeholders, creating the space in which communication based on the multilog concept allows for conducting discussions on the character of change at the time and in a way that the participants of that process accept thoroughly. What proves crucial is not only the leading topics connected with an implemented change but also "the tone of voice" perceived as a style of discussion and the "look and feel" identified with the general image of an enterprise or brand in a given medium. What remains of crucial importance is the fact that consumers observe what others do and copy their behaviour. Therefore, an accurate correlation of individual channels and instruments of social media with stages of change management process is required. Customer satisfaction requires meeting their expectations, but it is increasingly important, also in the process of creating and implementing changes, to provide stimuli that will exceed these expectations. It leads to more emotional experiences and can considerably condition the degree of involvement in the process of change management. The more often they are perceived as attractive, the more willing a customer becomes to share, while actively engaging into that process. So, customer endeavour must be present and understood in every single action, both outside as well as within its internal structures [Fisk 2009, p. 215]. It means that consumers, employees and other groups of stakeholders as well as processes and actions realised by them must concentrate on the realisation of mutual aspirations while consistently participating in the process of changes.

Social media are a perfect platform for the expansion of business in an interactive environment [Ahmad, Salman, Ashiq 2015, p. 1]. Their emergence has made it possible for one person to communicate with hundreds or even thousands of other people about products and companies that provide them. Thus, the impact of consumers communications has been greatly magnified in the market place. Therefore, managers must learn to shape consumer discussions in a manner that is consistent with the organisation's mission and performance goals [Mangold

2009, p. 357]. The customer has to be central to most of the decisions made by the company [Faulkner 2002, p. 13]. Businesses succeed when they meet the desires of customers more effectively than their competitors do. Technological change, new competition and changing desires make yesterday's solutions obsolete and create the opportunity for new answers [Doyle 2008, p. 4].

The culture of real virtuality in which we have to function means that social media can, due to their features, play an important role in the process of change management thanks to an opportunity to look at it from various points of view. It is worth being aware that social media are not a remedy, but only one possible element in the process of change management, whose effectiveness depends on the ability to use them in the initiated market actions. Their effective application in change management requires understanding the essence of social media, an enterprise's openness to having a conversation, the ability to listen to what is happening around, the ability to cope with criticism and initiating activities that will emphasise the efforts of all participants of that process – employees and customers in particular.

Bibliography

Afuah A., Tucci Ch. (2003), *Biznes internetowy. Strategie i modele*, Oficyna Ekonomiczna, Kraków.

Ahmad N., Salman A., Ashiq R. (2015), *The Impact of Social Media on Fashion Industry*, "Journal of Resources Development and Management", Vol. 7.

Appelo J. (2011), *Zarządzanie 3.0*, Helion, Gliwice.

Batra R., Keller K. (2016), *Integrating Marketing Communications: New Findings, New Lessons, and New Ideas*, "Journal of Marketing", Vol. 80 .

Carnall C. (2007), *Managing change in organizations*, Pearson Educated Limited, Ashoford Coloured Press, Gosport.

Cole G. (2004), *Management theory and practice*, South Western Cengage Learning, Geraldine Lyons, London.

Clayton S. (2015), *Change Management Meets Social Media*, "Harvard Business Review", No 10.

Dalbec B., *The Benefits of Internal Social Media? Engaged Employees*, http://www.apcoworldwide.com/blog/detail/apcoforum/2016/01/25/the-benefits-of-internal-social-media-engaged-employees(dostęp: 11.07.2016).

Dobiegała-Korona B. (2009), *Migracje klientów a wartość przedsiębiorstwa*, PWN, Warszawa.

Doyle P. (2008), *Value-based Marketing: Marketing Strategies for corporate growth and shareholder value*, 2nd Edition.

Drucker P. (1997), *The Future that Has Already Happened*, "Harvard Business Review", September-October, pp. 20–24.

Falls J., Deckers E. (2013), *Media społecznościowe bez ściemy,* One Press, Helion.

Faulkner M. (2002), *Customer Management Excellence,* John Wiley & Sons.

Fisk P. (2009), *Geniusz konsumenta*, Oficyna Wolters Kluwer Business, Warszawa.

Flinders K., *Social media for communication inside the enterprise,* http://www.computerweekly.com/feature/Social-media-for-communication-inside-the-enterprise (dostęp: 11.07.2016).

Gitomer J. (2011), *Społecznościowy boom*, Helion, Gliwice.

Gołębiowski T. (2001), *Zarządzanie strategiczne. Planowanie i kontrola*, Difin, Warszawa.

Joel M. (2010), *Sześć pikseli oddalenia*, One Press, Helion, Gliwice

Jue L., Marr J., Kassotakis M. (2010), *Social Media at Work: How Networking Tools*, Propel Organizational Performance, Jossey – Bass, San Fracisco

Jurkiewicz A., Majewska M., Sołtysińska B. (2012), *Kuszenie blogera*, „Marketing w Praktyce", nr 8.

Kaplan A., Haenlein M. (2010), *Users of the world, unite! The challenges and opportunities of Social Media*, "Business Horizons", 53.

Kasprzycki-Rosikoń J., Piątkowski J. (red.) (2013), *Crowdsourcing, Jak angażować konsumentów w świat marek,* One Press, Helion, Gliwice.

Kietzmann J., Hermkens K., McCarthy I., Silvestre B. (2011), *Social media? Get serious! Understanding the functional building blocks of social media*, "Business Horizons", Vol. 54, Issue 3, May–June.

Kos-Łabędowicz J. (2015), *Internet jako źródło informacji w decyzjach nabywczych konsumenta*, Wydawnictwo C.H.Beck, Warszawa

Kotler Ph., Kartajaya H., Setiawan I. (2010), *Marketing 3.0*, Wyd. MT Biznes, Warszawa

Kotler Ph., Kotler M. (2013), *Przez marketing do wzrostu. 8 zwycięskich strategii*, Dom Wyd. Rebis,Poznań

Kozielski R. (red.) (2011), *Wskaźniki marketingowe*, Oficyna Wolters Kluwer Business, Warszawa

Krawiec F. (2005), *Marketing w firmie przyszłości*, Difin, Warszawa

Kurtyka M., Roth G. (2015), *Zarządzanie zmianą. Od strategii do działania*, CeDeWu.pl, Warszawa

Li Ch., Bernoff J. (2009), *Marketing technologii społecznych*, MT Biznes, Warszawa

Malita L. (2010), *Social media time management tools and tips,*"Procedia Computer Science", Vol. 3

Mangold W., Faulds D. (2009), *Social media: the new hybrid element of the promotion mix*, "Business Horizons", Vol. 52, No. 4

Masri M., Esber D., Sarrazin H., Singer M. (2015), *Your Company Should Be Helping Customers on Social,*"Harvard Business Review", July 15.

Mazurek G. (2012), *Znaczenie wirtualizacji marketingu w sieciowym kreowaniu wartości,* Wyd. Poltext, Warszawa.

Mazurek-Łopacińska K. (2003), *Zachowania nabywców i ich konsekwencje marketingowe,* PWE, Warszawa.

McAfee A. (2011), *Firma 2.0,* Oficyna Wolters Kluwer Business, Warszawa.

McLuhan M. (2004), *Zrozumieć media,* Wydawnictwa Naukowo - Techniczne, Warszawa.

Mintzberg H. (2013), *Zarządzanie,* Oficyna Wolters Kluwer Business, Warszawa.

Morawski M., Niemczyk J., Perechuda K., Stańczyk-Hugiet E. (2010), *Zarządzanie. Kanony i trendy,* C.H.Beck, Warszawa.

Mruk H. (red.) (2002), *Strategie marketingowe,* Wyd. Akademii Ekonomicznej w Poznaniu, Poznań.

Mruk H., Stępień B. (2014), *Tworzenie wartości dla klienta z perspektywy konsumentów i przedsiębiorstw,* PWE, Warszawa.

Piotrowski W. (2013), *Dwugłos o zarządzaniu* [w:] Bogdanienko J., Piotrowski W. (red.), *Zarządzanie. Tradycja i nowoczesność,* PWE, Warszawa.

Probst G., Raub S., Romhardt K. (2004), Zarządzanie wiedzą w organizacji, Oficyna Ekonomiczna, Kraków.

Reeves M., Deimler M. (2013), *Adaptability: The New Competitive Advantage,* "Harvard Business Review", July - August.

Sadowski M. (2013), *Rewolucja social media,* One Press, Hellion, Gliwice.

Shih C. (2012), *Era Facebooka,* Helion, Gliwice.

Shuen A. (2009), *Web 2.0,* Helion, Gliwice.

Spector B. (2015), *Wprowadzanie zmian w organizacji,* PWN, Warszawa.

Todnem R. (2005), *Organizational change management: A critical review,* "Journal of Change Management" , Vol. 5, Issue 4.

Tomasello M. (2015), *A Natural History of Human Thinking,* Copernicus Centre Press.

Urbanowska-Sojkin E. (2008), *Praktyka zarządzania strategicznego,* PWE, Warszawa.

Verganti R. (2012), *Jak projektować przełomowe produkty,* „Harvard Business Review Polska", nr 7.

Wendt R. (2010), *Zarządzanie zmianą w polskiej firmie,* Dom Wydawniczy Zacharek, Warszawa.

Wright J. (2007), *Blogowanie w biznesie,* Wydawnictwa Akademickie i Profesjonalne, Warszawa.

Yawised K., Marshall P. (2015), *Social CRM: A Review of the Literature and the Identification of New Research Directions,* "International Journal of Virtual Communities and Social Networking", 7(1).

Żukowski M. (2016), *Twoja firma w social mediach,* Helion, Gliwice.

Żurek A., Brodka-Makara M. (2016), *Emocje i poszukiwanie sensu,* „Marketing w Praktyce", Vol. 4.

Zofia Patora-Wysocka
University of Social Sciences

Putting Daily Activities into *Practice*: a Practice-based Approach to Organisational Change

Abstract: The objective of the chapter is to introduce a practice-based approach to organisational change. The Practice Turn in management brings a new insight into the 'old' problems. The thesis posits that agency may be perceived as a category of twofold nature that is instantiated in practice schemas. The research applied an in-depth case study as well as non-participatory observation. The main findings are that agency and practice reproduction are based on routine and spontaneous activities. The temporal view on organisation implies the significance of questioning the split between stability and change in an organisation. A new perspective accounts for treating organisation as being in constant motion. The practice-based approach attempts to fill this cognitive gap. Routine activities are seen as practice reproductive categories of change while spontaneous activities may result in innovativeness and the institutionalisation of a new practice. The findings are of importance in the realm of a turbulent organisational environment.
Key words: practice-based approach, *Practice Turn*, organisational change, spontaneous actions, routines.

The chapter came into being within the project No. DEC-2011/03/D/HS4/01651 entitled 'Internationalisation as a factor initiating change in the enterprise', financed by the National Science Centre, conducted by the University of Social Sciences in the years 2012–2016.

Introduction

The practice-based approach is a relatively new stream of research within organisational and management studies. The focus of practice theories are mundane activities that provide a fertile ground for the exploration of the problems of organisational change. Aiming at the description of contemporary patterns of organisational environment, one may lock it in the notion of turbulence. This gives rise to the importance of 'ongoing temporality' (Hernes, 2014: 32). The practice turn in management is apt to explore organisational change in terms of fast and minute, yet influential daily recreated routines. Such activities are the loci of past, present and future structures and processes. Important references to the notion of routines within the practice-based approach are far from the common understanding of them as rigid and perfectly stiff categories of sustaining organisational life [Pentland, Feldman 2003]. Instead, they are perceived as basic units of changeability in organisational studies. The aim of this chapter is to invoke the practice turn ideas in an organisational change analysis. The thesis, illustrated by an in-depth case study, posits that agency instantiated in practice schemas is of a twofold character, i.e. it is based on routine and spontaneous daily activities. Routine activities are forces of the structure's reproduction while spontaneity stands for innovativeness and radical changes as well as new practice institutionalisation.

The practice approach to organisation and management often refers to the seminal work on the structuration process by Anthony Giddens [1984]. The title of this chapter is a reference to the work of Whittington [1992], who was one of the first to emphasise the coherence of the structurationist view with managerial agency and organisational issues. Structuration is aimed at linking agency and the system, and therefore it tends to be addressed within organisation and management studies through a practice-based approach. Although it may seem tautological, the leading inquiry in the structuration theory is the process of the creation and transformation of social systems. The basic domain of the structuration theory is practice:

- Everyday practices are engines of routinisation;
- Bodily induced practices institutionalise temporarily ordered schemas of acting;
- There is practical consciousness that is crucial for understanding the link between agency and structure.

These propositions tend to appraise the notion of agency as the carrier of organisational changes. Agency is instantiated in practice and enclosed with contextual knowledge.

The chapter is a result of theoretical and empirical studies. The theoretical part starts with epistemological considerations on the practice turn in management. It also draws on the processual orientation towards the notion of practice as well as organisational change. The empirical part explores the issue tackled with the use of a case study analysis. The observation was focused on an organisation from the apparel and creative industry.

1. *Practice Turn* in Management

The organisational world is in constant flux. This kind of change can be rigorously planned or spontaneous and unpredictable. Theoretical affordances to unbundle the organisational change process may be traced back to as early as the time when the management science started to develop. Stacey [2011] reached into philosophy, sociology and psychology to delineate the *ways of thinking* about organisational dynamics and managerial issues. Attempting to offer an alternative stream of thought, he contrasted the dominant systemic approach with the theory of complex responsive processes [Stacey 2011]. Kociatkiewicz and Kostera [2013] challenge the economical discourse in management, anchored in two main paradigms: functionalism and radical structuralism. In this sense, management draws inspiration from the natural science, and it is characterised by: verificationism, striving after generalisations and the accumulation of knowledge, and the determinist approach to the phenomena explained, based on the quantification methodology. Explanations of processes are based on striving after the objective, universal and quantifiable truth. Promoting the *homo oeconomicus* model, management theories gain predictive powers [Sułkowski 2012, pp. 114–116]. The cognitive vision of the humanist current places more emphasis on *getting to know and improving the fate of an individual in an organisation*, while the economic current focuses on increasing the organisation's effectiveness. Kociatkiewicz and Kostera emphasise that the humanist current does not oppose the economic approach, but it is characterised by different objectives of the research programme [Kociatkiewicz, Kostera 2013, p. 13]. Thus, challenging these two approaches represents the tension between societism and individualism, i.e. between macro- and micro-ontology, and this is why postulating the superiority of one discourse over the other is doomed to failure.

Many contemporary thinkers, such as Weick [1979], Jarzabkowski [2005], Whittington [2007], Orlikowski [2000], Shotter and Tsoukas [2011], Gherardi [2012], Garud et al. [2015] etc. argue that the dominant discourse should be abandoned, which might lead to a different understanding of organisational change. An alternative approach is important in the turbulent organisational reality. Organisational and social change is a complex circuit based on the continuous creation, disappearance and replacement of structures and processes. This may provide a new cognitive input into theory, bridging the gap between micro and macro views on the organisational reality. Therefore, the suggested theoretical shift may be achieved by relying on Giddens' influential work on structuration theory. The idea of duality of structure is "always the basis for the continuity of social reproduction in time and space" [Giddens 2006, p. 679]. Thus, it may be the departure point for an analysis of novelty and perpetuation as well as the collapsing of social systems. Structure has a character of "recursively organised sets of rules and resources that are out of time and space" [Giddens 1984, p. 25]. It is reproduced and preserved in the flow of routinely recreated daily activities.

However, there is the "absence of the subject" and "practical consciousness" that stands for linking macro- and micro-cognitive perspectives on social change. Individuals are "going on in the context of social life" [Giddens 1984, p. xxiii]. Their individual and discursive understanding has no influence on constituting social and organisational reality. Practices are the foremost categories that shape and recreate social systems. The ontological primacy of ordinary daily activities is the basic notion of theoretical propositions in the *Practice Turn* in management.

The practice stream of thought in management is relatively new and still underestimated.

Organisational change within the practice-based approach may be interpreted under several research strands that are rooted in philosophy and sociology. The seminal works of early precursors of the practice line of inquiry in management and organisation theory date back to the 1920s and 1930s. The key contemporary research tradition of practice-based studies is anchored in four cognitive strands:

1. Phenomenological inspirations are rooted in the philosophical works of Heidegger [1962] and Ingarden [1961], and they are mostly used to rediscover the notion of practice and to locate it in the realm of everyday life. Intelligibility and practical rationality (or consciousness) are of greatest significance to the way of thinking in the tradition of practice-based studies. Researchers rarely refer to the very fundamentals explicitly (on an operational basis). These are propositions 'kept in mind' by contemporary thinkers.
2. The interpretative-symbolic approach views organisational change as embedded in the process of enacting, post-factum interpreting. Everyday activities and the decision-making process are immersed in sensemaking, and they are determined by symbols and values. Mead [1934], Wittgenstein [1979], Foucault [1977], and Weick [1995] are the principal contributors to the development of this line of reasoning. It may be said that Jarzabkowski's concept of "strategising" in strategic management grew out of the interpretative schema of logics [Jarzabkowski 2005].
3. Pragmatic and neo-pragmatic lines of thinking are anchored in the works of James [1907], Mead [1943], and Dewey [1938]. In sociology, they were developed under the theory of action by Joas [1997], and in the realm of organisation theory they had a significant influence on the knowing-in-practice approach [Gherardi 2008].
4. The structuration theory by Giddens [1984] and, to a lesser extent, the practice theory by Bourdieu [1972, 2007]. The area of the structuration theory focuses on daily activities as basic categories of social changes, which greatly contributed to the practice-based stream of research in management science. However,

the Giddensian theory in its pure form has been poorly applied in empirical terms [Whittington 2011]; it serves as a kind of logical and well-reasoned line of inquiry to follow-up as part of empirical studies, especially in marketing, where the structurationist point of view is linked with the value co-creation process ([Echeverri, Skålén 2011; Baran 2013 etc.].

There are many possible ways of theorising practice developed within the framework of management and organisation theory. Gherardi [2012, p. 200] indicates five crucial strands of research:

1. *A cultural-aesthetic approach*, which is immersed in the interactionist view on social reality and emphasises the role of language and aesthetic knowing in everyday recreated tasks;
2. The *Situated learning theory*, which states that learning is embedded in daily routines and that the social reality and organisational structures are instantiated through routine activities;
3. The *Actor-Network Theory*, which is based on an assumption that socio-material networks and relations are built upon human and non-human agents;
4. *Workplace studies*, where practice is represented through tools, materials and bodies [Niccolini 2013, pp. 223–224] or perceived within the framework of *technology-in-use* [Orlikowski 1996].

The analysis of practice phenomena emerges in relation to the process of social change. The modern legacy of the practice approach is influenced by sociological and philosophical theories that are up to date with the processes of creation, transformation and collapse of behavioural schemas, institutions, values, rules and structures. By adopting the micro-cognitive perspective, it might be possible to observe the rapid pace of organisational change. The move from practices as hardly visible patterns of organisational processes to practices as basic units of analysis in an organisation is also the departure point for the methodological approach. Empirical studies on practice are heavily influenced by the interpretative turn in management, which is mainly based on the qualitative approach. The practice turn provides an alternative to traditional approaches in organisation and management studies.

2. Everyday Practices as Basic Categories of Analysis in Organisation Studies

Within the epistemological framework of references, there appear phenomenological, Foucauldian and Bourdieusian influences [Golsorkhi et al. 2011]. The use of the Heideggerian logic practices may be perceived as a derivative of bodily and agential locus of "everydayness" [Tsoukas 2010]. Reckwitz perceives practices as "routines of moving the body, of understanding and wanting, of using things, interconnected in a practice" [Reckwitz 2002, p. 255]. Therefore, structures and organisations exist in everyday use. Organisations are webs of daily activities and practices as such are "spatial and temporal loci of working, organising, innovating or reproducing" [Gherardi 2012, p. 2]. Shove et al. [2012] put forward two propositions that are important departure points for the analysis of the category of practice in an organisation:

1. Practices comprise interconnected elements that come into being when they are enacted.
2. Practices may emerge, persist and disappear – and these processes depend on the way they are enacted, i.e. whether the links between the elements are stable or eroding [Shove et al. 2012, p. 21].

Ad. 1 Attempting to unbundle the fundamental elements of practice in an organisation, one may start with Schatzki's basic notion of practice as "a diversity of doings and sayings (basic actions). But a set of doings and sayings constitutes a practice only if its members have an array of understandings, rules and structures" [Schatzki 1996, p. 106]. The collective nature of practice is evident. Meaning, understanding and intelligibility are important features of practice [Schatzki 1996]. Practice is a kind of interdependence between "forms of bodily activities, forms of mental activities, 'things' and their use and background knowledge in the form of understanding, know-how, emotional states and motivational knowledge" [Reckwitz 2002, p. 249]. Shove et al. reduce this catalogue to three basic elements:

a) Materials that represent tools, artefacts, physical and technical infrastructure, technology as well as the body;
b) Competence, which, according to Shove et al. [2012], accounts for tacit [Polanyi 1958] and explicit knowledge. Capabilities, i.e. know-how, skills, the Giddensian "practical consciousness" [1984] and "performative aspects" routines [Pentland, Feldman 2003] are purposefully mixed together to simplify the core logic behind the interdependence between elementary parts of practices.
c) Meaning, according to Shove et al. [2012], stands for "mental activities, emotions and motivational knowledge", as listed by Reckwitz [2002]. However, it is not limited to motives and drivers for recreating everyday practices in an organisation. Meaning is anchored in a historical setting and past experience that define the future orientation [Shove et al. 2012, pp. 23–24].

Ad. 2. Practice is a "routinised type of behaviour" [Reckwitz 2002, p. 249]. Routine captures behavioural schemas, values, norms, meanings as well as common and individual understanding. It comprises elementary categories of body, activity, agency and the contextual knowledge that are interconnected and then reproduced in daily organisational life. This is of importance to the understanding of the processual nature of links between the elements of practice. The routinisation process takes place where three constituents of practice are configured and similarly reconfigured in an active and effective manner. If the links between these elementary parts are no longer possible, then the practice collapses and disappears. Assuming that the practice is a category that puts an organisation into being, then it becomes clear that the disappearance of practice may result in the emergence of a new practice or organisational erosion. However, a simplified schema of the structure of practice does not show the inner context of practice creation and preservation [Shove et al. 2012, p. 24]. In order to identify and define the evolution of practice in an organisation, it is necessary to observe the details of daily organisational life. According to Giddens [1984], the observation of routinisation is crucial for the understanding of relations between individual characteristics of an agent, the way daily activities are recreated and the nature of institutions that are repeatedly reproduced through their practices. However, observing the routinisation process is a key element of grasping newness in an organisation only if a routine change reveals the "episodic character of encounters with the other" [Giddens 1984, p. 60].

To sum up, the concept of practice is coherent with the structurationist logic. Therefore, organisational structures consist of rules and resources, but Sewell [1992] substitutes the notion of rules for that of schemas [Sewell 1992, p. 8]. Structures are *work in practice.* The capability of resources to organise work and modes of everyday decision-making processes, and to influence agency, defines the way people act in an organisation. Rules (or schemas) evaluate the congruence of resources and the organisation. Structures as such are not tangible: they exist "virtually" [Giddens 1984, p. 17]. Material tools, the means of production and technology are devices important for the reproduction of practice in space. The organisational locus in everyday activities is the element that stands for the temporality and spatiality of given practices.

3. Organisational Change from the Practice-Based Perspective

The basic units of the analysis of organisational change are social practices. In a very broad sense, the practice-based approach is aimed at elucidating the micro-processual foundations of the perpetuation, change, and erosion of organisations, social structures and institutions. Human activities are central to the organisational life, and this basic assumption is the departure point for the dominant perspective in management and organisation theory. The *Practice Turn* bridges the gap between the notion of agency and structure, i.e. between human agents and processes, agency and structures. From this perspective, individuals and their agency are carriers of practice and organisational change. In Sewell's terms, agency is an individual capability to control and transform organisational relations and interactions, and it is instantiated in the contextual knowledge of behavioural schemas and routines (Sewell, 1992). However, the level of voluntarism in the case of agency is bounded by the participation of individual agents in (inter)organisational relations. Organisational structures are created and recreated in the course of everyday practice. Agency is embedded in "the performance of practices" (Reckwitz, 2002: 256). In the Giddensian view, there is "practical consciousness" that to some extent seems to be in opposition to the Rational Choice Theory. Instead, agency is located in the contextual knowledge and "arises from the actor's knowledge of the schemas", and so it can be reinterpreted and adapted to new circumstances. The vast array of cognitive schemas is located in habitus, work and personal experience, interactions and knowledge. Aldrich & Ruef (2006) exemplify person, role and "event schemas" that are influenced by different sources of knowledge [Aldrich&Ruef 2006, p. 119]. Schemas cultivate and at the same time constrain agency and practices. Agency is determined and "implied by the structure" [Sewell 1992, p. 20]. Sewell [1992] refers here to the metaphor of the capacity to use a language. Just like the speaking competence varies among individuals, agency is formed and bounded by schemas and resources, by organisational borders, identity and the continuum of managerial processes.

Agency seems to be a category of a twofold nature, which is instantiated in practice schemas. (Agential) enactment of practice may be performed on a routine as well as spontaneous basis. The routine way of practice reproduction arises from tacit knowledge and is performed automatically [Beck 1976]. However, automatic activities can be changed if they are performed in a conscious and reflexive manner. Lazaric [2010] assumes that humans display the tendency to apply procedural knowledge with a cognitive effort and in a deliberate and attentive way. Thus, repetitive activities are prone to be altered in-use. Changes of this kind are added to the everyday repertoire of practice. They have a marginal effect on the introduction of new practices as long as they are embedded in the shared understanding of schemas. On the other hand, a spontaneous manifestation of agency may be attributed to Sewell's notion of the "capacity to reinterpret or mobilise an array of resources in terms of schemas other than those that constituted the array" [Sewell 1992, p. 20]. A spontaneous enactment of practice may then result in opportunistic behaviour and initiate a radical shift in an organisation. However, such transformative actions are sometimes crucial for the sustaining of the organisation. In a turbulent environment, unplanned and innovative activities open up the possibilities of the organisational growth and therefore sustainability (Fig.1).

Fig.1. Agency and organisational change from the practice-based perspective

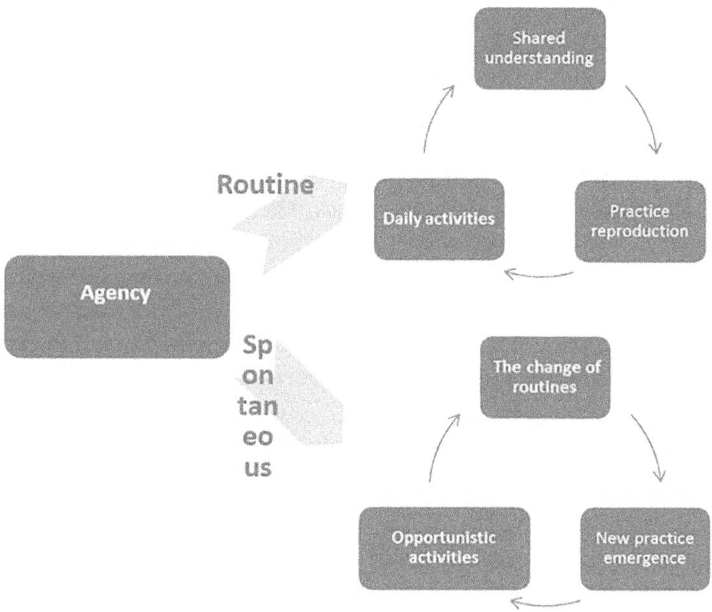

Source: Author's own work.

Agency is a crucial category that facilitates practice reproduction on a daily basis. The enactment and reproduction of structures arise from agency grounded in schemas. Schemas are carried by knowledgeable actors that are capable of acting on a routine as well as spontaneous basis. The salient features of the notion of agency within the practice-based approach form the basis for treating organisational change processes as a continuous stream of activities. The variety of ways of understanding *practice* imposes a different meaning on change in an organisation and management studies than the one present in the dominant discourse. In practice theory, it is assumed that organisational change can neither be strictly controlled nor independently introduced by individuals. Neither is organisational change perceived through the lens of practice placed within the discourse analysis or social interaction [Reckwitz 2002, p. 249]. It is built upon the routinisation process that serves consolidating and transformational purposes. The idea of spontaneous vs. routine agency is levelled within the discourse related to restructuring and emergent change in an organisation, i.e. planned and highly controlled changes vs. organisational amendments. Stability and change dilemma in organisational and management studies should not be perceived as unresolved but rather ill-formulated. Hernes [2014] calls for replacing the notion of organisational stability with that of continuity, and for drawing on the temporality of processes and structures [Hernes 2014, p. 31]. In the present activities, past routines, experience and knowledge collide. The temporality perspective raises the question of the generative impact of daily activities on structure.

The practice-based approach to organisational change poses a new cognitive challenge in organisational and management studies. Organisational change is located in ordinary actions performed daily. They are the routinely reproduced practices that "keep Giddens' immense wheel in motion" [Nicolini 2013, p. 45]. Agency, "practical consciousness" [Giddens 1984], situatedness as well as daily activities become the basic domain of inquiry into the "practical" coping with the 'old' management problems, and this opens up a possibility of understating organisational change in a turbulent and unforeseeable environment.

4. Organisational Change: Agency and Practice Reproduction

The chapter illustrates the results of an in-depth case study. The qualitative research was conducted on the basis of the case study method and non-participatory observations. An organisation from the apparel and creative industry was selected for the analysis. The selection of an organisation was purposeful and it was based on the researcher's knowledge of the local environment of young creative enterprises.

The study included a semi-structured interview that was complemented with the observation of the work entourage of the organisation as well as a 10-minute telephone call made shortly after the interview. Online sources like Facebook, press releases and websites were searched. The interview was recorded and supplemented with notes. The transcript was given to the informant, but she did not introduce any changes.

Since 2012, Zeta has been operating as a social cooperative – a screen printing and design studio. The logic behind the business model is based on cooperation with fashion brands, which are offered such services as imprints, graphics, clothes design and interior design. The production process is fully controlled. The cooperative workers include people with artistic education, characterised by a passion for creative activities, the effects of which are not always planned: their website deliberately provides information about creative 'experiments'. The cooperative is located in one of the former-factory buildings, transformed during privatisation into a kind of an artistic enclave, where young brands in the fashion and creative industry are created. The cooperative has a website and an online shop.

The following quotations from the interview illustrate how agency facilitates practice reproduction and the twofold nature of agency. Referring to Sewell [1992], the spontaneous path of the practice emergence arises from a capacity to reinterpret processual schemas in an innovative way. Therefore, as shown in Table 1, there are three crucial categories of practice enactment: opportunistic activities, the change of daily routines and new practice emergence (i.e. the institutionalisation of new practice).

Using the Giddensian [1984] notion, it is possible to show the way change "goes on" in an organisation. The routine path arises from everyday agential schemas and there are three categories crucial for the continuous change in an organisation: daily activities, shared understanding and practice reproduction (Table 2). The results of the study agree with the preliminary model shown in Figure 1.

Table 1. Key categories of agency in terms of a spontaneous stream of activities

Key categories	**Respondent's opinion**
Opportunistic activities (Zeta is a young brand on the market. Opportunism is very clear, any opportunity arising becomes an impulse to undertake creative activities. These activities are initiated by one person, and then all organisational actors get involved. Agency is of a collective character).	Z: (…) The recent collection, that's interesting, was a result of such playing (at printing). It was Natasza who somehow carried on with it (…) she just got an idea to take part in the Fashion Week first and to show such a presentation (…), it's a collection, right? As if… the very idea… because everything came down to getting it out somehow, just like you saw there… they are got out, and they… how to put it… This presentation as if… The presentation was a kind of a performance, those models were undressed there. We would put on a black dress, for example, a simple one, so that it was like a canvas and its printing area was as big as possible. And we printed on stage with a substance that could not be seen without printing. And when we put it on a model, it was still black. As if we hadn't printed it, right? But she only then came out and a chemical reaction after some time… ZPW: They would get revealed… Z: Yes. They just started to get out and appear, those flowers, you know?

Key categories	Respondent's opinion
The change of daily routines (Experimenting with the service is routinised. However, it is not connected with the disappearance of creative involvement in the integration of knowledge and resources, as the way of acting is routinised: the everyday practice is built upon experiments.)	Z: She just started to experiment with different things, play with them. She started to sew something, using these things. ZPW: (…) you need to do something with such a collection later, don't you? Sell it somehow. Z: Yes, we want to show it here because we've got a website… and we just want to sell it but in such a way… on order. Only if someone wants it.
New practice emergence (Creativity is the basis for the logic behind the cooperative's business model. The owners see new opportunities, which inspire them to new activities and finding new ways of providing services and products. Taking part in important events is a practice of showing collections and building the brand's identity.)	Z: If it's carried on, then it's a kind of an area of activity, right? Because it just emerged, because you did something well, a collection you showed, but what next? Will you repeat something like that? Of course, with a totally new idea but… (…) We would like to do things of this kind, so that it is on the borderline between art and clothing, just like that. This should be closely connected with printing. We haven't talked about it yet, perhaps we lack some kind of an impulse. Because it's easiest to make a decision when there is… ZW: An event? Z: (…) well, there's the Fashion Week, and the Fashion Philosophy.

Source: Based on Patora-Wysocka, Z., 2016.

Zeta is a young organisation operating in the creative industry. Opportunistic activities are factors initiating new practices. Spontaneity is a category of agency that may be considered as a collective and innovative configuration of resources, routines, knowledge and experience. Here, an individual actor employs their cognitive schema and creative capabilities in the context of a new opportunity. Shared understanding and interactions lead to the recreation of collective activities. All organisational participants start to experiment within the product development process. Creative activities are performed on a daily basis. A novel practice is institutionalised, defining the brand identity. The founders of Zeta perceive their unplanned participation in fashion events as an adopted way of practice reproduction.

Table 2. Key categories of agency in terms of routine activities

Key categories	**Respondent's opinion**
Daily activities (Zeta cooperates with many fashion designers on a daily basis. Orders are regular but they are very often time-consuming. The logic behind the service development process remains stable and is based on an artistic way of thinking.)	We simply earn from the orders for others. Very often, they are designers, but… how to put it… this is also something that consumes a lot of our time.
Shared understanding (Founders work as a team. They have the same understanding of the organisational aims. Practice diffuses through routines that arose around creative and artistic influences. There is the recurrence of work. However, the basic assumptions of the logic behind the business model contradict the aesthetics of mass production, which requires the development of specific solutions.)	We simply can't afford to… because such a collection (as the one for the Fashion Week) took a lot of time to prepare. This is hand printing. Sometimes even the customer, they're not interested in it. Because there are customers who come but they want everyone who sees it to know that it was handmade. Or there are things that can't be done with the use of a machine, and mostly these are our target customers. Because when a customer comes and says: 'We want it ideally printed, as if it had been made by a machine', then it defeats the purpose. I mean, we have certain reproducibility. It's not that we… we can print it well. It just defeats the whole purpose. You know what I mean?
Practice reproduction (The reproduction of practice is based on Zeta's relational resources. The maintaining of the business is possible due to cooperation with various creators: fashion designers, musicians and hairstylists. Every single enterprise or individual has different demands in relation to the value creation process).	Recently even a hairstylist (of the stars) Alfa came to us… he wanted to make some caps or something… I don't know… Beta, I don't know if you're familiar with Beta? (…) Well, Gamma, some companies, who else appeared… Epsilon, the new guy, who recently won the Project Runway, what's his name? Delta… I think.

Source: Based on Patora-Wysocka Z. 2016.

The service development process is of a recurrent character, but it is also based on creativity. Zeta's logic behind practice is built upon relations with top fashion designers who are very demanding in terms of quality and uniqueness. There is regularity and clear practice reproduction. Routines are embedded in the shared understanding, tacit knowledge and the common way of perceiving aims. Agency is derived from routines. It may be assumed that the process of practice reproduction stimulates individual actors of an organisation to grow. They perform daily activities in the realm of learning from their clients and through working with them within the value creation process.

Conclusions

The practice-based approach in management offers a new cognitive framework for organisational change issues. The Practice Turn is about thinking in processual categories. It is about routine daily activities that make organisational reality come into being. It is not about enumerating ordinary activities but observing how these everyday acts organise, transform and institutionalise structures. Sometimes, it may tackle the problem of organisational disappearance. I believe that the practice-based approach is aimed at locking the context of past, present and future directions of organisational development. It is of great importance from the perspective of the contemporary market uncertainty. Organisation change is instantiated in the recurrence of everyday practices. Practices impose and are imposed by behavioural and cognitive schemas. This kind of practice reproduction is based on agency. Agential enactment may be perceived as spontaneous as well as routine activities. However, an attempt at unbundling the category of practice reveals that it is not only about daily processes but takes place in the context of values, norms, rules, language, individual minds and bodies as well as artefacts. The organisational change is "going on" like the Giddensian structuration [1984].

The presented case study analysis pinpoints the duality of practice reproduction, considered from the agential perspective. However, observing organisational change from the practice-based perspective may result in getting to know the very mundane activities that are stimuli to innovativeness and the emergence of a new practice.

Bibliography

Aldrich H.E, Ruef M. (2006), *Organizations Evolving*, 2ed, London: SAGE.

Baran G. (2013), *Marketing współtworzenia wartości z klientem. Społecznotwórcza rola marketingu w procesie strukturacji interakcyjnego środowiska doświadczeń*, Instytut Spraw Publicznych, Kraków: UJ.

Beck A.T. (1976), *Cognitive Therapy and the Emotional Disorders*, New York: New American Library.

Bourdieu P. (1972), *Esquisse d'une théorie de la pratique, précédé de Trois études d'ethnologie kabyle*, Switzerland: Librairie Droz S. A.

Bourdieu P. (2007), *Szkic teorii praktyki, poprzedzony trzema studiami na temat etnologii Kabylów*, Kęty: Wydawnictwo-Marek Derewiecki.

Dewey J. (1938), *Logic: The Theory of Enquiry*, New York: Henry Holt.

Echeverri P., Skålén P. (2011), *Co-creation and co-destruction: A practice-theory based study of interactive value formation*, "Marketing Theory", 11(3): 351–373.

Foucault M. (1977), *Discipline and Punish. The Birth of the Prison*, New York: Pantheon Books.

Garud R., Simpson B., Langley A., Tsoukas H. (Eds.) (2015), *The Emergence of Novelty in Organizations*, Oxford: Oxford University Press.

Gherardi S. (2012), *How to conduct a practice-based study. Problems and methods*, Cheltenham: Edward Elgar.

Gherardi S. (2008), *Situated knowledge and situated action: what do practice-based studies promise?* [in:] Barry D. and Hansen H. (ed.), "Sage Handbook of the New & Emerging in Management & Organization", pp/ 516–527.

Giddens A. (1984), *The constitution of society: Outline of the theory of structuration*, Berkeley: California University Press.

Giddens A. (2006), *Elementy teorii strukturacji*, in: *Współczesne teorie socjologiczne*, opr. Jasińska-Kania A., et al., Warszawa: Wydawnictwo Naukowe SCHOLAR.

Golsorkhi D., Rouleau L., Seidl D. and Vaara E. (eds.) (2010), *Cambridge Handbook of Strategy as Practice*, Cambridge: Cambridge University Press.

Heidegger M. (1962), *Being and time*, Oxford: Blackwell.

Hernes T. (2014), *A Process Theory of Organization*, Oxford: Oxford University Press.

Ingarden R. (1961), *Spór o istnienie świata*, t. 2, wyd. 2 Warszawa: PWN.

James W. (1907/1995), *Pragmatism*, New York: Dover.

Jarzabkowski P. (2005), *Strategy as practice. An activity based approach*, London: SAGE Strategy Series.

Joas H. (1997), *Pragmatism and Social Theory*, Chicago: University of Chicago Press.

Kociatkiewicz J., Kostera M. (2013), *Zarządzanie humanistyczne. Zarys programu*, „Problemy Zarządzania", vol. 11, nr 4 (44), pp. 9–19.

Lazaric N. (2010), *Routines and routinization: an exploration of some micro-cognitive foundations* [in:] M.C. Becker (Ed.), *Hanbook of Organizational Routines*, Cheltenham, Northampton: Edward Elgar.

Mead G.H. (1934), *Mind Self and Society from the Standpoint of a Social Behaviorist* (Edited by Charles W. Morris), Chicago: University of Chicago.

Nicolini D. (2013), *Practice Theory, Work, and Organization. An Introduction*, Oxford: Oxford University Press.

Orlikowski W. (1996), *Improvising Organizational Transformation Over Time: A Situated Change Perspective*, "Information Systems Research", 7(1), pp. 63–92.

Orlikowski W. (2000), *Using Technology and Constituting Structures: A Practice Lens for Studying Technology in Organizations*, "Organization Science", 11(4), pp. 404–428.

Patora-Wysocka (2016), *The Twofold Nature of Spontaneous Actions: Insights From Practice Turn In Management*, "Studia Oeconomica Posnaniensia", accepted.

Pentland B., Feldman M.S. (2003), *Re-theorizing organizational routines as a source of flexibility and change*, "Administrative Science Quarterly", 48(1), pp. 94–118.

Polanyi M. (1958), *Personal Knowledge: Towards a Post-Critical Philosophy*, Chicago: University of Chicago Press.

Reckwitz A. (2002), *Toward a theory of social practices: a development in culturalist theorizing*, "European Journal of Social Theory", 5(2), pp. 243–263.

Schatzki T. (1996), *Social Practices: A Wittgensteinian Approach to Human Activity and the Social*, New York and Cambridge: Cambridge University Press

Sewell W.H. Jr (1992), *A Theory of Structure: Duality, Agency, and Transformation*, "American Journal of Sociology", 98, pp. 1–29.

Shotter J., Tsoukas H. (2011), *Theory as Therapy: Wittgensteinian Reminders for Reflective Theorizing in Organization and Management Theory*, "Research in the Sociology of Organizations", 02(32), pp. 311–342.

Shove E., Pantazar M., Watson M. (2012), *The Dynamics of Social Practice*, London: SAGE Publications.

Strategic Management and Organisational Dynamics: the challenge of complexity to ways of thinking about organisations. Pearson Education (6th edition), London 2011.

Sułkowski Ł. (2012), *Epistemologia i metodologia zarządzania*, Warszawa: PWE.

Tsoukas H. (2010), *Practice, strategy making and intentionality: a Heideggerian onto-epistemology for Strategy as Practice*, in: D. Golsorkhi et al., *Cambridge Handbook of Strategy as Practice* (pp. 47–62), Cambridge: Cambridge University Press.

Weick K. (1995), *Sensemaking in Organisations*, London: Sage.

Weick K. (1979), *The Social Psychology of Organizing*, New York: McGraw-Hill..

Whittington R. (1992), *Putting Giddens into action: social systems and managerial agency*, "Journal of Management Studies", 29(6), pp. 693–712.

Whittington R. (2007), *Strategy practice and strategy process: Family differences and the sociological eye*, "Organization Studies", 28(10), pp. 1575–158.

Whittington R. (2011), *The practice turn in organization research: Towards a disciplined transdisciplinarity*, "Accounting Organizations and Society", 36(3), pp. 183–86.

Wittgenstein L. (1979), *On Certainty*, Oxford: Blackwell.

Małgorzata Rozkwitalska
WSB University in Gdansk

Learning in Intercultural Interactions as an Antecedent of Organisational Change

Abstract: The aim of the chapter is to depict the role of learning in intercultural interactions as an antecedent of organisational change. The discourse refers to social learning and social cognitive theories, social-cognition models and cognitive dissonance. It also emphasises that learning in intercultural interactions is an inevitable component of thriving. The chapter first portrays intercultural interactions, then shows that learning, as a result of social interactions, can contribute to organisational change and finally discusses learning in intercultural interactions. Discussion, conclusions and directions for future research close the discourse. The chapter demonstrates that people learn since their representations are confronted with one another and they experience cognitive dissonance. They take an active role and witness thriving, where learning appears to be more salient than vitality. Furthermore, learning activates individual and organisational changes that are perceived as learning processes. The chapter supports the positive view in the literature on cultural diversity in organisations.

Key words: cognitive dissonance, intercultural interactions, organisational change, social-cognition models, social learning theory, social cognitive theory, thriving

Introduction

Globalisation has turned management into a multinational process and multinational corporations (MNCs) with their multicultural workforce have become an evident manifestation of this phenomenon [Groeppel-Klein et al. 2010]. It can be noticed that the companies encounter a growing need to internalise the international aspects into their boards and search for a more diverse staff with a broader knowledge base. As a result, the number of board members of different nationalities has grown [van Veen et al. 2014]. Furthermore, the unprecedented flow of immigrants, the short supply of professionals for certain key positions in organisations that has motivated some sectors, e.g. healthcare providers, to recruit immigrants, and global mobility of workforce have led to an increased presence of foreigners in numerous economies, mainly developed ones [Collings et al. 2007; Nolan 2012; Samnani et al. 2012; Harvey et al. 2004]. All these trends suggest that national diversity in organisations and states will probably rise in the future, leading to an increased number of employees working with culturally diverse others. Therefore, intercultural interactions, defined as contacts between people from a home country and other country nationals, are becoming and will be increasingly important in today's business [Abdul Malek & Budhwar 2013; Groeppel-Klein et al. 2010].

People involved in intercultural interactions face specific challenges such as e.g. the necessity to speak a foreign language or a cultural difference [Rozkwitalska & Basinska 2015a] that may lead to norm complexity or discrepancy. They can experience face threat, an identity conflict or performance ambiguity. Cultural diversity may result in a different perception of appropriate behaviour, negatively influencing intercultural interactions [Tanova & Nadiri 2010; Lauring 2009; Molinsky 2007]. Nevertheless, "when one interacts with another who is different and is faced with the novel worldview – perspective, thought process, values – that the other person presents", learning occurs [Davidson & James 2009, p. 139]. It, in turn, determines the quality of ongoing interactions and may facilitate an organisational change [Carmeli et al. 2009; Minbaeva et al. 2003; Antonacopoulou & Gabriel 2006]. Thus, learning is a vital aspect of individual and organisational functioning whereas individual learning behaviours are necessary for organisational learning [Carmeli et al. 2009][1].

The aim of the chapter is to depict the role of learning in intercultural interactions as an antecedent of organisational change. Although scholars highlight the importance of social contacts as facilitators of a learning process, still little is known about the phenomenon. Nonetheless, the nature of social interactions and their quality may be significant enablers of or impediments to learning in organisations [Carmeli et al. 2009]. As intercultural interactions present "doubled-edged sword" results [Stahl & Tung 2014], it is particularly interesting how such contacts may activate learning and contribute to organisational change.

To actualise the aim of the chapter, its structure is as follows: it first portrays intercultural interactions and outcomes associated with them, then shows that learning, as a result of social interactions, can contribute to organisational change and finally discusses learning in intercultural interactions. Discussion, conclusions and directions for future research close the discourse.

---

1 Organisational learning is perceived as a critical and complex process which enables organisations to adapt to changes in their environment, to grow, build and maintain their competitive advantage [Carmeli et al. 2009]. Individual learning and organisational learning are interrelated since "individual learning is always embedded in the organisational context and thus very much represents a social phenomenon" [Engelhard & Nägele 2003, p. 263].

The chapter emphasises a positive approach to cultural diversity in organisations. It augments the knowledge of the role of intercultural interactions, as a peculiar type of social interactions, in a learning process as an antecedent of organisational change.

1. Intercultural interactions and their effects

Working with citizens of various nations (e.g. peers in MNCs, expatriates or inpatriates, foreign contractors, authorities etc.) entails intercultural interactions [Shimoni 2011]. Such interactions refer to various types of contacts among culturally diverse people and include, for example, receiving feedback, negotiating with overseas partners, communicating via phone calls, answering emails, working in multicultural teams, etc. They can be momentary or enduring, short term or lasting ones [Molinsky 2007]. The literature uses the terms 'intercultural' and 'cross-cultural' interchangeably as an adjective, and 'interactions', 'contacts', 'relationships' or 'encounters' as the noun that it modifies. As a result, those contacts can be understood as interactions between/among individuals from a home country and other country nationals [Abdul Malek & Budhwar 2013; Colvin & Volet 2014; Harrison 2012; Peltokorpi 2010].

Intercultural interactions are very complex social interactions in which people exhibit mutually oriented behaviours [Rummel 1976] and interpret these behaviours using the lens of their own cultures and, as a consequence, different cognitive mechanisms. The complexity of intercultural contacts is the consequence of the impact of the cultures, personalities, professional background, type of the relationship and the context on the behaviours of interacting individuals [Müller 1998; Rozkwitalska 2014]. In a workplace, such contacts may include face-to-face and virtual interactions (e.g. working with an expatriate or with peers in other foreign subsidiaries in dispersed teams) as well as internal (e.g. superior-subordinate relationships) and external ones (e.g. negotiations with suppliers). Each intercultural interaction differs in terms of its intensity and frequency, depending on the particular situation, for example the degree of a company's internationalisation and integration or the type of staffing policy in MNCs [Cooper et al. 2007].

The review of the literature and research on intercultural interactions suggests that this type of social interactions presents the so-called "double-edged sword" effects [Mannix & Neale 2005; Stahl et al. 2010]. On the one hand, a significant body of research has documented that intercultural contacts may be detrimental and produce e.g. conflicts, process losses, ineffective communication, problems in social integration, barriers to knowledge sharing and changes, interferences in decision making process and dissatisfaction [Mannix & Neale 2005; Stahl et al.

2009; Björkman et al. 2004; Uhlenbruck 2004; Hernández-Mogollon et al. 2010; Engelhard & Nägele 2003]. On the other hand, there are also studies which present a more positive view of intercultural contacts and emphasise such positives as creativity and innovation [Mannix & Neale 2005; Stahl et al. 2010; Watson et al. 1993], less group-think, more perspectives, improved knowledge sharing and adaptability [Mannix & Neale 2005; Stevens et al. 2008; Stahl et al. 2010; Watson et al. 1993], more effective execution of complex organisational tasks [Stahl et al. 2010], more positive attitudes towards foreigners (White et al. 2011; Pettigrew & Tropp 2008), better communication within a team, satisfaction, forging social bonds, personal growth and development, self-efficacy and optimism [Stahl et al. 2010; Stahl et al. 2009; Rozkwitalska et al. 2014]. Some scholars also posit that intercultural interactions present learning potential that consequently improves learning abilities and enhances learning, which may lead to positive organisational changes [Stevens et al. 2008; Stahl et al. 2010].

2. Learning from social interactions and organisational change

Learning can be defined as a dynamic transformational process that is constantly extended and re-defined. It is determined by the context in which it happens. Learning reflects an organic growth of a person and has "an unleashing potential developing new ideas and outlooks" [Antonacopoulou & Gabriel 2006, p. 445]. Psychologists, while defining learning, refer it to the processes of acquisition or modification that are aimed at a representation of environment, namely mental states (such as ideas, certain concepts or beliefs, desires and knowledge) through which a person represents the world [Bartel-Radic 2006].

Learning is also seen as "a process that is often relational in the sense of relying on interactions between people to determine what needs improving and how to do it" [Carmeli et al. 2009, p. 81]. Therefore, learning in organisations requires interactions among their members and is a dynamic behavioural process that includes contacts and continuous exchanges among people [Carmeli et al. 2009]. To explain how social interactions may foster learning, social learning theory and social cognitive theory [Bandura 2001] are particularly helpful here.

In Bandura's social learning theory [1977], behaviour is learned from the environment since the process of observational learning takes place. Social interactions create learning opportunities – individuals may mutually observe others and consciously decide if they want to adapt or not, and learning occurs in both situations. Social cognitive theory [Bandura 2001] provides an even more thorough explanation of learning that occurs in social interactions. It posits that personal agency functions inside a wide network of social interactions. Agentic transactions involve people as producers and products of social systems, motivating them to be active, be agents and learn.

One of the key concepts linking learning and organisational changes are social-cognition models of change that originate from a phenomenological or social-constructivist view of organisations. They assume that learning "occurs as two pieces of conflicting information are brought together, in the phenomenon often labelled *cognitive dissonance*" [Kezar 2001, p. 45]. Cognitive dissonance is seen rather negatively as a state of uncomfortable arousal that results from an observed inconsistency between two cognitions, or between behaviour and cognition. Cognitive dissonance motivates individuals to reduce or eliminate it, which can help to facilitate a change [Maertz et al. 2009]. Since each person interprets his/her environment in a unique way, people are likely to reach a point of cognitive dissonance, which informs them that some actions or values clash, and they are impelled to change. Social cognition models try to explain how individuals' world-perspectives can be changed by learning. Change is only enacted by individual people and is seen as a learning process. Thus, interpersonal aspects of change, i.e. thinking, mental models and learning, are here emphasised and change is about individual learning [Kezar 2001].

3. Learning in intercultural interactions – intercultural learning

Social learning theory and social cognitive theory support the notion that intercultural interactions enhance learning [Davidson & James 2009]. With regard to social learning theory, it can be assumed that attention, which is seen as an antecedent sub-process of learning, may be even stronger in intercultural interactions since it is attracted by behaviours that individuals perceive as novel, while motivation for learning can be additionally induced by MNCs if they offer job resources that enable interactions [Bakker et al. 2010]. On the basis of social cognitive theory, it can be posited that individuals are compelled to be active and learn in intercultural interactions and be agents in such contacts since they are more demanding than common social interactions. Moreover, job resources, apart from facilitating agentic behaviours, strengthen collective agency by means of their accessibility [Bandura 2000].

Individuals, acting in intercultural interactions, demonstrate different representations which are highly influenced by their culture. It is the very culture that affects what correct behaviour is and what is deemed appropriate in a given situation. When a person interacts with culturally diverse others, his/her representations are questioned and changes in his/her mentality take place, initiating the process of learning, as demonstrated in prior research [Bartel-Radic 2006; Rozkwitalska & Basinska 2015; Basinska & Rozkwitalska 2016; Rozkwitalska 2014]. An individual observes inappropriateness[2] of behaviour, namely the observed behaviour of the other party that does not fit his/her behavioural norms [Cooper et al. 2007], and experiences cognitive dissonance. As a result, s/he is compelled to change, i.e. to manifest conflict behaviour, learning behaviour or separation [Davidson & James 2009].

Intercultural interactions leverage intercultural learning, namely "the acquisition or modification of the representations of intercultural situations" [Bartel-Radic 2006, p. 651]. Bartel-Radic [2006] holds that internal intercultural interactions have a higher potential for learning than interactions with external foreign parties. They can enhance intercultural learning if interactions are long-term and spontaneous, occur in a shared context and are accompanied by positive emotions or a conflict as well. Although a conflict may naturally arise in intercultural contacts, since mutual expectations are violated and cognitive dissonance and tensions come out, learning in such circumstances leads to high-quality connections or relationships [Davidson & James 2009].

Connections are rather momentary and short term interactions, whereas relationships are enduring and lasting. Nevertheless, both high-quality connections and high-quality relationships are marked by vitality, mutuality and positive regard. They can enhance organisational commitment, foster learning and growth [Wayne & Dutton 2009], contribute to individual satisfaction, improve commitment and performance [Kahn 2009].

Rozkwitalska and Basinska [2015], on the strength of case studies of intercultural interactions in two MNCs, infer that the multicultural workplace in MNCs is highly demanding, yet MNCs help their employees to cope with challenges, which boosts their learning and stimulates more positive than negative emotions. They demonstrate that individuals in MNCs experience thriving, i.e. conscious psychological states of vitality (the positive experience of energy and aliveness) and learning (the latter interpreted as an acquisition of applicable knowledge and

---

2 It is worth noticing that inappropriateness of behaviour, in view of prior studies, is associated with negative outcomes such as anger, rejection of those whose behaviour is seen as deviant and conflicts [Cooper et al. 2007]. Nevertheless, in this chapter, it is posited that although the observed discrepancy in norms in intercultural interactions causes negative effects, it also activates learning, which contributes to individual and organisational changes. People involved in intercultural contacts are motivated to reduce cognitive dissonance and acquire new or modify the existing representations of the environment.

skills) [Spreitzer et al. 2005]. The concept of thriving assumes that organisational learning only takes place in social interactions. Intercultural interactions may therefore expose areas for improvements and ways to implement them, which is the core of learning. Moreover, thriving reflects being agents in intercultural interactions at work. Rozkwitalska and Basinska posit that challenges that individuals face in intercultural interactions are a natural source of learning. Additionally, they indicate that the learning component of thriving in intercultural interactions is more salient than vitality [Rozkwitalska & Basinska 2015; Basinska & Rozkwitalska 2016].

Figure 1 summarises the discourse of the chapter.

Figure 1. Intercultural interactions, learning as a component of thriving and organisational change

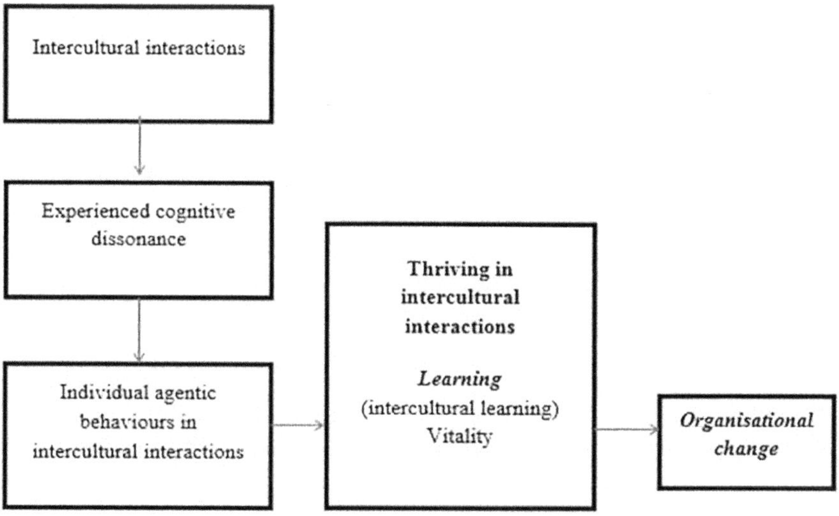

Source: own study.

4. Conclusions, discussion, future research

The discourse of this chapter demonstrates that learning is an immanent part of interactions with culturally different others. People learn since their representations are confronted with one another and they experience cognitive dissonance. They take an active role and witness thriving, where learning appears to be more salient than vitality. Furthermore, learning activates individual and organisational changes that are perceived as learning processes.

The notion that intercultural interactions facilitate learning supports the positive view in the literature on cultural diversity in organisations and the so-called positive cross-cultural scholarship research. *Positive cross-cultural scholarship* reflects an effort to apply a more positive approach to studying cultural diversity and was inspired by the stream known as Positive Organisational Scholarship [Stahl & Tung 2014][3]. The stream is recognised as an emergent field of study in the organisational sciences and is especially concerned with the positive outcomes, processes and attributes of both organisations and their members [Cameron & Spreitzer 2013]. In previous research, cultural diversity expressed in the behaviours of interacting people has been mainly presented as posing significant challenges that lower the quality of mutual contacts and negatively affect different aspects of management in MNCs [Björkman et al. 2007; Cooper et al. 2007; Luo & Shenkar 2006; Weber & Tarba 2012; Weber & Tarba 2010; Levin et al. 2012]. This view may suggest that intercultural interactions are an impediment to a learning process. Nonetheless, over the years, there have been attempts to portray the positive aspects of the employee cultural diversity [Dikova & Sahib 2013; Mannix & Neale 2005; Roberge & van Dick 2010; Stahl et al. 2010]. Yet, it still seems that this stream in the research is insufficiently documented, especially in the context of MNCs. Thus, the previous research appears to be biased and "the problem-focused view of cultural diversity is by far predominant in research" [Stahl & Tung 2014, p. 3]. Since there is far too little evidence about the positive aspects of intercultural contacts than about the problems, future research needs to "delve deeper" into the positive phenomena. The issue of learning in intercultural interactions as an antecedent of organisational change can add to this stream. Therefore, future research should provide more empirical grounds concerning learning in intercultural interactions as a facilitator of a positive organisational change in the specific context of MNCs. Furthermore, the comparison of learning in intercultural interactions with learning in social interactions among culturally similar people in the organisational context presents another promising avenue of future studies. It would be interesting and beneficial to the existing knowledge to know whether individuals in intercultural encounters learn more than in intraculture contacts. In other words, further empirical research may verify if a positive organisational change has more chances to occur in multicultural work settings or in a monocultural workplace.

---

3 Comparative research and applications of the ideas of a Positive Organisational Scholarship lens are another variation of positive cross-cultural scholarship studies. For example, they analyse how well-being is conceptualised and experienced among different cultures. See Sułkowski and Chmielecki [2017].

In this chapter, the focus was on individual learning in intercultural interactions and the case of how it contributes to organisational learning was omitted. Future studies should therefore delve into the role of interactions in a multicultural setting in organisational learning and how it translates into organisational changes. It could be particularly vital since previous research has revealed barriers to organisational leaning in MNCs [Engelhard & Nägele 2003]. Additionally, further research could explore factors inherited in individuals (not analysed in this chapter) as antecedents of a learning process in intercultural encounters.

Although the chapter is a theoretical/conceptual one, it allows for formulating some practical implications. Namely, the discourse indicates that, due to a learning potential embedded in multicultural work settings, managers need to enable intercultural interactions (i.e. increase their frequency and intensity as well as improve their quality) to enhance organisational changes and foster the thriving of their employees, which reflects their optimal functioning in the workplace. The frequency and intensity of intercultural contacts can be supported via e.g. establishing multicultural teams, geocentric staffing policy or a higher degree of internal integrations [Cooper et al. 2007]. The quality of intercultural encounters can be improved via e.g. cross-cultural trainings, conflict management techniques or information and communication enabling technologies [Rozkwitalska & Basinska 2015a].

Bibliography

Abdul Malek M., Budhwar P. (2013), *Cultural intelligence as a predictor of expatriate adjustment and performance in Malaysia*, "Journal of World Business", 48(2), pp. 222–231. Available at: http://dx.doi.org/10.1016/j.jwb.2012.07.006.

Antonacopoulou E.P., Gabriel Y. (2006), *Emotion, learning and organizational change*, "Journal of Organizational Change Management", 14(5), pp. 435–451.

Bakker A., van Veldhoven M., Xanthopoulou D. (2010), *Beyond the Demand-Control model: Thriving on high job demands and resources*, "Journal of Personnel Psychology", 9(1), pp. 3–16.

Bandura A. (2000), *Exercise of human agency through collective efficacy*, "Current Drections in Psychological Science", 9(3), pp. 75–78.

Bandura A. (2001), *Social cognitive theory: An agentic perspective*, "Annual Review of Psychology", 52(1), pp. 1–26.

Bandura A. (1977), *Social Learning Theory*, Oxford, England: Prentice-Hall.

Bartel-Radic A. (2006), *Intercultural learning in global teams*, "Management International Review", 46(October 2003), pp. 647–677.

Basinska B.A., Rozkwitalska M. (2016), *Psychological capital and challenge appraisal foster thriving in multicultural work settings*, "Procedia – Social and Behavioral Sciences", in press.

Björkman I., Barner-Rasmussen W., Li L. (2004), *Managing knowledge transfer in MNCs: the impact of headquarters control mechanisms*, "Journal of International Business Studies", 35(5), pp. 443–455. Available at: http://www.palgrave-journals.com/doifinder/10.1057/palgrave.jibs.8400094 [Accessed April 29, 2014].

Björkman I., Fey C.F., Park H.J. (2007), *Institutional theory and MNC subsidiary HRM practices: evidence from a three-country study*, "Journal of International Business Studies", 38(3), pp. 430–446. Available at: http://www.palgrave-journals.com/doifinder/10.1057/palgrave.jibs.8400267 [Accessed April 29, 2014].

Cameron K.S., Spreitzer G.M. (2013), *Introduction. What is positive about Positive Organizational Scholarship?* [in:] K.S. Cameron, G.M. Spreitzer (eds.), The Oxford Handbook of Positive Organizational Scholarship, New York: Oxford University Press, pp. 1–14.

Carmeli A., Brueller D., Dutton J.E. (2009), *Learning behaviours in the workplace: The role of high-quality interpersonal relationships and psychological safety*, "Systems Research and Behavioral Science", 98(November 2008), pp. 81–98.

Collings D.G., Scullion H., Morley M.J. (2007), *Changing patterns of global staffing in the multinational enterprise: Challenges to the conventional expatriate assignment and emerging alternatives*, "Journal of World Business", 42(2), pp. 198–213. Available at: http://linkinghub.elsevier.com/retrieve/pii/S1090951607000144 [Accessed May 28, 2014].

Colvin C., Volet S. (2014), *Scrutinising local students' accounts of positive intercultural interactions: A multidimensional analysis*, "International Journal of Intercultural Relations", 42, pp. 77–92. Available at: http://linkinghub.elsevier.com/retrieve/pii/S0147176714000601.

Cooper D., Doucet L., Pratt M. (2007), *Understanding "appropriateness" in multinational organizations*, "Journal of Organizational Behavior", 28(3), pp. 303–325. Available at: http://onlinelibrary.wiley.com/doi/10.1002/job.440/full.

Davidson M.N., James E.H. (2009), *The engines of positive relationships across difference: conflict and learning* [in:] J.E. Dutton, B.R. Ragins (eds.), Exploring Positive Relationships at Work. Building a Theoretical and Research Foundation. New York, London: Psychology Press, pp. 137–158.

Dikova D., Sahib P.R. (2013), Is *cultural distance a bane or a boon for cross-border acquisition performance?*, "Journal of World Business", 48(1), pp. 77–86. Available at: http://dx.doi.org/10.1016/j.jwb.2012.06.009.

Engelhard J., Nägele J. (2003), *Organizational learning in subsidiaries of multinational companies in Russia*, "Journal of World Business", 38(3), pp. 262–277. Available at: http://linkinghub.elsevier.com/retrieve/pii/S1090951603000221 [Accessed July 3, 2014].

Groeppel-Klein A., Germelmann C.C., Glaum M. (2010), *Intercultural interaction needs more than mere exposure: Searching for drivers of student interaction at border universities*, "International Journal of Intercultural Relations", 34(3), pp. 253–267. Available at: https://ezproxy.bibl.ulaval.ca/login?url=http://search.proquest.com/docview/613354753?accountid=12008%5Cnhttp://sfx.bibl.ulaval.ca:9003/sfx_local??url_ver=Z39.88-2004&rft_val_fmt=info:ofi/fmt:kev:mtx:journal&genre=article&sid=ProQ:ProQ:abiglobal&atitle=Inte.

Harrison N. (2012), *Investigating the impact of personality and early life experiences on intercultural interaction in internationalised universities*, 'International Journal of Intercultural Relations", 36(2), pp. 224–237. Available at: http://linkinghub.elsevier.com/retrieve/pii/S0147176711000393 [Accessed June 7, 2014].

Harvey M., Hartnell C., Novicevic M. (2004), *The inpatriation of foreign healthcare workers: A potential remedy for the chronic shortage of professional staff*, "International Journal of Intercultural Relations", 28, pp. 127–150.

Hernández-Mogollon R. et al. (2010), *The role of cultural barriers in the relationship between open-mindedness and organizational innovation*, "Journal of Organizational Change Management", 23(4), pp. 360–376.

Kahn W.A. (2009), *Meaningful connections: Positive relationships and attachments at work*. [in:] J. Dutton, B.R. Ragins (eds.), *Exploring Positive Relationships at Work. Building a Theoretical and Research Foundation*, New York, London: Psychology Press, pp. 189–206.

Kezar A.J. (2001), *Theories and models of organizational change* [in:] *Understanding and facilitating organizational change in the 21st century: Recent research and conceptualizations: ASHE-ERIC Higher Education Report*, Volume 28, Number 4. pp. 25–56.

Lauring J. (2009), *Managing cultural diversity and the process of knowledge sharing: A case from Denmark*, "Scandinavian Journal of Management", 25(4), pp. 385–394. Available at: http://linkinghub.elsevier.com/retrieve/pii/S0956522109000955 [Accessed September 17, 2014].

Levin S. et al. (2012), *Assimilation, multiculturalism, and colorblindness: Mediated and moderated relationships between social dominance orientation and prejudice*, "Journal of Experimental Social Psychology", 48(1), pp. 207–212. Available at: http://dx.doi.org/10.1016/j.jesp.2011.06.019.

Luo Y., Shenkar O. (2006), *The multinational corporation as a multilingual community: Language and organization in a global context*, "Journal of International Business Studies", 37(3), pp. 321–339. Available at: http://www.palgrave-journals.com/doifinder/10.1057/palgrave.jibs.8400197 [Accessed April 29, 2014].

Maertz C.P., Hassan A., Magnusson P. (2009), *When learning is not enough: A process model of expatriate adjustment as cultural cognitive dissonance reduction*, "Organizational Behavior and Human Decision Processes", 108(1), pp. 66–78. Available at: http://linkinghub.elsevier.com/retrieve/pii/S0749597808000708 [Accessed September 17, 2014].

Mannix E., Neale M.A. (2005), *What differences make a difference?: The promise and reality of diverse teams in organizations*, "Psychological Science in the Public Interest", 6(2), pp. 31–55.

Minbaeva D. et al. (2003), *MNC knowledge transfer, subsidiary absorptive capacity, and HRM*, "Journal of International Business Studies", 34(6), pp. 586–599. Available at: http://www.palgrave-journals.com/doifinder/10.1057/palgrave.jibs.8400056 [Accessed April 29, 2014].

Molinsky A. (2007), *Cross-cultural code-switching: the psychological challenges of adapting behavior in foreign cultural interactions*, "Academy of Management Review", 32(2), pp. 622–640. Available at: http://amr.aom.org/cgi/doi/10.5465/AMR.2007.24351878.

Müller C.V. (1998), *About differences and blind spots: A systemic view on an international, interdisciplinary research teams*, "Journal of Managerial Psychology", 13(3/4), pp. 259–270. Available at: http://www.emeraldinsight.com/10.1108/02683949810215066.

Nolan S. (2012), *Global mobility of human capital increasingly important*, "Strategic HR Review", 11(3).

Peltokorpi V. (2010), *Intercultural communication in foreign subsidiaries: The influence of expatriates' language and cultural competencies*, "Scandinavian Journal of Management", 26(2), pp. 176–188. Available at: http://linkinghub.elsevier.com/retrieve/pii/S0956522110000254 [Accessed June 7, 2014].

Pettigrew T.F., Tropp L.R. (2008), *How does intergroup contact reduce prejudice? Meta-analytic tests of three mediators*, "European Journal of Social Psychology", 38(6), pp. 922–934. Available at: http://doi.wiley.com/10.1002/ejsp.504.

Roberge M.-É. & van Dick R. (2010), *Recognizing the benefits of diversity: When and how does diversity increase group performance?*, "Human Resource Management Review", 20(4), pp. 295–308. Available at: http://linkinghub.elsevier.com/retrieve/pii/S1053482209000795 [Accessed January 28, 2014].

Rozkwitalska M. (2014), *Negative and positive aspects of cross-cultural interactions: A case of multinational subsidiaries in Poland*, "Inzinerine Ekonomika-Engineering Economics', 25(2), pp. 231–240.

Rozkwitalska M., Basinska B.A. (2015a), *Job satisfaction in the multicultural environment of multinational corporations,* "Baltic Journal of Management", 10(3), pp. 366–387. Available at: http://www.emeraldinsight.com/doi/10.1108/BJM-06-2014-0106.

Rozkwitalska M., Basinska B.A. (2015b), *Thriving in multicultural work settings* [in:] D. Vrontis, Y. Weber, & E. Tsoukatos, eds. Conference Readings Book Proceedings. Innovation, Entrepreneurship and Sustainable Value Chain in a Dynamic Environment. September 16–18, 2015, Verona: EuroMed Press, pp. 1897–1910. Available at: http://emrbi.org/wp-content/uploads/2015/11/euromed2015-book-of-proceedings-2015-11-02.pdf.

Rozkwitalska M., Chmielecki M., Przytuła S. (2014), *The positives of cross-cultural interactions in MNCs,* "Actual Problems of Economics", 57(7), pp. 382–392.

Rummel R. (1976), *Understending Conflict and War,* vol 2. In The conflict helix. Beverly Hills, California: Sage Publications. Available at: http://www.mega.nu/ampp/rummel/note9.htm.

Samnani A.-K., Boekhorst J.A., Harrison J.A. (2012), *Acculturation strategy and individual outcomes: Cultural diversity implications for human resource management,* "Human Resource Management Review", 22(4), pp. 323–335. Available at: http://linkinghub.elsevier.com/retrieve/pii/S1053482212000277 [Accessed September 4, 2014].

Shimoni B. (2011), *The representation of cultures in international and cross cultural management: Hybridizations of management cultures in Thailand and Israel,* "Journal of International Management", 17(1), pp. 30–41. Available at: http://linkinghub.elsevier.com/retrieve/pii/S1075425310000979 [Accessed September 16, 2014].

Spreitzer G. et al. (2005), *A socially embedded model of thriving at work,* "Organization Science", 16(5), pp. 537–549. Available at: http://pubsonline.informs.org/doi/abs/10.1287/orsc.1050.0153 [Accessed September 2, 2014].

Stahl G.K. et al. (2010), *A look at the bright side of multicultural team diversity,* "Scandinavian Journal of Management", 26(4), pp. 439–447. Available at: http://linkinghub.elsevier.com/retrieve/pii/S0956522110001028 [Accessed April 28, 2014].

Stahl G.K. et al. (2009), *Unraveling the effects of cultural diversity in teams: A meta-analysis of research on multicultural work groups,* "Journal of International Business Studies", 41(4), pp. 690–709. Available at: http://www.palgrave-journals.com/doifinder/10.1057/jibs.2009.85 [Accessed April 28, 2014].

Stahl G.K., Tung R.L. (2014), *Towards a more balanced treatment of culture in international business studies: The need for positive cross-cultural scholarship* "Journal of International Business Studies", pp. 1–24. Available at: http://www.palgrave-journals.com/doifinder/10.1057/jibs.2014.68.

Stevens F.G., Plaut V.C., Sanchez-Burks J. (2008), *Unlocking the benefits of diversity: All-inclusive multiculturalism and positive organizational change*, "The Journal of Applied Behavioral Science", 44(1), pp. 116–133.

Sułkowski Ł., Chmielecki M. (2017), *Positive cross-cultural scholarship research* [in:] M. Rozkwitalska, Ł. Sułkowski, S. Magala (eds.), *Intercultural Interactions in the Multicultural Workplace. Traditional and Positive Organizational Scholarship*. Switzerland: Springer International Publishing, pp. 19–35.

Tanova C., Nadiri H. (2010), *The role of cultural context in direct communication*, "Baltic Journal of Management", 5(2), pp. 185–196. Available at: http://www.emeraldinsight.com/10.1108/17465261011045115 [Accessed April 30, 2014].

Uhlenbruck K. (2004), *Developing acquired foreign subsidiaries: the experience of MNES in transition economies*, "Journal of International Business Studies", 35(2), pp. 109–123. Available at: http://www.palgrave-journals.com/doifinder/10.1057/palgrave.jibs.8400070 [Accessed April 29, 2014].

Van Veen K., Sahib P.R., Aangeenbrug E. (2014), *Where do international board members come from? Country-level antecedents of international board member selection in European boards*, "International Business Review", 23(2), pp. 407–417. Available at: http://dx.doi.org/10.1016/j.ibusrev.2013.06.008.

Watson W.E., Kumar K., Michaelsen L.K. (1993), *Cultural diversity's impact on interaction process and performance: Comparing homogeneous and diverse task groups*, "Academy of Management Journal", 36(3), pp. 590–602.

Wayne B., Dutton J.E. (2009), *Enabling positive social capital in organizations* [in:] J.E. Dutton, B.R. Ragins (eds.), *Exploring Positive Relationships at Work. Building a Theoretical and Research Foundation*, New York, London: Psychology Press, pp. 325–345.

Weber Y., Tarba S.Y. (2010), *Human resource practices and performance of mergers and acquisitions in Israel*, "Human Resource Management Review", 20(3), pp. 203–211. Available at: http://dx.doi.org/10.1016/j.hrmr.2009.08.007.

Weber Y., Tarba S.Y. (2012), *Mergers and acquisitions process: the use of corporate culture analysis*, "Cross Cultural Management: An International Journal", 19, pp. 288–303.

White D.W., Absher R.K., Huggins K.A. (2011), *The effects of hardiness and cultural distance on sociocultural adaptation in an expatriate sales manager population*, "Journal of Personal Selling and Sales Management", 31(3), pp. 325–338.

New Horizons in Management Sciences

Edited by Lukasz Sulkowski

- Vol. 1 Lukasz Sulkowski: Neodarwinism in Organization and Management. 2012.
- Vol. 2 Lukasz Sulkowski: Epistemology of Management. 2013.
- Vol. 3 Barbara Kożuch / Zbysław Dobrowolski: Creating Public Trust. An Organisational Perspective. 2014.
- Vol. 4 Konrad Raczkowski / Lukasz Sulkowski (eds.): Tax Management and Tax Evasion. 2014.
- Vol. 5 Michał Chmielecki / Łukasz Sułkowski: Metaphors in Management – Blend of Theory and Practice. 2017.
- Vol. 6 Łukasz Sułkowski (ed.): Management and Culture of the University. 2017.
- Vol. 7 Barbara Kożuch / Łukasz Sułkowski (eds.): Reflections about Contemporary Management. 2017.
- Vol. 8 Łukasz Sułkowski/Ewa Grandys (eds.): New Challenges in Change Management. 2018.

www.peterlang.com

www.ingramcontent.com/pod-product-compliance
Ingram Content Group UK Ltd.
Pitfield, Milton Keynes, MK11 3LW, UK
UKHW021832100926
8556IPUK00004B/302

9 783631 741139